SUMMERS ON THE SARANACS

By

MAITLAND C. DE SORMO

NORTH COUNTRY BOOKS
Utica, New York

SUMMERS ON THE SARANACS

Books written by the same author:

Told Around the Campfire (the Van Hoevenberg Story)
Noah John Rondeau, Adirondack Hermit
Old Times in the Adirondacks
Seneca Ray Stoddard, Versatile Camera Artist
The Heydays of the Adirondacks
John Bird Burnham — Klondiker, Adirondacker
and Eminent Conservationist

First Edition
Library of Congress Catalog Number: 80-81853
Copyright July 1980

First Paperback Edition
2002

ISBN 0-932052-87-8

NORTH COUNTRY BOOKS
311 Turner Street
Utica, New York 13501

DEDICATION
In Memory of Maitland De Sormo

Maitland's original dedication is reprinted below.

To the two of us — Sue and myself — who somehow survived the muss and fuss, the hustle and the hassle that have gone into the creation, production and promotion of our six husky hostages to literary fortune.

Unfortunately, my wife (8/27/1911-1/28/80) was not able to handle the seemingly endless chores and details that went into Opus No. 7 but nevertheless, her encouragement and persistence provided the necessary impetus that resulted in its publication.

Although she was no longer in the land of the living when the book saw the light of day, I consider it a fitting memorial to a sometimes restless but very productive and eminently satisfactory partnership of forty years duration.

At least we hope so!

Table of Contents

Dedication 3
Table of Contents 4
Acknowledgements 5
List of Illustrations 6
Preface 8
Chapter 1 — The Lure of the Saranacs Region 13
Chapter 2 — The Hotels: Martin's, Later Miller's Lake House. 31
Chapter 3 — The Hotels: The Ampersand 41
Chapter 4 — The Hotels: The Algonquin. 45
Chapter 5 — The Hotels: Bartlett's, Later The Saranac and Bartlett Carry Clubs . . . 51
Chapter 6 — The Hotels: Rustic Lodge, Later Swenson's and Indian Carry Camp . . . 63
Chapter 7 — The Hotels: Prospect House, Later Saranac Inn 69
Chapter 8 — The Hotels: The Wawbeek 89
Chapter 9 — Evidence of Indian Occupation of Saranacs Region 100
Chapter 10 — The Indian Carry Chapel. 103
Chapter 11 — The Ampersand Golf and Country Club 104
Chapter 12 — The Guideboat Builders: Willie Martin 110
Chapter 13 — The Guideboat Builders: Fred W. Rice 118
Chapter 14 — The Guideboat Builders: Theodore Hanmer 123
Chapter 15 — The Guideboat Builders: Willard Hanmer 126
Chapter 16 — The Guideboat Builders: Carl Hathaway and Others 131
Chapter 17 — Fred M. Rice and Martha Reben 136
Chapter 18 — The Saranac Guides: Sam Dunning 138
Chapter 19 — The Saranac Guides: Henry Martin 146
Chapter 20 — The Saranac Guides: Pete O'Malley 150
Chapter 21 — The Saranac Guides: Tom Peacock 153
Chapter 22 — The Saranac Guides: Herb Clark and Bob Marshall 160
Chapter 23 — The Saranac Guides: Ellsworth Petty 167
Chapter 24 — William Distin, Adirondack Architect 170
Chapter 25 — The Playgrounds of the Very Rich: Lewisohn's Prospect Point,
              Now Young Life Camp. 174
Chapter 26 — The Playgrounds of the Very Rich: Rockefeller's Camp Wonundra,
              Later Camp Cork 187
Chapter 27 — Dr. Ely and His Adirondack Map — George Marshall 191
Chapter 28 — The Hermit of Ampersand Mountain — Seaver Rice 205
Chapter 29 — The Saranac Sojourns of Stevenson and Twain 213
Chapter 30 — Edward L. Trudeau, M.D. — Dr. Gordon M. Meade 222
Chapter 31 — They Go to Church by Boat (Chapel Island) 241
Chapter 32 — Deer Island 251
Chapter 33 — The Church of the Ascension — Saranac Inn 257
Chapter 34 — Boat Races and Such on the Saranacs. 267
Chapter 35 — La Jeunesse, Premier Boys' Camp and the Blagdens 275
Chapter 36 — Deerwood. 285
Chapter 37 — The Psychology of the Lost 289
Chapter 38 — The Camera Artists: Seneca Ray Stoddard and Stoddard Miscellany . . . 295
Chapter 39 — The Camera Artists: William Kollecker and Miscellany 303

Acknowledgements

In compiling a book such as this it is necessary to include as many sources as possible — written history as well as oral tradition. In order to help preserve the latter, which of course perpetuates the sound of the individual voices as well as the information they impart, I have taped many interviews and thus given them longer life.

Many people have been generous with their time, recollections, photos and other personal items which have greatly enhanced the quality and quantity represented in this rather formidable effort. Among the contributors are the following: Ken Bennett, John Benson, Joseph Blagden, Sam Bodine, Steve Briggs, Velma Bristol, Mott Chapin, Clyde Cheesman, Kate Dacey, Ben Darling, Mrs. Fred Derby, George Donaldson, Alvin Doty, Dick Emperor, Will and Lorraine Green, Ed. Hale, Bessie Hanmer, Joe Harley, Mrs. Charles Harris, Warren Kay, Ludwig Keller, Mrs. J. Harmon Kirkendall, Mrs. Herbert Leggett, Bill McLaughlin, Greg Nowakowski, Mr. and Mrs. Ed. Patnode, Bill and Clarence Petty, Carl Prue, Mr. and Mrs. Francis Remington, Seaver Rice, Charles Ritchie, Mrs. Charles Roberson, Mrs. Irene Rushlaw, Percy Saumier, Clarence Savard, Mrs. Laurence Slaughter, Laurel Spina, Thomas Stainback, Frank and Eleanor Stearns, Maisie Wood and Jay Yardley.

A special expression of thanks is due Jim and Edna Finn for the use of their files of real estate sales brochures. Also to Willard Gilmette and Ken Bennett for their patient tolerance of my brain — picking efforts. Norman Dumas, Franklin County Clerk was especially helpful in researching property transfers.

I am also appreciative of the digital dexterity and thorough cooperation of Sally Wallace, who was responsible for the script preparation. For the excellent photographic work of Barbara Parnass I am also most grateful.

Obviously, a lot of people were involved in this wide-ranging project. Without their special kinds of assistance this book would never have seen the light of day.

If anyone has been left out please accept my apologies and the assurance that the oversight was both unintentional and regrettable.

Maitland C. De Sormo

List of Illustrations

Frontispiece: *Te Deum Laudamus* (We Praise Thee, God) painting by Elizabeth R. Fulda
An Adirondack Stream 12
Map of Franklin County Showing The Saranac Lakes 1858 15
Alexander Macomb and William Constable 16
Map of the South Woods Showing Harrietstown 1876 17
Rev. William H. H. Murray (photo) 19
Moses St. Germain (Sanjemo) 21
An Up-to-Date Portage 21
Paul Smith's, Lower St. Regis Lake in 1880's (Stoddard) 22
Guide House at Paul Smith's (Stoddard) 22
Guideboats Galore 23
Lunch at Half-Way House 24
Modern Invasion of the Woods 24
An Adirondack Fire Trap 25
Forest Aflame 25
Attacking a Fire in Time 25
Plowing Furrows to Stop Progress of a Ground Fire 26
Fire Under Control 26
The Fire Fighters' Cook 26
Packing in Food for the Fire Fighters 26
Anglers' Camp in the Forest — Discussing the Catch 28
Venison for Supper 29
Lower Saranac Lake. Wood Engraving by Harry Fenn 32
The Saranac Stage (Stoddard) 35
Martin's, Later Miller's on Lower Saranac Lake (Stoddard) 35
Martin's, Later Miller's from the West Shore (Stoddard) 36
William F. Martin 37
Mary H. (Mrs. Ferd) Chase 37
Loon Lake House in Its Heyday — 1925 38
Ampersand Hotel, Lower Saranac Lake (Stoddard) 40
View South from Ampersand Porch — Miller's Hotel Opposite (Stoddard) 40
Hotel Ampersand Office (Stoddard) 43
Hotel Ampersand Parlor (Stoddard) 43
Tent of Tubercular Guest at Ampersand Hotel (Stoddard) 43
The Alexander, Later Algonquin House 46
The Algonquin from the East (Stoddard) 47
John Harding 48
Bartlett's Village, Middle Saranac (Round Lake) in Background 52
Bartlett's, Saranac River in Foreground (Stoddard) 52
Virgil C. Bartlett 54
Caroline Greene Bartlett 54
Saranac River End of Bartlett Carry (Stoddard) 55
Dr. Romeyn on Bartlett's Rapids June 1887 57
The Saranac Club (Stoddard) 59

Interior of Saranac Clubhouse 59
Merritt Cottage, Bartlett Carry Club 61
A Fascinating Study 62
Corey's Original Rustic Lodge, Upper Saranac Lake 64
Jesse Corey (Stoddard) 64
Corey's Rustic Lodge in the 1880's (Stoddard) 64
Indian Carry, Upper Saranac 65
Indian Carry Landing at First Stony Creek Pond 66
Hiawatha House, First Stony Creek Pond (Stoddard) 66
Rustic Lodge Cabins, Later Moved to Lake Clear 66
Swenson's 67
Prospect House, Upper Saranac Lake (Stoddard) 70
Prospect House, Blagden's "Cabin" (Stoddard) 70
North from Prospect House, Upper Saranac Lake (Stoddard) 71
Stage Departing from Saranac Inn 73
Saranac Inn in 1903 (Stoddard) 73
Daniel W. Riddle, Supt. at Saranac Inn 73
Saranac Inn Guidehouse (middle) and Annex right 1903 (Firth photo) 74
Saranac Inn Store with Cooler in Background 1903 (Firth photo) 74
Saranac Inn: L to R Carpenter Shop, Blacksmith Shop, Paint Shop 1903 (Firth photos) 74
Saranac Inn Laundry and Windmill 1903 (Firth photo) 74
Saranac Inn Woodyard, Forest Home Road 1900 (Firth photo) 74
Saranac Inn Sawmill, Forest Home Road 1903 (Firth photo) 74
Map of Saranac Inn Locations in Early 1920's (courtesy William Hord 76
Aerial View of Saranac Inn in its Heyday — 1920's 77
Altemus — Mills Wedding Party at the Inn 79
Mr. and Mrs. Willard Boyce, Harrington Mills, Judge Paddock at Boyce Retirement Party 9/29/28 79
Dining Room of Saranac Inn in 1930's 80
Drawing Room of Saranac Inn in 1930's 80
Saranac Inn from the Lake 81
Lounge at Inn in 1960's 81
Buffet at Inn in 1960's 81
Fire Photos June 17, 1978 84-85
The Buyer — Ralph Bowles; the Seller — Charles Vosburgh 87
Captain James H. Pierce 89
Christopher F. Norton 89
Sweeney — Daniels Cabin 91
Wawbeek End of Sweeney Carry (Stoddard) 92
Wawbeek Hotel in 1895 (Stoddard) 93

"The Loon" Freight Boat on Upper Lake 94
Some Upper Saranac Lakers (Stoddard) 94
The Second Wawbeek 94
The Second Wawbeek. Painting by Iskat c. 1970 96
Fire Photos 3/1/80 97-98
Indian Carry Chapel 103
View from Ampersand Clubhouse 105
Tennis at Ampersand Clubhouse 1900 106
Ampersand Golf and Country Club 1978 109
Aerial View of Lower Saranac Lake, Looking South 110
A Difficult Carry 111
A Carry — The Start 112
A Carry — The End 112
A Complicated Passage 113
Some of Willie Martin's "Eggshells" 115
Probably the "Water Lily" (Stoddard) 117
Fred W. Rice and Family 119
Fred Rice's Boathouse (left) and Studio (right) 119
Dr. Charles Peabody's Cottage, Moss Rock Point, Upper Saranac Lake (Fred Rice photo) 121
Theodore Hanmer at 83 122
Theodore Hanmer (right), Willard (left) 124
Truman Hanmer and Friend 125
Willard Hanmer at Ease 127
5 Stages of Guideboat Construction 128
A Finished Hanmer Product 130
Carl Hathaway (Ed Hale photos) 132, 134-5
Martha Reben and Fred M. Rice 137
Saranac Guides at Sportsmen's Show, N.Y.C. 1904 139
"Goyd' by Clayton Seagers 140
Typical Guide's Cabin and Occupant 141
Sportsman and Guide — A Friendly Chat 143
A Swim for Life 144
Roughing It — Homer D. Martin 146
Trouting 147
A Successful Hunt 147
Lean-to Life in the Tall Timber 148
Successful Hunters — Pete O'Malley (guide) and Charles Oblenis (sport) 151
In Camp — A Sticky Wicket 151
Tom Peacock, Indian Guide and T. R. in Ontario 156
Close-up of T. R. and Trophy Moose 156
Tom Peacock and Friends 158
Last Photo of Peacock 159
Herb Clark 161
Bob Marshall in 1925 165
Map of Bob Marshall Wilderness Area, Montana 165
Ellsworth Petty 168
William G. Distin, Sr. 172

Home of William Distin, Glenwood Park, S. L. 173
Camp Pine Knot on Raquette Lake 174
Dr. Thomas C. Durant 175
William West Durant at Camp UNCAS 175
Adolph Lewisohn and Granddaughters 176
Prospect Point Boathouse 177
Stairway to Main House 177
Main House at Prospect Point 178
Dining Room at Prospect Point 178
Summary of Accommodations at Prospect Point 179
Sekon Lodge or Fish Rock 181
Seligman Family Reunion at Fish Rock 181
Aerial View of Bache's Wenonah Lodge 182
The Game Room at Bache's Wenonah Lodge 182
The "Margaret". Launch Given by Seligman for Ambulance Use 7/3/17 183
The Charles G. Harris Camp on Lower Saranac 184
Young Life 4 Views 185
W. A. Rockefeller's Camp Wonundra (Camp Cork) 188
Dr. William W. Ely 192
Round Lake from Bartlett's 194
Ampersand Lake 194
Verplanck Colvin 196
Ruins of Colvin Homestead on Western Ave., Albany 197
Colvin Surveying Equipment 197
Mills Blake, Colvin's Chief Asst. 198
Plan Showing Method of Mountain Measurement 200
Forest Surveying 203
The Great Corner 203
Capt. Pliny Miller 206
Van Buren Miller 206
Walter Rice, The Hermit of Ampersand Mountain 207
Villa Dorsey 208
Seaver Rice and His Catch of Northerns 209
Seaver Rice (left) and His Father 1912 210
Walter Rice and Visitor on Ampersand Mt. 1916 210
Saranac Lake Village and Lower Lake from Mt. Baker 213
Woodcut of R. L. Stevenson by Henry Wolf 214
Baker's Cottage, where R. L. Stevenson Stayed 214
Saranac Lake Stevenson Memorial Plaque 215
Mark Twain Camp, Lower Saranac Lake 217
Mark Twain at Duryee Camp in 1901 218
The Clemens Family 218
Dr. Gordon M. Meade Birdwatching 222
Dr. Edward Livingston Trudeau 1885 223
Mrs. Edward L. Trudeau 1910 223
The Old Hotel at Paul Smith's in 1884 224
Saranac Lake Village in 1875 (Stoddard photo) 224
Trudeau on His Way to Visit a Patient 227

Dr. & Mrs. E. L. Trudeau 228
Adirondack Cottage Sanitarium (Trudeau) in 1900 (Stoddard) 230
Early Saranac Lake from Lake St. Hill 230
Laboratory at Trudeau in Early Days 230
Taking The Cure — Rest Period in 1900 (Stoddard) 235
Exercise Phase of the Trudeau Cure in 1900 (Stoddard) 235
Three Leaders in T. B. Field — Drs. Brown, Heise and Baldwin 236
Gloria Victis — Mercié 237
Edward L. Trudeau Memorial Statue by Gutzon Borglum 237
Trudeau Sanitarium in Its Heyday 238-9
Trudeau Institute on Lower Saranac Lake (Kirstein photo) 240
View West Over Lower Saranac Lake from Trudeau Institute (Kirstein photo) 240
The Island Chapel, Upper Saranac Lake 241
Mr. and Mrs. Charles I. Marvin 244
The Marvin Wedding Party 244
Baptism of Carolyn Alethea Robinson 245
Sunday Service in Original Church 245
Destruction by Fire of Original Church — Aug. 1956 247
The Island Church in Winter 248
Edmund Lyon 252
Carolyn Talcott (Mrs. Edmund Lyon) 252
"Bircholm", Deer Island 252
Capt. Philo Talcott 254
"The Chug-Chug" 254
Mr. Lyon and His Three Daughters 255
Lisa R. Dietal and Her Mother, Mrs. W. M. Dietal 256
Celebrating the 50th Anniversary of "The To-N-Fro" 256
Church of the Ascension in 1893 (Frank Firth photo) 257
Rev. Dr. Leonard W. Richardson (Firth photo) 259
"The Birches" Main House (Firth photo) 259
Elizabeth Morgan Serving Tea at "The Birches", 1904 259
"The Saranac" (Stoddard photo) 260
Duncan LeClaire, Capt. of "The Saranac" 260
John Clark, Mate of "The Saranac" 260
Upper Saranac Guides: Arlo Flagg, Jim Patterson, Duck Derby, Jim O'Malley Earl Torrence, Bert Chase 263
Probably the Way "The Eagle" Flew 268
Saranac Inn Dock on Regatta Day 268
Douglass Blagden, "Albatross" Winner 8/10/07 269
Frank Firth's "Nan" 8/10/07 269
Wide-Open Inboards on The Lower Saranac 270
"Adios II" on Lower Saranac in 1922 Race (Kollecker photo) 271
"Adios II" with Mrs. J. C. Kane, Pilot and Mrs. Charles C. Harris

(Kollecker photo) 271
"The Poker Dot", Mrs. Charles C. Harris, Pilot 272
Dr. Albert Einstein on Lower Saranac Lake 1936 273
Sailboat Race on Lower Saranac Lake c. 1920 (Kollecker photo) 274
Thomas Blagden and Sons 276
Mr. and Mrs. Joseph Blagden at Beaverwood Cabin 278
"The Cabin", Also Known as "Camp Alpha" and "President's Cottage" 279
"The Lodge" 280
La Jeunesse 1951 281
"Hank" and Mary Blagden at Fish Pond Nov. 1955 (Bodine photo) 282
The Harry Blagden Family (Christmas card) 282
"Camp of the Winds" 284
Thomas Blagden in Whimsical Mood 286
A Blagden Picnic 286
Aerial View of "Deerwood" 287
"Deerwood" — Adirondack Music Center 287
Boathouse at "Deerwood" 288
Easy Country to Get Lost In 290
Part of a Search Party 291
Lost In a Snowstorm 293

STODDARD MISCELLANY:
Female Golf Form Then and Now 296
Running the Rapids Between Middle and Lower Saranac 297
Kiddies' Day at The Loon Lake House 297
Blue Mt. Lake Hotel 299
Prospect House, Blue Mt. Lake 299
"Homeward Bound" Lake George 1879 300
Seneca Ray Stoddard (1844-1917) 300
Adirondack Hunters 302
Wild Adirondack Game 302
Fletcher Farm, Bloomingdale, N.Y. 303
Mr. and Mrs. William F. Cheesman 304
Cheesman Store Interior, Kollecker Behind Counter 304
Kollecker and Friends, 1926 304
Kollecker in 1933 305
Kollecker Message on Lake Placid School Blackboard 1903 305
Hannah Clarke, The Girl Kollecker Never Forgot 305

KOLLECKER MISCELLANY:
Mouth to Mouth Resuscitation 308
Four of a Kind: Riverside Hotel in Background 308
A Girl and Her Friends 309
Come A Runnin' 309
Cats Aren't the Only Curious Creatures 310
Almost September Morn 310
In the Good Old Summer Time 311
There's Nothing Like a Picnic 311
That Guy on The Right 311
Croquet Adirondack Style 312
Much Ado About Something 312
Aeroplane vs. Automobile Oct. 6, 1912 312
Loon Lake House in 1920's 313

Preface

This particular writing project — Opus Number 7 — lingered an unconscionably long time in the gestation period and thus nearly died aborning. In fact there were many times during the prolonged parturition period when I was almost convinced that it would never hatch at all. However, after other somewhat less formidable but nevertheless higher priority products had seen the light of day, been spanked into alertness and launched on their merry way to the marketplace, the main obstacle to progress became primarily a problem of overcoming inertia and generating enough enthusiasm, momentum and sense of involvement to compensate for what the Lambs (brother Charles and his sister Mary) aptly described as "The Agony of Composition," the frantic sometimes frenetic search for les mots justes.

Then too I was constantly nudged into action by the oft-quoted Chinese proverb — "A journey of a thousand miles starts with but a single step," and, in my case, but a single word, then a sentence etc., etc. By also reminding myself that I really didn't deserve a night's sleep until I had ground out a reasonably satisfactory stint, I gradually got the mental gears out of reverse, then out of neutral and into a forward slot which in turn produced appreciable and appreciated so-called progress.

Over the years and during my various writing efforts, which have so far yielded six books and 55 articles, I had slowly acquired a fat file of miscellaneous material pertaining to the Saranacs — Lower, Middle (Round), Upper and the River. Besides my research library there were many ephemeral items such as clippings from newspapers and periodicals, photo albums, scrapbooks, hotel brochures, postcards and the like.

These were supplemented by my very impressive accumulation of vintage photographs, so I knew that that essential ingredient was well taken care of. My stock of Stoddards alone could have adequately filled the bill but fortunately I was also able to supply an extra dollop of serendipity by including some of Kollecker's most representative work as well. Since, nowadays, no literary product stands the proverbial Chinaman's chance or that of a snowball in Hades without superior illustrations — which I had in considerable quantity — I decided that I had no acceptable or logical reason for stalling any longer. So I got busy and here it is such as it is.

That mental green light signal was later on strongly reinforced by a segment of the "60 Minutes" TV show which featured Mike Wallace's interview with one of the Soviet dissidents. The real clincher came in this paraphrased response to Wallace's question: "Knowing the fate of so many of your people who had dared to protest publicly, how did you ever muster up the courage to put your life on the line — or if not that risk life imprisonment at hard labor?"

The Russian's reply was short and memorable: "Yes, I suppose it did take a lot of courage but I looked at it this way: "If not I — who? If not now — when?" Listening to that really shook me out of my lethargy and supplied the missing motivation.

Obviously, there is no direct comparison between the Russian's situation and mine, but nevertheless there is a certain modest degree of correlation. While many other people have more knowledge of the three Saranacs, few have had the time, the opportunity and the sense of obsession to undertake the seemingly endless chore of collecting, digesting and producing a verbal and pictorial history of this alluring region which has evoked so much literary and artistic enthusiasm since in the mid 1850's and 60's. Hammond, Headley, Street, Van Dyke, Murray et al among the writers; Homer Martin, Sanford Gifford, A. W. Tait and A. B. Frost among the painters. . . .

My first impression of the storied Saranac Section came quite early in life — in 1911 at age 5 to be exact. My father, who owned a small general store in Hermon, N.Y., had contracted consumption — bovine tuberculosis it was termed — while butchering diseased cattle. This necessitated a period of complete rest and, hopefully, recuperation and eventual recovery in a tent at Wanakena, near Cranberry Lake. However, since there was not appreciable improvement in his condition the following Spring, he either went or was taken to Saranac Lake.

St. Mary's of the Lake (Woods), on the crest of the hill on Ampersand Ave., was one of the largest of the more than 150 such cure-cottages then operating in this village, which at the time and until the 1950's owed much of its prosperity to the health industry. Long since torn down, St. Mary's overlooked Ampersand Bay, the head of Lower Saranac Lake.

At that time the intervening area was mostly open pasture-land so the view from the top of the hill above what is now called Schroeter's field was unobstructed and, to my young and eager eyes, was downright spectacular and deeply moving.

As I recall the scene through the mist of the years, the late August sun seemed to shimmer as it was being reflected and refracted by the wave-broken surface of the Bay. The low forested hills on either side framed several middle-distance islands and rocky points. In the farther background loomed the serrated silhouettes of what I later learned were the Seward Range, Scarface and Ampersand mountains.

That indelible visual delight made a profound and long-lingering impact upon a youngster then accustomed to the far tamer rural scenes of St. Lawrence county — so strong an effect in fact that I impulsively promised myself that someday, somehow I, like MacArthur, would return for keeps to that strangely fascinating area.

Even though that initial impression was later darkened by the death of my father, in January 1912, I nevertheless never relinquished that desire to come back. A love of place, seemingly, that to natives can be aptly called "the return to the womb."

However, it took nearly forty slow-drifting, school-teaching years — first in a Florida prep school and later in Long Island and Westchester systems — before I could see my way clear to realize that deep-seated yearning and personal promise. . . .

Late afternoon on January 29, 1967, just ahead of Madden's movers and amidst a raging blizzard my wife Sue and I drove into Saranac village. After several years in a rented apartment and one Winter in a house on Trudeau Rd. we bought the rapidly deteriorating clubhouse of the long-defunct Ampersand Golf and Country Club.

Even though it only too obviously called for major maintenance attention, expensive alterations and improvements, the well-designed old building (vintage 1897) had plenty of potential and was redolent with history, character, charm — and carpenter ants! Moreover, its two-acre wooded location and backyard brook provided added visible assets.

Using the place as a base of operations and o.p. book business I gradually increased my knowledge of the Lakes by frequent guideboat trips and occasional speaking dates, mostly at the Wawbeek Hotel on the Upper Lake and at the annual Summer conferences on the Adirondacks sponsored by St. Lawrence University. All the while I was also gleaning information by picking the brains and tapping the recollections of year-round residents and

Summer people. Whenever convenient I also taped the interviews and thus built up an extensive oral history library as an extra desirable dividend.

Early in my research campaign I was not surprised to discover that my affinity for the Saranacs was not a personal monopoly but one that was also almost an addiction for a host of other reasonably discerning visitors who had frequented this entrancing area over the long span of years from the 1800's onward — Indians, surveyors, sportsmen, land agents/ would-be developers, authors, artists, photographers and, of course, sportsmen and health-seekers (spiritual as well as physical). Many of these gifted individuals had already made names for themselves elsewhere but recorded their memorable impressions of this fabulous region in outbursts of purplish prose, with colors and inspired photographs. Present-day readers usually label the writing style of the era as so much sloppy emotion, but there are many of us who rather like such shows of honest sentiment and feel that it never requires apologies or qualifications.

By using excerpts from the work of those early writers and adding chapters featuring guides (a vanished breed), the guideboat builders, the early hotels, the regattas, the famous Summer residents such as Mark Twain and Albert Einstein, the wealthy camp owners and Bill Distin, the architect who built many of them, I have provided a wide-angle perspective on the picturesque and historic aspects of the alluring lake region of the Saranacs.

Although I have no first-hand knowledge of Camp La Jeunesse and Deerwood, the renowned Summer music center, I have decided to include them because of their pronounced impact upon the culture and economy of the general area.

Henry Van Dyke's classic "Ampersand" article and George Marshall's tribute to Dr. Ely, who literally put Ampersand Mountain on the map, were mentioned or included to give this book a touch of class. The same criterion applied to the use of Dr. Gordon Meade's fine biographical sketch of the incomparable Dr. Edward L. Trudeau.

All in all the purpose and hoped-for result of all this shared effort should be a sort of literary smorgasbord with a generous helping of photography for dessert. Like a well-stocked buffet table it has all sorts of assorted goodies to titillate the tastebuds. But best of all it should evoke numerous nostalgic nuggets for those familiar with those long-gone, good and-for some-not-so good-old days.

For others less acquainted with that era and the area's past this compilation is planned to provide an introduction to a repository of recollections pertaining to this particular region — The Saranacs — a choice section of the "beautiful bedeviled Adirondacks."

Samuel Johnson, probably the greatest talker in the history of the English language, was equally eloquent when he stated: "The only end of writing is to enable readers better to enjoy life, or better to endure it."

If this book comes even half-way close to accomplishing either of those objectives, I shall consider it well worth the seemingly endless hassle and hustle, muss and fuss, mental and physical sweat that went into the production and promotion of Opus #7, my lengthy hostage to literary fortune.

Many times, in recent years especially, I have been asked to explain my motivation — why I let myself become virtually obsessed by the urgency to put into print the gradually garnered accumulation of shared records and recollections. Basically it's been the strong feeling of something bordering on responsibility — obligation even — or sense of mission to put all the acquired material on cassette and in print. The oral tradition is of course every bit as important as the written so here's the aftermath of countless hours of talking and writing.

Two quotes express the feeling far better than I can.

The first gem is lifted from an interview with Norman Lear (creator of Archie, the indestructible Archie Bunker), during which he was asked the age-old question — the definition of personal happiness. "The finest definition I ever have come across was that of an anonymous Greek who stated, 'Happiness is the exercise of one's vital abilities along lines of excellence in a life that affords them scope.' "

The second, from the Preface to George Bernard Shaw's *Man and Superman*, puts it this way: "This is the true joy in life — the being used for a purpose recognized by yourself as a mighty one; the being thoroughly worn out before you are thrown on the scrap heap; the being a force of Nature instead of a feverish, selfish little clod of ailments and grievances and always complaining because the world will not devote itself to making you happy. . . . And also the only real tragedy in life is being used by personally-minded men for purposes you recognize as base. All the rest is at worst mere misfortune or mortality."

And that sums it up beautifully and memorably.

Maitland C. De Sormo

An Adirondack Stream

Chapter 1

The Lure of the Saranacs Region

The late T. Morris Longstreth, in his widely-read *The Adirondacks* (1917), accurately assessed the special charm of this uniquely endowed — if for water and forest assets alone — northern section in this perceptive statement: "The Adirondack region is so full of beauty, so rich in historical association that it is easy to believe that as a fountainhead of literature it will be of increasing value to American writers."

Longstreth certainly knew whereof he spoke and his optimistic prediction has been at least partially fulfilled. Since his time Donaldson contributed his landmark two-volume vade mecum — *The History of the Adirondacks* (1921) and twice reprinted; Hochschild's virtuoso *Township 34* (1952); Dunham's unforgettable *Adirondack French Louie* (1952); White's memorable *Adirondack Country* (1954); P. Fosburgh's first-class *The Natural Thing* (1959); Durant's in-depth *Guideboat Days and Ways* (1963); Jamieson's comprehensive *Adirondack Reader* (1964); Manley's well-documented *Rushton and His Times in American Canoeing* (1968) — these are very likely the best representatives of a steady stream of books featuring the Adirondack scene.

Not to be overlooked are the outstanding coffee table pictorial products exemplified by Eliot Porter's *Forever Wild: The Adirondacks* (1966); the late Lincoln Barnett's *The Ancient Adirondacks* (1974) and Clyde Smith's *The Adirondacks* (1976). Each one contains color photography at its very best.

As Barnett noted: "The primary paradox is that this wilderness lies close to the most densely populated section of the United States — scarcely 250 miles north of New York City. Yet a great part of it was virtually unknown, save to parties of warring Indians, Frenchmen, Englishmen and the Americans until the 1830's. The headwaters of the Columbia River in the Far West were discovered more than a half century before the highest headwaters of the Hudson. Stanley had found Livingston in darkest Africa before most New Yorkers knew much about the wilderness at their back door."

That provides but a small facet of the historical aspect mentioned by Longstreth. A far-famed Catskill visitor in 1863 epitomized yet another phase of its appeal. Burroughs recalled: "Our campaign in the Adirondacks seems almost like a dream; it has idealized itself already and my life will always be sweeter and richer for it. How it enhances the value of living, does it not? To have something sweet to remember!"

The great naturalist also commented on still another quality that makes the region so special: "It is not in the woods alone to give one this impression of utter loneliness. In the woods are sounds and voices and a dumb kind of companionship; one is little more than a walking tree himself; but come upon one of these mountain lakes, and the wilderness stands revealed and meets you face to face. Water is thus facile and adaptive, that it makes the wild more wild, while it enhances culture and art."

And as for the general misconception of the wild places Thoreau said it best — "A howling wilderness seldom ever howls. The howling is chiefly done by the imagination of the traveler." Acute inflammation of the imagination is the usual diagnosis.

Right at this point perhaps some of the restless readers are wondering why the succession of quotes and the relative absence of personal contribution to the progress of this all-important opening chapter. In answer to that here's yet another borrowing and this one from Alexander Pope:

"True wit is Nature to advantage dressed,
 What oft was thought but ne'er so well expressed."

In other words the author of this opus has been around long enough to know that "You can't gild a lily," that it's well-nigh impossible to compete in the word game with the acknowledged knowledgeables, and that clumsy paraphrasing is a poor counterfeit compared with the contemporaries — therefore why try? Go with the best and in this special case the very best is what is called for in this verbal analysis of the lure of what is universally considered to be the most visually appealing and memorable Adirondack waterways — the Saranacs. Admittedly a somewhat chauvinistic and parochial assertion but one that has had the endorsement of most of the qualified writers of their time. Among these were Charles Hoffman, who first visited the general region in 1837, Farrand Benedict two years previously; Ebenezer Emmons in 1839; Rev. John Todd, who traveled via the Saranacs in 1841, to Long Lake; Rev. Joel Headley in 1849; Samuel Hammond in 1848; Lady Amelia Murray in 1855 with Gov. Horatio Seymour and Harvey Moody, guide and Alfred B. Street in 1854 on his first trip here and Ralph W. Emerson in 1857-8.

Still further evidence of the lingering longing for the woods was aptly expressed by William James in what he termed an "organic-feeling need. We of the highly educated classes (so-called) have most of us got far, far away from Nature. We are stuffed with abstract conceptions and glib verbalities and verbosities; and in the culture of these higher functions, the peculiar sources of joy connected without simpler functions often dry up. . . . The remedy under such conditions is to descend to a more profound and primitive level. . . . Living in the open air and on the ground, the lop-sided beam of the balance slowly rises to the level line. The good of all the artificial schemes and fevers fades and pales, and that of seeing, smelling, tasting, sleeping and daring and doing with one's body grows and grows. . . . I am sorry for the boy or girl, or man or woman, who has never been touched by the spell of this mysterious sensorial life with its irrationality, if so you like to call it, but its vigilance and its supreme felicity."

Besides its beauty, historical associations and solitude the Adirondack region which included the Saranacs also exerted a potent attraction in the form of great potential profit through land speculations. The state of New York appropriated a large part of what is now the Adirondacks when in 1779 the Legislature passed a bill which declared that all the lands belonging to the Crown before 1776 were "forever after to be vested in the people of this state." However, the "forever" lasted a very short while indeed because just five years afterward the Legislature, prompted by its customary urgent need of cash to stoke the law-making furnaces, passed a follow-up measure which called for "the settlement of the waste and unappropriated lands within the state and providing for this "speedy sale." The main bait was not the land itself but its piddling price tag. While the terrain in other less formidable areas sold readily, that in the Adirondacks attracted nary a purchaser despite the extra bonus that no taxes would be levied for seven years.

Included was the so-called Old Military Tract of 650,000 acres in Clinton, Essex and Franklin counties which the state offered to its Revolutionary War veterans, who to a man opted for the more desirable land in the Mohawk Valley. Speculators finally acquired that northern tract for about nine cents per acre.

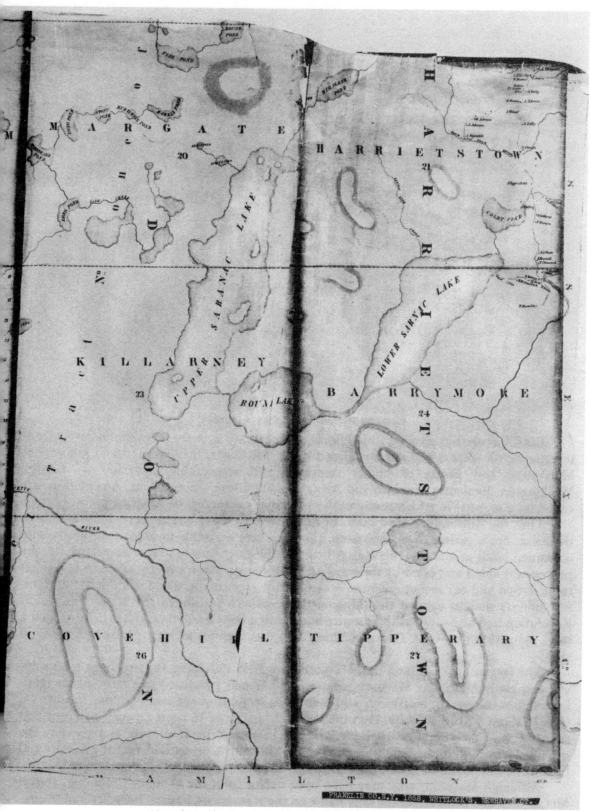

Map of Franklin County Showing The Saranac Lakes 1858

Alexander Macomb and William Constable

Land speculation resulted from efforts by every state as well as the federal government to compete for settlers and sell unclaimed lands. Moreover, the "Harpy Land Jobbers" of Manhattan had plenty of highly respected and respectable associates — George Washington, Benjamin Franklin and Alexander Hamilton among them. A contemporary called it "a scandal in which many of the principal characters of America are invol·.ɔd!"

Thus the Adirondack land sales, in Eighteenth Century terms, were unusual only in their size. For a variety of valid reasons it seemed very desirable to unload the apparently unwanted lands at any cost, no matter how low the price and how much conveniently the process was aided and oiled by the legislators. Moreover, the frontier with Canada was yet to be settled and our recent enemies — the British — were there and seemingly entertaining military designs against the thinly-settled northern section of the State. The recent Revolution had also saddled the Empire State with a debt burden of $1,167,575 — such a huge obligation that Gov. George Clinton hoped to pay off at least partly by state land sales.

The largest buyer of land in the Totten-Crossfield Purchase, the first huge tract sold, was nominally Alexander Macomb, who was apparently interested in almost all the lands included in the North, Northwest and Southwest sections of the mountainous region — a total of about 3,816,960 acres. His offer was eight pence or 16 cents an acre, two cents less than that for which other comparable land had brought official refusals. Nevertheless, the deal was made and immediately screams of "Graft" and "Corruption" rent the Albany and New York City skies. In spite of the justified outburst no one was ever prosecuted.

Although Macomb, who may have been only a front for William Constable, Daniel McCormick and others, was the only name on the transaction papers, he never had the opportunity to exploit the situation because still another of his schemes went sour; he was

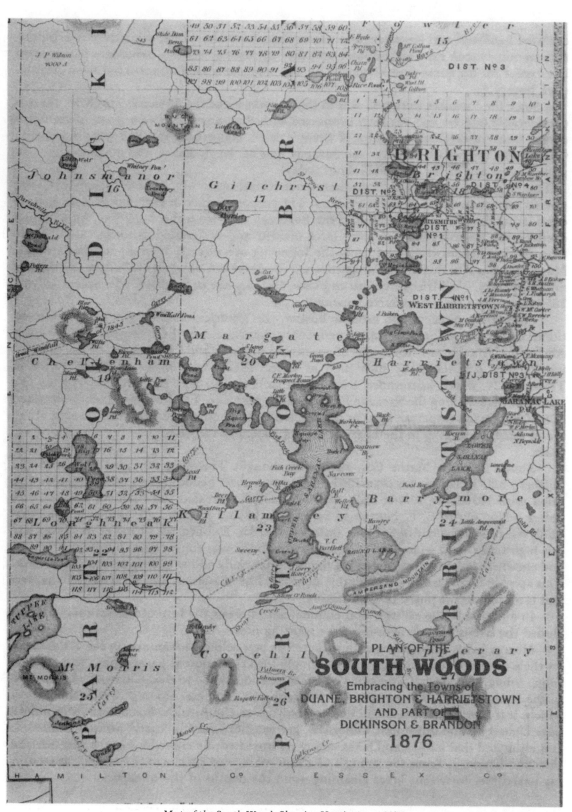

Map of the South Woods Showing Harrietstown 1876

declared bankrupt and imprisoned to protect him from the wrath of his victims. His partners seemingly took care of him later and they themselves made a handsome paper profit but except for his name forever placed on the map, he totally disappeared from Adirondack history.*

Since the Saranacs were well within the boundaries of the Macomb Purchase, there is considerable interest and curiosity connected with the names that were given to the towns carved from the original townships of Great Tract I, comprising 821,819 acres in Franklin County, the one which contains the Saranac and St. Regis Lakes, the most popular and populous section of the Adirondacks of today.

This huge tract was divided into twenty-one townships to which, besides numbers, were given a smorgasbord of fascinating names. The preponderance of Irish names is no surprise considering that all three involved in the Purchase were from the Auld Sod. Although all twenty-seven townships, which were later divided and designated as towns, are of more than passing historical interest, only the following are directly relevant to the Saranacs: Margate, a place in England; Harrietstown, a daughter of Constable; Killarney, Barrymore and Tipperary — all Irish of course and Cove Hill, a place in England. The accompanying 1858 map shows their respective locations. . . .

Beyond the physical and esthetic beauty, the historical and literary attributes mentioned by Longstreth and the purely mercenary connivances of the "Harpy Land Jobbers of Albany and Manhattan" there was of course the invasion and exploitation by the lumbering interests dominated by such men as Orson Richards, who in 1847 bought all of Township 24, which surrounded Lower Saranac Lake, to take full advantage of the law passed in 1846 making the Saranac River a public highway. The first drive, which consisted of 50,000 markets (separate logs) or ten million feet of lumber, marked the opening of the era of intensive logging in the heart of the Adirondacks and continued unabated for forty years.

About 1850 the Maine Co., of Boston, bought Township 20, which encircles the northern half of Upper Saranac Lake, and set up their headquarters where Saranac Inn stood until 1978. The Maine Mill, as it was called, operated full blast for several years before selling out to C. F. Norton of Saranac Lake and Plattsburgh, the man who eventually controlled the entire Saranac waterway system. Dubbed the "King of the Saranacs" this high-roller cut a wide swath not only through the vast timberlands but also in Albany and elsewhere before he overextended himself financially and would up a virtual bankrupt. This episode is covered in considerable detail in The Wawbeek and Saranac Inn chapters and is an important phase of area history.

In addition to the esthetic and commercial interests the lure of the Saranacs also included the irresistible attractions of the sporting life.

Murray in his extremely popular, therefore best-selling *Adventures in the Wilderness,* set the scene most compellingly and alluringly with these potent paragraphs: "On the very ridge — board of the vast watershed which slopes northward to the St. Lawrence, eastward to the Hudson, and southward to the Mohawk you can enter upon a voyage the likes of which, it is safe to say, the world does not anywhere else furnish. For hundreds of miles I have boated up and down that wilderness, going ashore only to "carry" around a fall. . . . It is estimated that a thousand lakes, many yet unvisited, lie embedded in the vast forest of pine and hemlock. From the summit of a mountain, two years ago, I counted, as seen by my naked eye, forty-four lakes gleaming amid the depths of the wilderness. . . .

---

*The Macomb Purchase was covered in much more detail in Chapter 13 of my *Heydays of the Adirondacks.*

Rev. William H. H. Murray (photo)

"And yet thousands are in Europe today as tourists who never gave a passing thought to this marvelous country lying as it were at their very door. . . ."

Even though Murray, as he himself insisted, did not actually start the headlong rush to the woods — that had been accelerating gradually over at least a decade — as a matter of fact he joined it and thereby sold thousands of his books: these most emphatically did not *discourage* anyone by his romantic picture of ease of travel and sporting pleasures. His N.Y. *Tribune* 10/23/1869 explanation and self-vindication is thoroughly logical and understandable: "Hundreds visited the region expecting to "do the wilderness" in a week or ten days at the most. The pace at which parties, composed of both sexes, have been pushed through the woods was appalling to old Adirondackers. Ladies, fresh from Saratoga, schoolgirls delicate and fragile, and even invalids were hurried from Martin's up to Blue Mountain Lake and back at a rate which would have endangered a divorce [that came later] in my family had I attempted it. And all this at the request and entreaties of the tourists themselves. Parties had only so many days to devote to the excursion, and their chief desire seemed to be to go as far and suffer as much as possible. Guides were charged by such people with laziness if they did not make their 30 or 40 miles a day, regardless of wind and weather, and abused because they had not made a better camp at night. . . . A guide is a very convenient scapegoat.

"A certain class of sportsmen are indignant because their sporting has been spoiled and the woods filled with people. To such I have only to reply that I am glad if the woods are filled with people and I trust that thousands will visit them yearly. . . . I do not look at the Wilderness as belonging to the sportsmen or any other class. Its magnificent mountains, its thousand lakes are for all. We sportsmen can go elsewhere for game." Bien dit!

The peripatetic Parson (Murray) was constantly forced to defend himself from such verbal blasts as this excerpt from an article by "Wachusett" in the *Boston Daily Advertiser* dated 7/1879 from Martin's on Lower Saranac:

"Mr. Murray's pen has bought a host of visitors into the Wilderness such as it has never seen before — consumptives craving pure air, dyspeptics wandering after appetites, sportsmen hitherto content with small game and few fish, weary workers hungering for perfect rest, ladies who thought that climbing the White Mountains the utmost possible achievement of feminine strength, journalists and lecturers of both sexes looking for fresh material come in parties of twos and dozens and make up in the aggregate a multitude which crowds the hotels and clamors for guides and threatens to turn the wilderness into a Saratoga of fashionable costliness."

Nevertheless, along with the guides Murray was bombarded with a burden of unreasonable reproach from poor sports and silly tourists. Even though his book was a mélange of practical hints enlivened with dollops of unadulterated Gothic phantasy, his tall-tale telling was no more balderdash than some of the concoctions of his fellow clergymen — Todd and Headley. In Murray as Charles Hallock, editor of *Forest and Stream* noted, "There was a toothsome flavor of fact."

To add a felicitous, almost serendipitous tone to the opus here's a pleasant passage from A. J. Northrup's *Camps and Tramps in the Adirondacks* (1880): Locale: The St. Germain, or Sanjemo (its corruption) Carry between Upper St. Regis and Big Clear Pond. "We were met here by a party of two gentlemen, two handsome ladies and three or four little children with their guides who were on their way from the Saranac to Paul's [Paul Smith's Caravansery]. It was a right merry party and they laughed and chatted and drank St. Germain's "pop-beer" [obviously Coca Cola and Pepsi were still fairly far in the future] with a charming air of confidence in its integrity — as delighted with everything as if they were en-

Moses St. Germain (Sanjemo)

An Up-to-Date Portage

joying a late lunch at Delmonico's. The last we saw of them they were setting off — ladies, children and all — on their two-mile walk over the country with light, tripping steps and the merriest laughter as if walking down the lawn at home, after tea, for a boat ride on the river. [Can't resist the temptation to comment about two missing elements — the apparently accommodating blackfly population and the convenient absence of liquid sunshine — alias rain — which can put a very effective damper on the dispositions of all but the most effervescent and incurable optimists.

Moreover, the Five, Seven or Nine Carries jaunt from Saranac Inn to Paul Smith's is unquestionably the easiest and most pleasant water and land passage in the northern Adirondacks.]

"This is not quite the sort of sunshine and romance one would be looking for on a carry, but it is precisely the thing not uncommon on these forest thoroughfares among the St. Regis and Saranac Waters — a region which has charms of its own for the gentler sex and all others who want to see the woods and waters in their primitive state — with "improvements." The sportsman is crowded every year into remoter regions; but there is room enough for him, and he ought not to begrudge some little portion of his realm to beauty and childhood. He must, however, heed the "move on!", which the increasing multitudes utter all along his favorite haunts. If he is a sensible, generous and gentle-hearted sportsman, he will not grumble at this and talk of "Murray's Fools," but will rejoice that it is possible for so many to share with him the forest and its benefits to health and heart. The unexplored wilderness is close at hand, and it is his if he will but seize it. Let the wife and children journey over, and enjoy the favorite old ways even if their presence frightens the deer to remoter regions and the trout are to be sought in more secluded haunts.

Paul Smith's, Lower St. Regis Lake in 1880's (Stoddard)

Guide House at Paul Smith's (Stoddard)

Guideboats Galore

"One of the prettiest pictures at Paul Smith's [Martin's, The Ampersand or the Wawbeek] is when after sunset, a dozen or a score of boats filled with ladies and children, push out onto the lake — each boat manned by a strong oarsman who knows how to row a genuine Adirondack guideboat with swiftness and handle it with safety. Indeed the commingling there of gaiety and sobriety, fashion and simplicity, sportsman's life and social life, excites constant interest in the mind of a looker-on in Venice" as I was. "Dolce far niente," sweet do-nothing at its very best!*

"This lake country is a network of rivers, ponds and lakes as far as we know unique in its character, offering to the summer tourists or sportsman a thousand miles of boating, varied by occasional land carries. This part of the Adirondacks is best known and oftenest visited, both by sportsman and pleasure-seeker. Its attractions are: being paddled [rowed mostly, the paddler is in the stern and steers] day after day, in a light boat, over waters embosomed in the silent woods, with occasional magnificent mountain views, and such added enjoyment as can be gained from camp-life and the very uncertain hunting and fishing.

"The draw-backs are: the exposure to the changeable summer climate, the misery of mosquitoes and blackflies in the woods and the crowning affliction — the extortions of hotel-keepers, guides, boatmen and the general riffraff of the wilderness. As there is only a watery highway through this paradise, only as expert can safely venture into it; the ordinary tourist is completely in the hands of this army of assistants. . . . The most moderate rate of expense considerably exceeds that of a first-class New York hotel.

"This is a state of transition; but while it lasts the charms of the Adirondack lake

---

*A far less euphoric viewpoint was taken by Amory D. Mayo in the *Unitarian Review* for Nov. 1875.

region are practically hidden to all but two classes — the wealthy and willing to disburse, and the sportsman prepared for labors and exposures more severe than those of an ordinary New York State farmer. . . .

"The huge crop of summer diseases that always follows the brigade of camping-out young ladyhood, to say nothing of the social side of this free life in the woods, is attracting the attention of the small class of old-fashioned mammas who still insist on knowing where their daughters are at in their vacation rambles." Prudish, a spoil-sport or just a man who really knew the score?

Charles E. Whitehead in the New York *Evening Post* 8/30/1858 added yet another unpleasant item to the litany of use and over-use of the few good campsites along the water-ways: "These portages, or carries as they are termed, form the great delay to quick or easy traveling in this country. . . . Where they do occur, there are usually to be found the re-mains of former campfires [stripped evergreen trees, burned-over areas etc], antlers of deer, bits of rope, broken bottles indicated the passage of other travelers. . . . and lest they be overlooked, the fore-runners have enshrined their names on some blazed tree. Curious records of men's taste for solitude and freedom! There are to be found Gov. Seymour's name, the poet Lowell, the artist Coleman and a few of the inevitable [ubiquitous] Browns and Joneses who would be unknown to fame even if heroes, so buried is their individuality in the species.

"There was a time when this place was unvisited except by the trapper. But alack and a-day! in the train of Gov. Seymour — and who wouldn't follow a governor? — came Tom and Dick with bottles of brandy, and George and Pete from college with volumes of Moore and Byron and, horrors of horrors to timid deer that abhor flaunting colors and merry

Lunch at Half-Way House

Modern Invasion of the Woods

laughs! There came Miss Murray, the Queen's waiting-maid and many other misses in Balmorals!"

Slobs and yahoos and visual and visible pollution — even then — 1858!

Yet another writer — Thaddeus Norris — added his tale of exasperation in this short excerpt from the *American Angler's Book in 1864:* "At the mouth of Ampersand Brook (a tributary of the Raquette River) our guides put our boats within easy cast of the best places and we thought we would have a good, quiet, lovely time. The trout were dimpling the water all around us and we had made a few successful casts when faint from further distance borne was heard the clang — of something like a tin canal horn. Looking up toward the head of Stony Creek Pond, a boat rounded the point, a flag flying at the bow, and two red-shirted "Boweryboy-fellows" in the middle of it, approached us, each flourishing an empty bottle and singing "Old Dan Tucker!"

Just one further final quote to round out this chapter — a mixed bag, a literary smorgasbord if there ever was one. It is/was a statement made by the deservedly renowned, frequent Adirondack visitor — author, artist, mystic, and the person responsible for the Philosophers' Camp on both Follensby and Ampersand Ponds in 1858 and 1859. Writing in his ill-fated literary publication *The Crayon* in September, 1855 he made these rather surprising comments and observations about the Lower Saranac Lake at a time when the entire region was supposedly well-nigh pristine and primitive [redundant I know but used for emphasis].

He had been delayed at Martin's and, in order to kill time, had mentioned to the owner that he would like to go fishing. Season being over, the bossman himself volunteered to take Stillman out. Here's Stillman's description of the desecration he saw as they moved down the Lower Saranac Lake, Lake of the 52 islands (if you count the protruding boulders), Lake of the Clustered Stars. "This lake has suffered much disfigurement from fires, which have burned over most of the islands and immense tracts on the mainland, leaving the trees dead and blackened, wringing their mutilated limbs against the sky or, when time had had a longer work, bare and white skeleton-like, while the rocks beneath, denuded of their drapery of moss and the scant soil which had accumulated droppings of the leaves of ages, and which gave rooting to shrubs and ferns innumerable and luxuriant, were grey and ashen in the morning sun when we passed by that day. Here and there white birches had sprung up in thickets and covered acres with a dense drapery of intense green, now just warming into golden yellow in places. This tree, quick of growth, seems to come first to recruit the mould, and thus give a place to the slower-growing trees, to which they yield when their brief existences are finished. And the pines and beeches, the maples and the hemlocks of the aftergrowth push their heads into the light and warmth. Then again the mosses and ferns, planted by some mysterious seeding, come and drape the rocks and cover all traces of the old devastation.

"Here were burnings of all dates. On some all was yet black and dead, on others the first few birches had struggled in, and on still others the pines had begun to protrude through the gay green of the birch thickets.

'Careless hunters,' Martin said, 'have built fires on the shore and neglected to put them out.' He cursed them bitterly and well he might because they have injured the beauty of the Lake beyond measure.

"The noblest pines have been rafted from the Saranacs these last half-dozen years." Fire and logging, the twin nemeses of the forestland everywhere! And to listen to the descendants of some of those careless guides claim that all their ancestors were true-blue conservationists long before the term became either cursed or applauded — stalwart lovers

Anglers' Camp in the Forest — Discussing the Catch

28

Venison for Supper

and staunch protectors of their great wilderness heritage! Malarkey!!

Furthermore, it wasn't only the dim-witted Saranac guides who were extremely careless with fire: the 1903 holocaust that destroyed Henry Van Hoevenberg's palatial Adirondack Lodge was directly traceable to stump-burning and timber-clearing activities at Wood's Farm, only a few miles east, and Ben Brewster's heedless and deliberate incendiary projects on Bear Cub Road farther west in North Elba. Incidentally, the South Meadows prong of that same conflagration was also attributable to land-clearing chores.

A further example of the old-timers' characteristic carelessness with matches can be pinned on Orson (Old Mt.) Phelps of Keene Valley who, with Charles Dudley Warner in tow, abandoned a campfire which destroyed ten or fifteen shoreland acres at Clear now known as Heart Lake.

Early issues of the famed *Forest and Stream* magazine carried recurring comments on pollution and the desecration all along the hundred and more miles between Old Forge and the Saranacs. That's one aspect of the so-called "good old days" that most emphatically wasn't all that good. . . .

In this chapter probably the most potent allure of all has been almost entirely omitted for the very obvious reason that coverage of such a broad-gauged topic would have necessitated the exclusion of much of the lesser aspects of vacation delights. The hunting and fishing adventures and misadventures were delineated almost ad nauseum by Hoffman, Lanman, Headley, Street, Chittenden, Hammond, Northrop — and of course Murray and his spoofer, Charles D. Warner. For that reason the less gory and more anemic highlights of summer travel are featured.

As an ex-hunter and present wildlife watcher, I derived much vicarious pleasure from such accounts away back when, but enough can often become more than sufficient. One man's meat is indeed another man's poison and of course there's really no accounting for tastes. Whatever, over the many years since the 1830's the area has exerted an attraction almost tantamount to a compulsion for the thousands who then, and even more-so nowadays, seek — and find — their own special kind of wilderness experience in this incomparable, storied region of the Saranacs.

Chapter 2

Martin's, Later Miller's, Saranac Lake House

In his much maligned but nevertheless amusingly imaginative and history-making *Adventures in the Wilderness,* published in 1869, the Rev. W. H. H. Murray listed only five so-called hotels along the unusually scenic water passage extending from Paul Smith's on the St. Regis chain nearly 45 miles to Uncle Palmer's on Long Lake. For reasons known only to the flamboyant preacher he left out Hough's Prospect House (later Saranac Inn), built in 1864 and Corey's Rustic Lodge (1850) on either end of Upper Saranac Lake and both on direct route south.

Those Murray did mention besides Pol's (Apollos, Paul) place, built in 1859, were Martin's on Lower Saranac (c. 1850), Bartlett's on the Saranac River between Middle Saranac (Round Lake) and the Upper Lake, built in 1854; Mother Johnson's (originally a loggers' camp c. 1850) and Palmer's (date unknown) on Long Lake.

Smith's and Martin's establishments were by far the most convenient, most fashionable and most publicized. Never known as being sparing with words Parson Murray, credited in the same bracket with Stoddard and Colvin as the men mainly responsible for popularizing the Adirondacks, composed a rather fetching commercial for both the hostelry and its owner:

"Martin's is located on Lower Saranac Lake and is the terminus of the stage route from Keeseville, (close to Port Kent, steamboat stop on Lake Champlain). It is, therefore, the most convenient point at which to meet your guides. Its appointments are thorough and complete. Martin is one of the few men in the world who seem to know how to keep a hotel. At his house you can easily and cheaply obtain your entire outfit for a trip of any length. Here it is that the celebrated Long Lake guides with their unrivaled boats [the Rev. was very partial to "Honest John" Plumley, a Long Laker] principally resort. Here too, many of the Saranac guides, some of them surpassed by none, make their headquarters. Mr. Martin, as a host, is good-natured and gentlemanly. His table is abundantly provided, not only with the necessaries but also with many of the luxuries of diet.

"The charges are moderate and the accommodations for families, as well as for sporting parties, are in every respect ample. Martin's is a favorite resort to all who have ever once visited it, and stands deservedly high in public estimation."

Wallace, in the 1875 edition of his *Guide to the Adirondacks,* the best (most complete) such book ever compiled, updated Murray and contributed many other complementary and complimentary flourishes:

"Martin's," one of the far-famed gateways to the Wilderness, is a most desirable tarrying place for all in quest of health or sporting recreation. The house has recently been greatly enlarged and now affords apartments for 250 guests. The parlors are 64 ft. and the dining hall 84 ft. in length. The rooms are generally large and airy, and are furnished with taste and neatness, and while occupying them one can enjoy most of the comforts of the St. Nicholas or Fifth Ave. (N.Y.C.) here together with all the rare and dainty viands the region

Lower Saranac Lake. Wood Engraving by Harry Fenn

yields, and at the same time command an exquisite view of the varied beauties that lake, mountain and forest ever give.

"For the interest of ladies we will say that the fine croquet ground connected with the premises will afford them agreeable diversion when weary of boating. Stages arrive and depart daily and triweekly for Paul Smith's, Hough's (Saranac Inn), Point of Rocks (the old terminus of the railroad before it came to Ausable Forks), North Elba [no Lake Placid village then], Wilmington Notch, Keene, Elizabethtown and Westport. Mail and telegraphic communications are complete; parties, including a goodly sprinkling of ladies, assemble here in large numbers during the Summer months, some of whom make Martin's their headquarters, while others proceed to Bartlett's, Corey's, Moody's [Big Tupper] and Grave's [now American Legion Camp]. Dukett's [Hiawatha Lodge on Stony Creek Ponds], Kellogg's [Long Lake] Cary's [Forked Lake] or to camp on some of the many delightful ponds and lakes that form a vast network in this romantic wilderness. Martin furnishes the sportsman with a complete outfit, comprising boats, guides, tents, and all the requisites of camp life; as do also all the hotels above noted.

"Some 22 or 23 years ago Mr. Martin located here at the head of this charming bay [Ampersand]. The spot at that time was entirely wild, but he has lived to see the forest immediately around him "blossom like the rose." He is a thorough sportsman as well as a landlord, and can throw a fly or secure a deer with a skill equal to that of the most finished disciple of Izaak Walton or the fabled Nimrod."

Some, however, were not totally or even partly charmed. One of these, a correspondent for a Boston paper* whose sobriquet was Wachusett, expressed his dissatisfaction in words somewhat reminiscent of Dr. J. P. Lundy's more pungent sarcasm in *Saranac Exiles:*

---

*Boston Daily Advertiser, July 17 and 19, 1869

"When you quit your wagon at the door of Martin's, lame, soiled and hungry as you are, the chances are ten to one that you postpone the sofa, the supper table and the washbasin that you may catch the extended hand of the hospitable proprietor of the inn and selfishly strive to get ahead of the occupants of the next team by whispering eagerly in his ear, "How about a guide?"

"Perhaps you have written to Mr. Martin a month in advance to serve you in this respect; perhaps you have come in trusting to luck. In either case the answer is the same: 'You will have to wait! — there are some people in the house who have waited several days already and who must be supplied ahead of you. But guides are coming in every day, and the delay will probably not be long. Meanwhile, there is excellent fishing in the neighborhood and everything will be done to make the time pass pleasantly'. . . .

"As you mingle with the guests of the inn, you discover that one thought is dominant with all. People collect into knots to talk over their chances of getting guides; they form combinations to secure the desired end; they watch each other jealously to see that no individual gets an unfair advantage; they stand guard on the pier to catch the first glimpse of an incoming boat; they make furtive expeditions up the Lake on the dim chance of catching a disengaged guide coming down. Arrivals at first indifferent catch the fever, as sober people at Baden get infected with the passion of the place for gambling. One would think that Mr. Martin's pleasant hostelry was a prison-house by the eagerness of its inmates to secure the means of getting away.

"If it were a simple question of four times as many tourists wanting guides as there are guides open to engagement, and the lists long since closed, there would be room only for despair and none for excitement in the pursuit. But there are other elements to the problem. Mr. Martin himself has about forty guides in his employment, and there is no more certainty when any of them will come in than into what number the ball on the roulette board will come to a stop. Parties who go off for four weeks will come back after three days, moaning about the blackflies or some other annoyance, and throw their guides upon the market. Parties who have engaged six guides for a certain day will arrive in diminished numbers and only want four, releasing the surplus men to be snapped up by those in waiting. And, on the other hand, parties once off for the woods will overstay their time, throwing the most elaborately arranged slate into confusion. Once away from Martin's wharf there is no communication. No telegrams nor letter can send a summons or an inquiry; nor can a messenger find a particular party in the vast expanse of lake and woods much more easily than a hunter can find a particular deer. Thus there are all the elements of an exciting chase in search of guides, and the people at the hotels enter into it with a zest which they will not feel for the pursuit of deer or trout. . . .

"I have spoken of the prevalence of the mosquitoes. With these must be included the blackflies. Either these insects have not read Mr. Murray's book; or they have mislaid their almanac; or, what is probably more probable, the lateness and wetness of the season has prolonged their term of life; for certainly the first week in July finds them here in undiminished numbers. Mr. Murray makes light of these insect pests; and from my own experience I shall not venture to contradict him; but I can simply tell what I have seen and heard. I have seen parties hurrying back to the haunts of men from camps which they had sought but a few days before with high hopes of pleasure, but driven away solely and simply by the infuriating insects.

"I have heard of a gentleman — a sportsman and journalist, who came into the woods for a long stay, bringing four hundred pounds of baggage, and who discharged his guide after five days and sped back to the city to tell how a reverend author had gulled him and the public. I have seen a gentleman so disfigured by mosquitoes that he sought a resting place where his bites might heal before he would present himself to his friends. I have known those temporarily deprived of sight and hearing by mosquito bites. I have been told by these sufferers that they used every ointment prescribed by guide or apothecary and had resorted to every variety of net for the head, window and lodge front without the least relief. I have seen people going through lovely scenery with heads muffled up, like those of the assassination [Lincoln's] conspirators in the Washington prison, and yet the faces thus enveloped were covered with mosquito bites!

"And yet it seems to me that Murray is in the right when he asserts the possibility, by proper management, of avoiding and defying the stingers and biters. There are some people so physically constituted that the bite of a mosquito is as serious a matter to them as the sting of a scorpion. These people should never come into the woods; or, having unwisely come, they should hasten away as soon as their tenderness of skin and blood is discovered. But the majority of people can get along without serious inconvenience. . . .

"In the chronic habit of grumbling which the famine of guides and the surfeit of mosquitoes has created at Martin's, growls are aimed at the sporting, and indeed it is not to be wondered at that some discontent is generated by the condition of things in this respect at the outer edge of the wilderness. The deer, with all their foolishness, have learned not to venture into the neighborhood of Lower Saranac Lake and venison is about as rare there as it is in Boston. One hears of good fishing, but one sees only gentlemen going out laboriously for all day and returning half-ashamed of a scanty string of little four-inch trout such as they would have thrown contemptuously back into the water had any larger fish risen to their flies. . . ."

"With the sportsmen there mingles this year a larger proportion than ever before of invalids attracted here by the reports of marvelous healing properties in the air, of especial benefit in case of lung diseases. The great majority of these people derive invaluable benefit from their visit because the great majority are those who come in time, in the first stages of a malady at first capable of cure. The singular sweetness of the air is apparent to all.

"But there is another class who come here this Summer equally filled with hope of thorough recovery who find nothing but the bitterest disappointment, bringing perhaps an accelerated death in its train. These are the consumptives in the later stages who have tried everything else in vain. It is the saddest of sights to see some of these sufferers arrested in the forest by the coming of death, the comforts with which home would surround him absolutely unattainable by any expenditure of money, no means at hand of summoning friends, no physicians to be found, even departure by the route of entrance impossible now that the stimulus of hope has been withdrawn. . . .

"The table at one of the hotels the other day was greatly entertained by the torrent of indignation poured forth by a lady who considered that she had been induced to come into the Adirondacks on false pretences, and promised to 'show up Mr. Murray in the New York *Herald.*' But I cannot join this crusade. I think there is no lady who could not heartily enjoy the tranquil row from Martin's to Bartlett's, comfortably established in a light boat, conscious of the becoming novelty of a Highland costume with natty boots and red stockings, graceful sash and jaunty cap, and the unaccustomed but fascinating ornaments of pearl-handled pistols, a glittering hunting knife, and a chased silver drinking cup hung about the waist, with a coquettish ivory whistle suspended from the neck.

"But I think I have known ladies who would not enjoy, even in the same array, crossing a carry in a rainstorm, face and hands dripping with tar and oil, mosquito bites smarting and the boots soaked through and through, the reserved stockings in the carpet bag equally

The Saranac Stage (Stoddard)

Martin's, Later Miller's on Lower Saranac Lake (Stoddard)

wet, guide and escort so loaded with bag and baggage as to be incapable of rendering assistance, and a slippery log tempting to tumble into a shallow pool with a muddy bottom. Ladies who can pass such an ordeal without a loss of temper which would make all its evils tenfold worse — can safely make their plans for the Adirondacks."

These excerpts from Wachusett's articles, while admittedly somewhat lengthier than such quotes usually are, nevertheless certainly "Tell it like it is — was," as our obnoxious friend, H. Cosell, would say. In my frankly biased opinion these superbly written segments represent just about the best ever written about the Adirondacks region as it was a century plus a decade ago.

The "Murray Rush," triggered by that controversial landmark book, caught the region unprepared and caused all kinds of regrettable incidents and accidents not only at Martin's but also at Paul Smith's as well. People accustomed to Saratoga and Lake George and their luxurious accommodations were understandably disappointed, dismayed and frequently disgusted by what they found at the fringes of the wilderness.

Ten years later things were much different in every respect — except for an even more noticeable absence of deer and trout within reasonable travel distance from the hotels. Such sections had been literally hunted out and fished out by market hunters but potential Adirondack visitors by then had been given a far more muted and much less hyped understanding of just what to expect in the Lakes country.

At this point it has been convincingly established that by 1870 there was a flourishing hotel at the north end of Lower Saranac Lake, but what about the man responsible for bringing it into being? Since the logical and chronological place to start is at the beginning, William Fortune Martin's father (same first name) from England, lived for awhile in Connecticut, married there and moved to Westville, a suburb of Malone; from there the family

Martin's, Later Miller's from the West Shore (Stoddard)

William F. Martin

Mary H. (Mrs. Ferd) Chase

went to Bangor, where his parents later died. Not content with life on the farm the venturesome William and his two tall and powerful brothers — Henry and Stephen — came to the backwoods settlement of Saranac Lake in 1849. Lundy's "miserable little hamlet" at that time had about a dozen houses scattered along the primitive Northwest Bay (or Old Military Road), which led from Westport on Lake Champlain to Hopkinton in St. Lawrence County.

In the late 1840's Capt. Pliny Miller, who had arrived in Saranac Lake about 1822, built a small hotel opposite his sawmill; the site is now occupied by the village office building. Miller leased the modest inn from 1849 to 1850 to Martin. For the next two years it provided Virgil Bartlett, another hotel pioneer, who rates a chapter of his own, with hotel management experience.

Both Martin and Bartlett were readily convinced that the area had a definite future as a recreational resort. Having seen and talked with the occasional city sportsman who stopped off there, they were confident that if good food and comfortable accommodations were provided, the better-heeled outlanders and their families would flock to the mountain and lake country.

Before the year was over Martin had bought a choice tract of land on the Lower Lake and began to build the first hotel in the Adirondacks designed to attract the leisure class. The first stage of the project was low and L-shaped but eventually enlarged and raised to three stories and a mansard roof. Still later another large addition was constructed over the road and forming a tunnel which became the famous "hole in the house," the lounging place for guests and guides.

The place prospered from the start and many of the patrons came back year after year. Moreover, most of them became staunch friends, entertained the Martins in their city homes and treated them as honored guests.

The most tragic incident in the life of the family occurred in March 1862 when Laura, their 11 year-old daughter became seriously ill. It had been an exceptionally severe winter

37

Loon Lake House in Its Heyday — 1925

and a raging blizzard made travel hazardous and well-nigh impossible. Nevertheless, as the child's condition was deteriorating rapidly, Martin hitched up his best horse to his pung, a homemade box-sleigh, tossed in an axe and a shovel and headed for the nearest doctor — Romeyn of Keeseville — 45 miles away.

Hacking his way through drifts sometimes 12 feet high and getting help from neighbors along the route, he finally covered the seemingly endless distance to his destination, where he located the doctor, replaced his exhausted horse and started back to Saranac Lake. The homeward trip was far less formidable but their combined efforts were futile because the little girl had died only fifteen minutes before their arrival. The mother, the first Mrs. Martin — Laura Hunkins — never recovered from the shock; she died August 13, 1864.

Like Mary Howe Chase, the wife of Ferd and the one mainly responsible for the success of the Loon Lake House; Lydia Martin Smith, wife of Paul Smith and Caroline Greene, Virge Bartlett's life partner, both the wives (he married Sarah Lamson in 1865) of William Martin were remarkably pleasant, tactful and competent managers. Furthermore, all three husbands willingly acknowledged their spouses' contributions.

After his daughter's death, which the father felt was due to the remoteness from medical help, Martin, always an omnivorous reader, decided to learn as much basic medicine as possible in order to prevent similar tragedies. This program was supplemented by the experienced advice of several of the physicians — particularly Dr. J. Savage Delavan* of Albany — who considered Martin to be a very quick learner. Within a short

---

*Dr. Delavan, on 8/8/85 met a tragic fate in the waters of Big Tupper Lake; while on a trip with his wife and guide, he stood up in the guideboat to shoot a hawk. The recoil of the shotgun caused him to lose his balance and capsize the boat. His wife, tangled in the mesh of fishing tackle managed to right the boat and save herself, but her husband and guide, A. C. Clark, were drowned.

time his services were sought and given free to many from the village and nearby logging camps.

Although Martin was a very intelligent man he was anything but money-minded and lacked business sense. Always happy-go-lucky and an "indefatigable optimist" he, like Mr. Micawber, always expected that everything would turn out right even when his financial condition was shaky. Even though his hotel was popular and apparently successful he died a poor man. Mainly because of his generosity, trustfulness and honesty — characteristics not reciprocated by his debtors — early in 1881, as a result of a mortgage foreclosure, Martin lost his hotel and under ironic circumstances. The mortgage holder was Silas Arnold of Keeseville, a regular guest and close friend of Martin. Elisha, his eccentric son, was a different breed of cat, and promptly started proceedings to recover the fairly small amount even though the distraught Martin assured him that the required money was on its way. The mails were delayed, the sale of the property went on as scheduled and Martin's became Miller's Saranac Lake House, when Milo B. Miller bought it.

Having lost the fruits of his lifetime's labors Martin decided to try once again and built the Edgewood, a smaller place, nearby. However, things were never the same and in spite of temporary success it was a losing struggle. His health failed appreciably along with the declining business and on October 3, 1892 he died.

Although Miller, the new owner, made many expensive improvements and alterations — including converting the "hole in the house" into a lavish office, the far-famed old hotel was apparently jinxed. In March 1888 the main building was totally destroyed by fire. The large guidehouse, which had thirty bedrooms was saved and used for hotel purposes, but it too went up in smoke and flames nine years later (1897).

Thus passed into history what was in its day the oldest, finest and most spacious hotel in the Adirondacks — Martin's on Ampersand Bay of Lower Saranac Lake.

Ampersand Hotel, Lower Saranac Lake (Stoddard)

View South from Ampersand Porch — Miller's Hotel Opposite (Stoddard)

Chapter 3

The Ampersand Hotel

There were three hotels on Ampersand Bay of the Lower Lake and their locations formed a rough right triangle. Martin's (later Miller's) main building, which burned in 1888, was located on the east shore and represented one corner of the base. On the same shore, less than a mile south and on the site now occupied by the Trudeau Institute was the Algonquin, originally the Alexander House. Directly opposite Martin's and diagonally across the narrow Bay from the Algonquin was the most luxurious and last built of the three — the Ampersand, so named probably because of its distant view of Ampersand mountain.

Constructed in 1888 for year-round occupancy it attracted many of Martin's/Miller's former guests as well as many others who sought deluxe accommodations.

Wallace's Guide to the Adirondacks, 1894 edition, supplied the following ecstatic description of the famous hotel and its array of facilities. "On the sloping heights at the northern end of Lower Saranac, nestling in the foliage of the sweet-scented pine, balsam and hemlock, brightened by the sugar maple and the silver birch, stands Hotel Ampersand, the "Queen of the Trossachs." This grand establishment is elevated 50 feet above the water and commands a magnificent view of this island-gemmed inland sea with the adjacent mountains, whose most conspicuous figure is the stately tower* from which the house got its name.

"From the spacious piazzas in the Summer time a delightfully animated scene may be witnessed. The surface of the lake is then dotted with every variety of small craft from the swift steam-launch glittering with gay colors and the flying white-winged yacht, to the graceful little shallop [guideboat] peculiar to the Adirondack waters.

"This hotel is provided with all the appliances of a modern resort. Among the adjuncts are elevator; electric bells; steam heat; gas illumination; two large fireplaces in the main office; fireplaces in about 60 of the apartments; general bathrooms; many private bathrooms; reading, writing and cardrooms; men's and ladies' billiard parlors; ladies' writing-room; elegant public and private dining rooms; barbershop; guiderooms; sumptuous parlors; luxurious equipment; broad verandas extending the length and width of the house; several commodious cottages; a large annex building for athletic and amusement purposes; a general store furnishing complete camping outfits; telephone; telegraph and post office — Ampersand, N.Y.

"The cuisine and service are unexcelled. From the Ampersand farm the usual supplies are obtained and every delicacy attainable in the markets of the great cities will be found on the table. Pure water and thorough sanitary arrangements are included in the appurtenances. Music every afternoon and evening is furnished by a select orchestra.

"The beautifully ornamented and park-like grounds present a combination of lake-

---

* Removed in 1978. See "The Hermit of Ampersand" chapter for more on this much-visited mountain and its tower.

side and woodland charms not often surpassed. There, various means of diversion are offered, including games on the ballfield and lawn tennis court, and delectable wanderings under the trees, where at convenient intervals comfortable seats in the leafy shade will be found.

"Many delightful excursions by boat or carriage may be made in the neighborhood. Hotel Ampersand has already become famous as a Winter resort, especially for those afflicted with consumptive tendencies. In that season of the year the verandas are enclosed in glass. Its faultless management has won the highest encomium of its numerous patrons. Upon the whole, this is doubtless one of the more important and palatial of all the mountain hostelries, and is as complete as the most exacting could demand. It receives 300 guests.

"Tally-ho coaches connect with every train at Saranac Lake Village 1 mile East. Fare 50 cents."

Now that is what could correctly be called the Good Housekeeping stamp of approval — and then some!

From Stoddard's *The Adirondacks Illustrated,* 1900 edition, come these other items of information: "The Saranac Hotel Co. proprietors, and C. M. Eaton, the manager. Rates $4.00 per day and upwards. For special rates address the manager."

This posh place saw many prosperous seasons but, like all resort hotels, also experienced some lean years as well when the weather was unfavorable and reservations were cancelled. Like all businesses dependent almost entirely on the sun's munificence, such setbacks had a devastating impact upon the area economy because unless there was a full house many employees who relied on that source of vital income were suddenly unemployed. Moreover, the management which had to spend a great deal of money for supplies in anticipation of a banner season found themselves in financial trouble or worse — possible bankruptcy.

All too often large vacation resort owners, who might be financed soundly enough to weather one unprofitable season, suddenly realized that they were feeding a very large white elephant — and took the obvious way out.

Since it is so difficult to prove, the arson route has undoubtedly been taken by many desperate proprietors who are understandably desirous of salvaging at least part of their bank accounts. Many fine old hotels, Loon Lake House for example, went up in flames under extremely suspicious circumstances shortly after the place had closed at the end of the 1956 season. How many others met the same fiery fate is a matter of pure speculation, but there is not too much doubt about what happened to the Ampersand.

On the night of September 23, 1907 that hotel was torched and completely destroyed by the flames. When the word was spread that the fire was raging, crowds of villagers converged on the scene. Those with boats got as close to the conflagration as was safely possible, while others sat or stood on the opposite shoreline to take in the spectacle. People who were there that night said that a circus atmosphere prevailed and that it was the entertainment high point of that year.

Since the season had just closed, there were no guests in the hotel when it burned. Some of the cottages escaped the flames and were, like the Greenough House and cottages, able to stay in business for years afterward.

The Saranac Lake local paper dated 3/2/08 contained some interesting information about the Ampersand incendiary incident. Apparently copied from a N.Y.C. newspaper it featured the following headlines and article:

Hired to Burn Ampersand

Hotel Ampersand Office (Stoddard)

Hotel Ampersand Parlor (Stoddard)

Tent of Tubercular Guest at Ampersand Hotel (Stoddard)

Two Prisoners in Alleged Insurance Plot

"Two men arrested on Saturday and remanded in Court yesterday to Police Headquarters are accused of having conspired with others to burn Ampersand Hotel on 9/23/07.

Prisoners, according to Inspector McCafferty, claim that they and the partners not yet apprehended engineered the burning on "behalf of a man who is a member of the hotel organization who said the place must go because it was losing money."

Arrested were Herman Vanderwell, chiropodist at 978 E. 169th St., formerly of the Hotel Plaza, and Vanderwell's son-in-law, Morris Newmark, a clerk at 126 W. 136th St. Complainant is W. J. Green, insurance agent at 46 Cedar St. Vanderwell was captured at 42nd St. and 6th Ave. and Newmark at 334 Broadway by Detectives Van Twistern, Mc-Cormick and Butts. Magistrate Droege signed warrants. Brought in ignorant of each other's arrest prisoners at first claimed that they knew nothing about the hotel and its destruction but Newmark suddenly opened up [became garrulous]. Sometime before the fire his father-in-law broached chance of making some easy money. "There's a hotel up there is Saranac Lake that must come down" is the way he put it.

"Down?" asked Newmark. Vanderwell replied, "Yes, torn down or burned down some way and there's $500.00 in it for you."

In a saloon on 106th St. near Madison Ave. Newmark found two men willing to do the job for $100.00 apiece and expenses both ways. Contact was then made with Vanderwell and at that point Newmark dropped out of the story. Negotiations continued and date set for September 21. Two days prior Vanderwell saw hirelings at 125th Street Station on New York Central, bought their tickets and advanced $100.00 each for 'trouble' and $25.00 each expense money.

All said farewell with utmost assurance that Vanderwell would soon hear from them.

According to the police, stooges then went to the ticket counter and tried to redeem the tickets but the agent refused to oblige.

Thereupon the two men, confident of their employer's silence, decided to bring suit against the Railroad and saw a lawyer in re same. Moreover, they spilled the whole beans about the plot to burn down the "$100,000 hotel — The Ampersand."

Lawyer contacted the Board of Fire Underwriters of whom W. J. Green is a member. Letter complained to Magistrate Droege and warrants were issued. Investigators were then assigned — best men available."

While all the evidence was and is unavailable one fact remained: the hotel did burn and the owners involved in prolonged litigation to collect the $100,000 insurance coverage. A final decision — in favor of the hotel company — was not reached until April 1914, nearly seven years after the fire.

In 1920 the property, comprising 450 acres, was sold by C. M. Eaton, who had owned it for 33 years, to S. D. Matthews.

Subsequently the property was acquired by the Little family who, using as the nucleus the largest building that survived the fire, operated a cottage colony for the next several decades.

So, two out of the three Lower Lake hotels passed out of existence and into virtual oblivion. The third, The Algonquin, had a more ordinary lifespan.

Chapter 4

The Algonquin Hotel

The third of the three hotels on Lower Saranac Lake was located at the apex of the right triangle of which Martin's and The Ampersand formed the base. The hypotenuse was the diagonal across the water of Ampersand Bay. Built in 1884 by Jabez D. Alexander of Vermontville on the bluff overlooking the widest part of the Lower Lake, it offered a vista of great breadth and beauty and featured, in the foreground, Eagle and the Sisters islands. Alexander and his son Percy sold the hotel, originally named after them, and moved to Tupper Lake, where they built and operated the Waukesha, later owned for a short time by Mart Moody.

John Harding, the new owner, bought the place in 1890 and changed its name to The Algonquin. Harding, who had learned the hotel business thoroughly from long experience first at Paul Smith's and later at The Ampersand, made it one of the most popular resorts in the mountains.

E. R. Wallace's *Descriptive Guide to the Adirondacks* has this to say, in the 1894 edition, about the hotel: "The Algonquin is delightfully situated on an eminence half a mile south of the Saranac Lake House (Martin's, later Miller's), commanding a noble view of lake, forest and mountain scenery. This fine hotel is replete with modern conveniences. Large, high and well-ventilated rooms, appropriately furnished; electric bells; open fireplaces; spacious balconies, pure spring water; large wall tents, with carpeted floors, conveniently near; and the best of sanitary arrangements are among its desirable features.

"The table in all its details deserves the highest praise. The connecting farm furnishes abundantly the choicest dairy and vegetable supplies. The grounds, with a grand waterfront of three-fourths of a mile, embraces many acres of verdant lawn, interspersed with flowers and shrubbery and prettily fringed with evergreen trees. Among the various amusements afforded should be named croquet, lawn tennis, boating, and rambles on the ground and through the surrounding woods. Orchestral music for dancing is furnished tri-weekly. The hotel livery offers every suitable conveyance for riding.

"The proprietor, John Harding, was an apt pupil of the great master, Paul Smith, and prides himself on his ability to provide for the wants of sportsmen and the travelling public. The Algonquin's four-horse stagecoaches meet all trains at the station, one and three-quarters miles distant. Fare 50 cents. Telegraph and post office in the hotel."

Early in 1913 the hotel was leased to a syndicate which converted it into a sanitarium. The new owners were exploiting a much bally-hooed cure for tuberculosis based on turtle serum. The discoverer — Dr. Friedman of Berlin — created a sensation among medicos and started a raging warfare of words. The controversial German and his brother came to this country and sold the bottling rights to his nostrum to a gullible American company, which rented The Algonquin and promoted it as "The Lower Saranac Lake Health Resort."

As could be expected the quackery was soon exposed and the ill-advised scheme died

The Alexander, Later Algonquin House

an early death because, on January 21, 1914, the curtain rang down on the con operation.

Harding resumed operation but, at that period in his busy career, he established other priorities so the hotel had several other managers before its sale in 1920 to William N. Hanes, owner of the Winston-Salem, N.C. textile firm.

Hanes, who had been curing in Saranac Lake, owned a camp not far from the Algonquin. Whether he saw it — the hotel — as an investment possibility or as its being an intolerably noisy neighbor, he broke the news of its purchase to his wife in a rather amusing way. Mrs. Charles C. Harris, during an interview, provided the details. Hanes went home one evening and casually remarked to his wife, "I bought a camp today. As a matter of fact I bought two. And for that matter I also bought a hotel!"

Apparently Hanes did not want to be bothered with the management routine and, when he found that he would have to be involved, decided to call it quits. The famous old hotel closed its doors later that year — 1920 — and became just another part of the local legend and the playground for area youths.

Eleanor Rice Stearns, who lived nearby, told me that the abandoned landmark was like a magnet — the thick carpets, its rickety cupola room, the kitchen equipment still in place, keys in the slots behind the front office desk, and seemingly everything ready to start up again on short notice. Vandalism of course changed that considerably over the years until about 1957, when the contents were auctioned off that August and the buildings demolished.

Adirondack Pioneers, a scarce pamphlet written by John H. Titus of Bloomingdale and published in 1899, provides additional information about the many-sided John Harding, who was born in Prescott, Ontario, October 19, 1862 and went to Paul Smith's in 1878 where he worked as telegraph operator before becoming head clerk and assistant manager. In 1888 he went to the newly-opened Ampersand, where he stayed until 1890, at which time he bought out the Alexanders.

Harding also was very active in local politics and government and was mayor of Saranac Lake for several terms. Moreover, he headed a regional division of the New York State Conservation Department for a number of years. *After selling the Algonquin, Har-

---

* * After selling the Algonquin he also managed the Berkeley Hotel in the village before buying the Van Ness and the Vermont

46

ding bought the Van Ness and the Vermont, two leading Burlington, Vermont hotels and closed out his career in that city.

"Jack" Harding, according to Titus, was very fond of jokes and, while still at Paul Smith's, was credited with this one: "It was coach-time during the peak of a busy season. All the rooms were full when the loaded stagecoach pulled up and, of course, all the fatigued and famished occupants were eager to sign in and be given their rooms. They crowded up to the desk and demanded immediate service. Harding was trying his best to oblige them when a young guide walked behind the counter, touched him on the shoulder and said, 'Say Jack, can you tell me where I can get an axe?'

"'Yes,' said Jack, somewhat menacingly, 'I just used one in the parlor and left it on the piano!'" That somewhat gruesome and evocative remark intimidated the new arrivals and gave Harding all the time he needed to handle the situation properly.

My friend Watson Harding, a retired U.S. Rubber official, of Wykoff, N.J. supplied the following recollections of the days when his father owned and managed the renowned hotel: "It was a four-story, rectangular structure with wide verandas on the front and one side facing the Lower Lake; with its two cottages it accommodated about 100 guests. The rooms had no private baths but each floor was provided with three bathrooms.

"Specimens of wild animals were on the office walls, and over the dining room fireplace were mounted local birds, a wildcat, and elk and moose heads. Many pictures of Adirondack scenes were displayed on the walls. One of my jobs was cancelling the stamps of the outgoing besides stamping and sorting the incoming mail. Our private telegraph line was an important method of communication those days.

"When I was very young our four-horse tally-ho met the morning and evening trains at the Saranac Lake railroad station. Many times I went along just for the ride on the seat beside the driver.

The Algonquin from the East (Stoddard)

John Harding

"It seems incredible that, in the early 1900's, a guest could stay at the Algonquin on the American plan of room and meals for $21.00 a week. But it must be remembered that waitresses received $3.00 per week wages — plus tips of course — and all other costs were in proportion. The breakfast menu included tenderloin and sirloin steak, lamb-chops, bacon, eggs and broiled Spring chicken. On Sundays there were also all kinds of freshly baked hot breads and pancakes with maple syrup. Syrup sold then for 85 cents a gallon [1979 price: about $16.00].

"My father learned the hotel business at Paul Smith's, the most famous [along with Loon Lake House and Saranac Inn — all three in Franklin County] of the Adirondack resorts. He insisted on excellent food, service and all other factors. No waitress for instance, was ever permitted to serve guests until she had been trained at our, the family, table. At dinner the headwaiter wore a tuxedo. My father practiced, as did others, some discrimination with respect to the guests he would entertain. Many of them were families who came for the entire Summer, from all over the eastern United States; some from as far west as Chicago and as far south as Atlanta.

"Father hired cooks through a New York City employment agency. They included a meat cook, one responsible for vegetables, a baker and a head chef. They were usually German or French. Sometimes we were fortunate enough to hire good ones who stayed for two or three years. Others lasted only long enough to assure the arrival of a new team before being fired.

"One chef — I remember him well! — liked to please my father with special dishes to demonstrate his culinary skill. One evening he served us a large platter of small birds very attractively prepared. They were delicious! After dinner Father went out to the kitchen to compliment the chef and to find out what kind of birds they were. They were robins! It was explained to the cook that killing robins and other songbirds was illegal in America. The amazed chef informed us that in the Old Country — France to him — robins, thrushes, larks and such were sold in all the markets. However, you can be sure that we never again ate tasty robins! . . .

Fire Protection

"We took precautions against fire by installing two firehoses on each floor and by hiring a night watchman. There were no fire-escapes. The watchman had 20 timeclocks to punch between 10 p.m. and 7 a.m. If his chart showed that he had missed any, he was promptly fired. However, his schedule did allow him a little time between rounds. One husky fellow from New York would sit on a box on the lawn during his spare time. One morning there were two dead skunks, one on each side of his box. Strangely enough, there was no odor of mephitis mephitis in the air. We wondered how come.

"When he came on duty the next night Father asked him how he had managed to kill the skunks without malodorous results. 'Oh,' he exclaimed, 'Were they skunks? I thought they were cats. I just grabbed them by the neck and strangled them!' Thus we discovered his intense dislike of cats.

"A device for chimney fires was a serrated glass globe filled with extinguishing liquid. When the globe was broken at the base of the fire, it would put out not only the chimney blaze but the one in the fireplace as well. There was always the danger of sparks igniting the tinder-dry roof of the hotel so such fires were a constant cause for concern.

"One day I recall that a particularly pushy and obnoxious salesman was given permission to demonstrate his product. A bonfire was built in the backyard and a crowd gathered to hear his pitch. 'Ladies and gentlemen,' he exclaimed, 'I want you to know that no other similar substance can put out that fire with only one bottle of my patented fluid. Watch closely and I'll show you how it's done!'

"Then with a flourish he proceeded to toss the glass container into the eager flames. However, the show didn't turn out exactly as planned — and expected — because, instead of drowning the fire, there was instead a great burst of flames and the bonfire flared up more furiously than ever. Someone who had decided to give the overbearing, bumptious salesman his come-uppance had replaced the contents of his bottles with kerosene! . . .

Saranac Guides

"The Adirondack guide had reached the peak of his importance long before my time. During that early period when long trips by guideboat were necessary and popular, one of the most famous treks was from Old Forge on First Lake of the Fulton Chain to the upper end of Lower Saranac Lake — to Martin's. The guides had to be familiar with a wide but narrow territory including carries, and campsites all along the 100 mile route. With the coming of the railroad from Utica, however, in 1892 and by 1900 such trips had lost some of their appeal and purpose.

"It's understandable that the average guide had a very limited knowledge of the region other than his own bailiwick because he customarily traveled by boat, on foot or by horse and buggy. Moreover, roads were few in those early days.

"The guides that I knew retained two characteristics shared by the best of the old-timers: (1) they insisted that they be treated as equals, even by millionaires, and (2) they just plain could not tolerate a sport who was tight with his money. If they liked a man the hunting or fishing trip could be most enjoyable. If they didn't — God help him! There were many ways of getting even.

"One guide I'll never forget, who lived near us on Algonquin Avenue and who often went with us deer-hunting, invariably had a couple lapses of sobriety every Summer and went on what to him were — at least temporarily — glorious sprees. At the end of each bender instead of going home, thoroughly plastered, to his much-enduring wife he showed up at the Algonquin, where I was room clerk. Each time he would hand me his big gold watch and heavy chain plus sometimes as much as $100.00 in cash. Then a bellboy would assist him on his meandering way to his room and there he would sleep off his drunkenness.

"Next morning, without fail, he would excitedly come to the desk and report the loss of his valuable watch and all his money. Each time I would stop him abruptly, go to the safe and, much to his surprise, would hand over his missing possessions. On every such occasion he would pour out his relief and profuse thanks. Moreover, it was typical of him and others so afflicted that, in spite of repeated practice, he never seemed to remember that this had happened before. . . .

Home Remedies

"Although there was a good doctor available for such things as removal of tonsils, we seldom called him for anything less serious. We had never heard of tetanus shots but we applied salt pork to any foot pierced by a rusty nail. The pork slab was tied on for a few days and on several instances proved effective for me. I don't think I'd try that same remedy nowadays however.

"For croup we sucked a lump of sugar with a few drops of turpentine on it. Headaches we merely endured or we might get relief with a stiff dollop of castor oil. We treated sore throats by cold compresses.

"For coughs the prescription was wild cherry rum. We made this mixture each August when the wild black cherries were ripe. Sheets were spread on the ground and it was my job to climb the tree and shake down most of the fruit. These were packed into a five-gallon demijohn and rum was added right up to the neck. The cherries were so small that actually there was very little space left for the rum. Made in late Summer this elixir was dispersed chiefly in Winter. The dose for youngsters was half a wine glass. The grown-ups of course required considerably more to insure certain results. Although I can't accurately say that the concoction ever stopped coughs, but I can assure you that it tasted downright good! good!"

The End of an Era

"By the Fall of 1917, the Algonquin was leased to others and the Harding era was over. In 1920 it was sold to W.M. Hanes and shortly afterward closed its doors forever. Automobiles had changed the nature of the resort business so that hotels were no longer profitable. The Algonquin buildings deteriorated for 30 years until at last they were torn down in 1958-9. I never went near the spot because I wanted to remember the hotel as it had been [much like some people's unwillingness to view a corpse]. I hoped sincerely that the site would be used for some activity appropriate to the Algonquin's useful and distinguished past, but I knew that another hotel would never stand there again.

"Happily, on September 17, 1960 ground was broken for the million-dollar Trudeau Research Laboratory, which was dedicated in August, 1964 with, I understand, impressive ceremonies. It is gratifying to know that the well-remembered site now has such a dignified and dedicated future.

"The era in which the fine old hotel was at its prime is gone forever. Nevertheless, the beauty of its views will never fade from the pages of my memory. I'll forever cherish those happy days of 50 years around the Algonquin."

Chapter 5

Bartlett's, Later the Saranac and Bartlett Carry Clubs

Unquestionably, the three best-known names in early Adirondack hotel history were William F. Martin, Apollos (Paul) A. Smith and Virgil C. Bartlett, and all three became legend material as did their creations — Martin's on Lower Saranac, Smith's on Lower St. Regis and Bartlett's on the Saranac River, between the Upper Saranac and the Middle (or Round) Lake. By far the smallest of the three, Virge's unpretentious place nevertheless provided clean, cozy and comfortable accommodations for hundreds of sportsmen and tourists from 1854 until his death thirty years later.

Bartlett, like Martin, learned the business during the two or three years that he leased Capt. Pliny Miller's small hotel on the river in Saranac Lake. Like Martin too he apparently realized that the steadily increasing number of well-heeled city hunters and fishermen represented a golden opportunity for an enterprising fellow like himself. After all, his friend Martin was already faring well so why shouldn't he?

So, with that in mind, he invested most of his money in 267 remote acres of strategically located land, built his "Sportsmen's Home" and was soon ready for business. The two-story spread — out structure, which could take care of about fifty guests, was successful from the start and, except for the addition of a wing, barns, boathouses and other outbuildings it stayed the same throughout the years.

Unlike other resort owners the Bartletts never yielded to the expansion obsession — the downfall of so many more venturesome proprietors. Quite content with a reasonably generous return from their combined labors they preferred to spend their money in travel, benefactions and creature comforts.

One of the first travelers to show up at the new inn was Alfred B. Street, historian, state librarian and author of the emotionally embellished *Woods and Waters* and *The Indian Pass*. Accompanied by Harvey, head guide, and three other Moodys — Mart, Cort and Phin — Street described the place as it looked in late 1854.

"The clearing contained but an acre or so, on the north bank of the river. Here stood Bartlett's two-story, unpainted frame tavern and its shadow lay cool and black upon the gentle, glassy slope as I passed toward the entrance. Our guides were clustered at the open door of a log hut at one side.

"A huge, savage-looking bulldog, with porcupine quills clinging to his coat and his black lips curled over his white fangs, stalked near the hut, looking powerful enough to bring down a moose. Bartlett himself, a short but strong, square-built man, with a hat that seemed made of dingy jackstraws, talked to one, laughed with another and kicked the hounds generally out of his way with expletives more emphatic than pious.

"In the sitting-room I found my comrades louder than usual in conversation for which the empty glasses, telling clearly of punch, probably accounted.

"The boats and luggage having been carried on wheels over the portage to the Upper Lake, we followed, leaving Bartlett in the act of applying his right foot to the ribs of an

Bartlett's Village, Middle Saranac (Round Lake) in Background

Bartlett's, Saranac River in Foreground (Stoddard)

unlucky hound and the bulldog gazing after us with a face grim enough to darken daylight."

William Stillman, who masterminded the philosophers' camps at Follansbee and Ampersand, left this record of a stop-over at Bartlett's. Guided by Steve Martin, the artist and an unnamed companion docked their boats there on a sunny day in October, 1855:

"Some huge dogs sauntered around the landing and the carcass of a bear hung nearby. We landed, ordered dinner and then the guides commenced the ungrateful task of carrying the lading and boats. One shouldered a boat and the other its cargo and, having deposited them in the lake (Upper Saranac) at the head of the falls, returned to await dinner previous to carrying the other moiety of their burdens. They calculated all the steps and took none in vain. There were three miles yet to go on the Lake, and then our journey was finished for the day. We here purchased some stores which we had been unable to procure at Martin's. It (the trip) ended at the head of a deep bay of the Upper Saranac Lake, which sets up within a mile of a tributary of the Raquette, leaving a carrying place of that distance on which is a cabin, at which we lodged that night. [That cabin was probably Jesse Corey's first home, on the Sweeney Carry, which he built about 1830.]

Virge Bartlett's volatile temper and command of an impressive arsenal of profanity made him the foremost regional celebrity. Titus in *Adirondack Pioneers* called him a "show in himself." Hilariously amusing for the audience but extremely humiliating for the victim. Delivered in a high-pitched nasal voice, which often cracked under the emotional strain, the outburst of sarcastic abuse poured from his mouth like lava from a newly erupted volcano.

But unlike most other vitriolic, short-fused individuals Bartlett soon simmered down, recovered his cool and became a congenial companion again. Moreover, he had a sharp sense of humor and could even take a joke on himself with seeming relish, as shown by this Titus anecdote: "One Sunday night in 1864 we were there and stayed overnight. He had just bought a new cutter, which was nicely cushioned and lined throughout. He had the cutter taken up to his front piazza and tipped up against the house to keep it out of the storm. During the night several of his many dogs crawled under it and decided to amuse themselves with the expensive lining. In the morning the porch was covered with scraps of cloth.

"His guidehouse was a little way above the house on a direct line with the piazza. Several of his men were up before he was that day and, seeing the damage, eagerly anticipated the coming explosion and kept on the lookout for him. Before long he came out, took it all in, and decided to cheat his men of their fun. 'Well, boys,' he commented, 'You can go on with your work. I'm going to put this off until I'm alone.' With that he turned and went back into the house."

The bullet-headed Bartlett was somewhat of a despot and ruled his little realm with remarkable efficiency. Since he was a workaholic himself he demanded much more than a merely fair day's work for a fair day's pay and the results and rewards were proportional. The honest workers admired and respected him and the goldbrickers never lasted long. Those who were reliable could always be sure of a square deal, a square meal and all-out help when that was required.

One of his former employees, a lumber-jack, found that out when he became seriously injured on a remote logging job. Bartlett heard about it and immediately went into action. He prepared a bed in one of his pungs, a box-sleigh contraption, drove the long bumpy trip back into the lumber camp, brought the sick man to their home and sent a man to get Dr.

Virgil C. Bartlett   Caroline Greene Bartlett

Romeyn of Keesville who, incidentally, was a guest and frequenter of the old hotel and its successor the Saranac Club for forty-five consecutive years. Mrs. Bartlett nursed the man back to health, a gesture that proved that for them loyalty was a two-way street.

Virge, also unlike many fiery-tempered, vindictive men, and in spite of the unfavorable comments of Street and Stillman, was passionately fond of small animals — pet fawns, raccoons, weasels, flying squirrels etc. if not certain dogs. Their particular pet was a parrot which had been taught to say "Good night, Mrs. Bartlett!" [Mrs. Chase of the Loon Lake House also enjoyed the companionship and antics of a gaudy parrot named Drexie, who had a very extensive vocabulary including one expression which I heard often. It was "Tip the bellboys! Don't forget to tip the bellboys!" Since I was one of them I rather fancied that phrase but the Mrs. apparently thought it both vulgar and unnecessary because she banished the bird from the front desk area.] Having no children of their own they adopted Carrie Niles, Mrs. Bartlett's niece, and provided a home for several years for two other young girls. When her sister married Tom Haley, a local guide, Mrs. Bartlett and her husband eventually adopted the young son, who was christened Bartlett Haley; and "Virge" made him his constant companion and spoiled him rotten, as the saying goes. According to friends the only things little Barty didn't have were the things he didn't think to ask for.

Although Bartlett never sought or held public office he nevertheless was a power in local politics. Moreover, he fully expected and insisted that his help vote as instructed as a condition of continued employment. The outcome of any Harrietstown election hung in the balance until the boatloads from the "Solid South" showed up at the booth. In those days twenty or thirty votes could determine the difference between victory and defeat for the candidates. . . .

Bartlett and Paul Smith, staunch friends, met one day in Plattsburgh and exchanged pleasantries.

"Virge," declared "Uncle Paul," "I've got the best and wealthiest people in the country staying at my place this Summer."

"That so?" replied "Virge." "Well now, I'll tell you that I've got the best for their weight out at my place but the trouble is they don't weigh very much."

"Yup," continued Paul, "The class of men at St. Regis each Summer is so good that I saw an unusually good opportunity for my three sons [Henry, Phelps and Paul Jr.]. I've raised them to be stage robbers."

"How did it work out?" inquired Bartlett, leading with his chin and straight into the verbal trap.

"Not so good I'm sorry to say. You see at times they made the stupid mistake of holding up the stagecoach outward bound from Bartlett's and damned near starved to death!"

Much has been said and made about "Virge" Bartlett but almost as much should also be recorded about Caroline Greene, his wife. An ex-teacher, she was a large, refined, handsome woman who was an excellent cook and manager. She also had the ability to manage people through diplomacy, compassion and affection. Like Mary Howe Chase, Lydia Martin Smith and the two Mrs. Martins — Laura Hunkins and Sarah Lamson, their maiden names — Mrs. Bartlett was the real power behind the throne of their respective realms and everybody — including their husbands — was well aware of the domestic situation. Each of these women was better educated, more refined and more competent than their men and therefore wrote the contracts, handled the money, did much of the hiring and firing, the settling of arguments and the soothing of damaged egos. These women and many others less humble have never been given anywhere near the credit they so richly deserve for their incalculable contributions to the area history. Their men, invariably the rough and tough, mighty hunter, yarn-spinning, back-slapping, typical frontier type have been prime subjects for the praises and brushes of writers and artists from the opening of the Adirondacks. These included authors Hoffman, Webber, Street, Chittenden, Stillman, Murray, Headley, Hammond etc. and artists and such as Winslow Homer, Tait, Homer Martin, A. F. Frost and others of varying competence. . . .

Saranac River End of Bartlett Carry (Stoddard)

One of the many testimonials to the excellence of the menu provided at Bartlett's was the remark recorded by a visiting lady who rated Mrs. Martin's food as second only to Mrs. Bartlett's. Another traveler, a Mrs. Dunning, nearly drowned in a rough crossing of often dangerous Round Lake, remarked that "The discomfort was not too high a price to pay for a meal of Mrs. Bartlett's brown bread."

Another story, typical of Bartlett's era, had for its featured character a cantankerous old guide, a relative of the owners who was whiling away his declining years as a freeloader. On one occasion a large party from the Boston area arrived and found the supply of guides somewhat short-handed. In order to get at least some return for his ample board, booze and lodging from the grumpy old parasite, "Virge" assigned him to go out with a short, gruff, bossy and generally uncongenial Dr. — and he reluctantly complied. . . .

Late that afternoon all the other parties had returned and had sat down to dinner when someone noticed that one of their group was missing. The proprietor was notified and went down to the boathouse to find the guide — who, sure enough, was there rocking away in an armchair, whittling, smoking his pipe, and generally letting his evening meal settle.

Virge didn't waste any time. "Where's Doc so-and-so?"

No answer. Just shrugged shoulders.

"Bill, where's the man you went out with this morning?"

"Down in Round Lake," was the reply.

"In Round Lake? What's he doin' there?"

"Wa-a-ll," and slowly he extracted this explanation. "Him and me set out and right away I knowed that we wouldn't get along nohow. He kept bossin' me and givin' orders. I took it as long as I could and — you know that big rock down near Bullrush Bay?

"Yup," said Bartlett, "what about it?"

"Wa-a-ll, that's where he is — and if you want him go down and git him yerself! I won't!"

Someone else was dispatched, the ornery, irked medico rescued and brought back to the fold — a disgruntled but subdued and wiser man. Wiser in the democratic ways of the woods, that is. . . .

To draw the curtain on the career of "Virge" Bartlett I have never found a better and more apt eulogy than this passage from Dr. Henry Van Dyke's chapter called "Ampersand" in *Little Rivers:* "Fields were cleared, gardens planted, half a dozen log cabins were scattered along the River, and the old house having grown slowly and somewhat irregularly for twenty years, came out just before the time of which I write in a modest coat of paint and a broad-brimmed piazza. But Virgil himself, the creator of the oasis — well-known by hunters and fishermen, dreaded by lazy guides and quarrelsome lumbermen — "Virge" the irascible, kind-hearted, indefatigable, was there no longer. [He died in 1884.] He had made his last clearing and fought his last fight; done his last favor to a friend and thrown his last adversary out the tavern door. His last log has gone down the River. His camp-fire has burned out. Peace to his ashes. His wife, who had often played the part of Abigail toward travelers who had unconsciously incurred the old man's distrust, now reigned in his stead; and there was great abundance of maple syrup on every man's flapjack." . . .

Mentioning Bartlett's without including the name of Dr. J. R. Romeyn of Keeseville would be doing a disservice to his memory and of that memorable place because his connection with the resort covered a period of 45 years — from 1855 until 1900. Donaldson's tribute to the good Doctor is expressed eloquently in this manner: "The last years of his pilgrimage were filled with the keen sadness of change but the routine of a lifetime held dominion over him. He continued to do the thing which for years had been his greatest

Dr. Romeyn on Bartlett's Rapids June 1887

pleasure, even though he knew there could be only sorrow in its repetition. He outlived the regency of Virge and the vice regency of Virge's wife. He saw their domain of blended personality change into a soulless "club." He wandered over the familiar ground when the familiar landmarks and people had disappeared. His recurrent presence became the one thing changeless in the midst of change. He became a last and lonely link with the past — the avatar of Bartlett's — perpetuating in his tall and gaunt but kindly person the half-forgotten memories and associations of its heyday.

"There is no more lovable or pathetic figure in Adirondack story than Romeyn of Keeseville for a lifetime casting his fly in the Bartlett rapids — outliving not only the friends on the bank but the run of trout in the waters. At last in the Spring of 1901, he came no more and early in the following year he died; but we who knew the lonely fisherman will always think he died because he could not come." [Donaldson at his very best]

The Saranac Club

[This section is based on the minute books of the club. Courtesy of Jay Yardley of Bartlett Carry Club, its present owner]

At an informal meeting held at Davies' Restaurant, Orange, N.J. on January 17, 1889 the principal topic of discussion was the desirability of buying a tract of land, owned by Mrs. Virgil Bartlett, in the Adirondack Mountains near Upper Saranac Lake. Several of those present having been guests there had developed a strong affinity for the place and expressed a keen interest in its purchase as a private club for themselves and their friends, while also offering transient privileges to the traveling public.

One of those present, E. A. Cruikshank, was delegated to revisit Bartlett's to make arrangements for the possible acquisition of the property for a sum not exceeding $15,000 for its 267 acres, buildings and improvements. Mission was accomplished but not as successfully as hoped for. Even though the property was available at the stipulated price and a $500.00 binder given, there was nevertheless a complicating factor. George Fowler, who had been managing the hotel for Mrs. Bartlett since her husband's death in 1884 had a lease, refused to settle for less than $1000.00. Moreover, there was also a mortgage on the property held by an E. Fetherstone of Plattsburgh which had to be satisfied.

In spite of this and because the title search had favorably checked out, the group more or less jumped the gun by setting up a corporation to be known as The Saranac Club and designated as directors for the first year the following members: Theodore Fitch, Charles Reed and S. Hedding Fitch, all of Yonkers; Charles Alford, Jonathan Broome, Robert Douglass and William Riker Jr., all of Orange, N.J.; Edwin and Warren Cruikshank of Brooklyn.

Knowing that the still not-completely-resolved-situation required face-to-face dickering, a so-called Fowler Committee was appointed. These were G. Alford, chairman; Charles Reed, E. A. Cruikshank and F. P. Fiske. This delegation went to Glens Falls on April 15, 1889 to meet attorney Beaman of Malone, who had done the title search. His failure to show up on time plus other snarls of varying nature and degree of difficulty made the committee's eight-day trip anything but monotonous.

However, lawyer Beaman finally arrived as did an attorney named Trumbull, representing Mrs. Bartlett, who collected $11,500 in her behalf. The group than proceeded to Plattsburgh by train where Fetherstone, the mortgagor, claimed more accrued interest than anticipated, a development that required a second participation by Trumbull but which was reached agreeably by paying Fetherstone $3,640 in principal plus interest.

While still in Plattsburgh the delegation heard to their consternation that Fowler, the lease-holder, had died but were relieved to learn upon arrival in Saranac Lake that the report was an ill-founded rumor.

Nevertheless, Fowler was indeed seriously ill, according to his legal representative, named Kendall; therefore very fast action was called for and provided.

"When we attempt to describe our journey from Saranac Lake to Bartlett's over what was then known as the Winter road, language fails us but, suffice it to say, it will linger very long indeed in the memories of your Committee." [That's the way it is recorded in the minutes.]

Fortunately, Fowler was still in the land of the living so they were able to close the deal to their mutual satisfaction. In fact the delegation found that even though the fouled-up inventory required three days of concentrated effort, the outcome was serendipitous because the expected $3,000 personal property listing actually turned out to be worth more than $4,500 broken down as follows:

Household furniture of all kinds and descriptions	$1428
Groceries and supplies exclusive of liquors	$1496
Liquors of all kinds and brands	$ 431
Livestock — horses, cows, sheep, pigs, poultry, barn and farm implements	$1162
Total	$4517

As a counter-balancing factor the committee soon discovered that certain repairs and improvements were urgently needed — costs of which could not be readily estimated.

Besides Mr. and Mrs. Fowler, the resident managers, it was felt that at least 15 other people would be needed to properly staff the Club, with a payroll of about $85.00 per week.

So much for the acquisition phase and earliest days of the Saranac Club. In order to

The Saranac Club (Stoddard)

Interior of Saranac Clubhouse

59

raise the capital necessary to cover the essential repairs, several members assessed themselves the sum of $250; other members half of that amount. Further assessments, in addition to organization and initiation fees of $1000.00 each, had to be made with predictable regularity as the years went by and the Club developed its property. Such self-imposed taxes plus resignations, deaths, steadily increasing overhead and correspondingly decreasing interest and involvement among the original membership constituted an ever-recurring problem situation as well as an unfavorable augury for the organization, which never numbered many more than twenty families.

In the Spring of 1891 the old "Sportsmen's Home" was expanded and refurbished and a new twenty-room annex was put up nearby. In July, same year, the old hotel was totally destroyed by fire; but the annex was saved.

In 1893 a large clubhouse was constructed to accommodate not only the members but also travelers, who were still permitted to use the carry and wanted a meal or overnight lodging.

By 1903 the decision, somewhat reluctantly, was made to obtain a $27,000 mortgage, the bonds to be purchased by a majority of the members. In 1909 a second mortgage was negotiated with Alfred B. Jenkins, of the Jenkins Valve Co., to advance the money and both obligations due to mature on January 1, 1913.

A short nine-hole golf course, built about 1905 and lasting well into the 1930's can still be traced although natural reclamation has almost obliterated most of it.

On January 12, 1912 four members and Farnham Yardley, by invitation representing his father-in-law, Jenkins, showed up for two informal meetings. Then on January 22 the secretary mailed out the long-anticipated communication which read as follows: "As the Club is without funds and the managers have no means of the paying the premiums on the $29,600 insurance coverage carried by the Club, this notice is sent for you so that you may take whatever steps which you deem necessary in order to protect your own interests."

On November 19, 1912 at a poorly attended meeting those present regretfully voted that the mortgages be foreclosed and the property sold.

Here are the final entries in the minute books:

January 28, 1913

Memo: Owing to the present financial condition of the Saranac Club the annual members' meeting scheduled for today was canceled.

Mr. B. Douglass Jr. stated that Farnham Yardley had been designated as Treasurer protem, Mr. A. B. Jenkins certified having been transferred to him (Yardley).

Then the terminal item:

New York April 15, 1913

"In consequence of the absence of the necessary quorum a regular meeting of the Board of Managers of the Saranac Club, scheduled for this day, at the office of the Secretary, was not held."

With that ringing down of the curtain on the activities of the Saranac Club the foreclosure proceeded according to schedule in order to satisfy the claims of the various members. The purchaser was Henry B. Corey and the sale price was $22,000. It is not known whether he was acting for the Club or as an agent for someone else.

On September 24, 1913 he sold the 267 acres to the Bartlett Carry Realty Co., Inc., a group which included some of the old members — such as Jenkins, Douglass and Schuyler Merritt, who later became governor of Conn. — and several newer individuals. These stalwarts then gave their organization the name of Bartlett Carry Club and operated it through "feast, famine and fires" until the general demise of such large clubs after World War II.

About the turn of the century when the Club was still operating, it was said that some very desirable property owned by Pauline Shaw of Boston, a Club member, was on the market. Mr. Jenkins and a member named Kingsford both had long been interested in acquiring the same choice chunk of real estate on the Middle Lake and there had been a friendly rivalry over that terrain.

Apparently both men heard about the deal almost simultaneously so, since each knew that time was emphatically of the essence, they climbed into their guideboats and raced down the River to Round (Middle Saranac) Lake. Jenkins proved to be the stronger oarsman and faster-footed so he got there first and closed the deal pronto. Jenkins, having his choice of location, chose the south and more accessible point. Kingsford settled for Caper Point just opposite, but reached only by boat.

This lively competition did not shake the friendship between the men, however, and they entertained each other regularly — once each Summer. Moreover, every night they kept in touch by a signal system. They would stand on their respective docks and slowly wave railroad brakemen's lanterns — one red, the other green — back and forth several times to report that all was well and to wish each other a symbolic, slightly psychedelic good-night.

Eventually the Kingsford holdings — a large cottage building and several others — were acquired by the late Harry Duso of Crescent Bay Marina, Lower Lake, who spread the smaller structures to the good locations along the shoreline and, during the 1950's sold most

Merritt Cottage, Bartlett Carry Club

61

A Fascinating Study

of them but retained at least one for his own use. A very good deal for a very enterprising Harry.

The Bartlett Carry Club

The recreational resort tradition started by Virge and Caroline Bartlett and the next owners, The Saranac Club, is still going strong even if on a smaller, more sociable scale. Its owners, Jay and Fran Yardley, the fourth generation to enjoy the superb vistas offered by this well-wooded, mountain, lake and river setting, have available a limited number of comfortably furnished lodges for rent during the Summer season.

Situated on a thousand acres the Bartlett Carry Club is surrounded by the Adirondack Forest Preserve yet is only 11 miles from Saranac Lake and its excellent airport. The Bartlett Carry itself is one link in the historic 86 mile Saranac Lake to Old Forge canoe and guideboat route.

In these days of rapid change, which is not always to be confused with true progress, it is very reassuring to know that there still are people, like the Yardleys, who are totally unconvinced that space and numbers are valid criteria by which to judge the observable qualities and values of places or people.

Too bad there aren't more same-minded people and fewer rapacious, quick-buck developers and other assorted characters with little or no respect for either the landscape or tradition.

Since the principal purpose of an historian is to protect the past from the abuses of the present, I hope that this book accomplishes at least one thing: by photos and narration it will perpetuate the so-called aura generated by some truly remarkable people, their accomplishments and their affection for Bartlett's and the Saranacs.

Chapter 6

Rustic Lodge, Later Swenson's and Indian Carry Camps

Very little is known about Jesse Corey, very likely the earliest permanent settler in the Upper Saranac Lake area, but what information there is leaves little doubt that he rated considerable historical importance. No one seems to know where he was born and spent his youth and his newspaper obits have yet to surface. Moreover, the leading guidebooks of the period — Wallace's *Descriptive Guide to the Adirondacks* and Stoddard's *Adirondacks Illustrated* — provide skimpy notes indeed about either the man or his creation — The Rustic Lodge on the Upper Lake and of the original and ancient Indian Carry.

What is known is that Corey arrived in the region, liked what he saw and built his first log home about 1830 somewhere on The Sweeney Carry, the alternate route to the Raquette River. There he lived for at least several years before he, like Alvah Dunning, was smitten by wanderlust and wound up in the West. How far west is plain supposition but he apparently satisfied his curiosity, soon got his fill of sun, sagebrush and sand, and headed back to his bailiwick on the Upper Saranac.

Somewhere along the line he married and set up housekeeping about 1850 in a small, typically frontier log cabin. Soon the Coreys became sharply aware that they were, like Martin and Bartlett, owners of a most favorable location and that prosperity was not only just around the corner but knocking resoundingly on the door.

Besides doing a brisk business at the hotel, the enterprising Corey also hauled guideboats, canoes, baggage and camping parties over the Indian Carry to nearby Stony Creek Ponds or the three miles farther to Axton on the Raquette River. Prices varied according to cargo but the passengers in 1900 paid 75 cts. each if they preferred not to depend upon "shank's mare."

Alfred B. Street's fascinating *Woods and Waters or the Saranacs and Racquette* (sic) mentions Corey several times as the party's hired hunter and the Moodys as their guides during the state historian's first trip with four companions through the interlocking waterways in 1854.

Even during its best years the Rustic Lodge was never a pretentious place. Although it was given a second floor and expanded lengthwise, it was still a primitive, squared-log and plaster-chinked structure. Nevertheless, in spite of its rusticity in very shortly acquired a reputation for comfort, good cheer and "woodsy brotherhood" and remained so until 1894, when Corey leased his modest hotel and retired to nearby Axton [Axe-town]. There he died May 28, 1896 and was buried in the Pine Ridge cemetery, Saranac Lake and not as local legend has it on the pine knoll overlooking the Axton landing. Some other Corey was buried there.*

He selected his successor well because Charles H. Wardner, his lessee, not only continued the thriving business with noteworthy success but also made it even more popular

---

* Marian, Corey's wife died October 20, 1859, aged 25, and is buried beside him in the Pine Ridge Cemetery.

Corey's Original Rustic Lodge, Upper Saranac Lake

Jesse Corey (Stoddard)

Corey's Rustic Lodge in the 1880's (Stoddard)

Indian Carry, Upper Saranac

than before. Furthermore, to meet the increased demand for accommodations, he added to the line of cottages on the knoll north of the Lodge until they numbered at least nine.

In 1897 E. P. and S. A. Swenson, former guests at Saranac Inn, bought the Lodge and approximately 500 acres of property, including the Carry, from the Corey estate; but they continued to lease the Rustic Lodge to Wardner.

Stoddard's 1900 edition of his *Adirondacks Illustrated* noted that there was a golf course at Rustic Lodge, laid out where, according to local tradition, once were the cornfields of the ancient Adirondack people who gave the place its name. How this small nine-hole course came into being is also noteworthy and amusing. One of the Swenson brothers occasionally played at nearby Bartlett's or Saranac Club layout. One day when he, a relatively deliberate and therefore exasperatingly slow player was enjoying a round of golf, another player's shot came dangerously close to Swenson.

Although the second person had ceremoniously yelled "Fore!" and asked to play through, Swenson refused the request, stalked off the course in medium high dudgeon with the loud remark: "By God! I'm going to build me a course of my own!" And so he did, probably in 1898 or 9.

The Swensons, however, never monopolized their private links and it became very popular among the Summer residents of the Upper Lake. The green fees also helped defray maintenance costs. It was also a welcome source of spending money for the young boys of the Corey's area — Bill, Clarence and Archie Petty — among others.

The picturesque little nine, in use until after World War II, can be readily traced today.

In 1911 Wardner, having been alerted to expect substantial changes, relinquished his lease and bought Rice's Lake Clear Inn. Before he left he arranged to purchase the cabins,

Indian Carry Landing at First Stony Creek Pond

Hiawatha House, First Stony Creek Pond (Stoddard)

Rustic Lodge Cabins, Later Moved to Lake Clear

slated to be demolished. The following Winter he had them cut into three sections, loaded them onto big sleds and hauled them across the ice of the Upper Lake, over the carry to the outlet of Lake Clear and on to their destination at Rice's. There, the well-built cottages can still be seen lined up and ready for vacation pleasure as of yore.

In 1913 the Swensons decided to restrict the use of the Indian Carry for the traveling public and gave orders to have torn down the old lodge and the remaining service buildings — the well-patronized little store, the laundry and the boathouse. About all that was left was the caretaker's cottage.

The owners also had the Saranac Lake — Tupper Lake road, which originally ran right past the Lodge, relocated a considerably more convenient distance away, and thereby gained added privacy.

The Swenson Era

Most of the time that they owned the Rustic Lodge the Swenson family stayed at the far more luxurious Saranac Inn. However, E. P., whose family income came mostly from a banking, oil and sugar importing interests, finally decided to build on his own property. So, with architect Bill Distin and contractors Branch and Callanan of Saranac Lake, work was started during 1928 and the thirty-room mansion was ready for occupation for the Winter of 1931. A low — rather rambling building with shingled walls and roof and heavy timbers for ornamentation, the structure blends well with its impressive surroundings.

As the accompanying photo shows there are two main wings — one containing the six master bedrooms, and the other the service section. Between these are the library, the large

Swenson's

living room and the octagonal, quilted-ceiling dining room, both having magnificent views of the Upper Lake.

Probably the most noteworthy feature is that each bedroom had its own bathroom and each of these had its separate fireplace — 19 in all, five with Delft tile borders. To provide heat during the two years of Winter occupation, which included the 1932 Olympics at Lake Placid, there were five furnaces, originally wood-burners. These of course, had to be manned around the clock so two and three-man crews were kept busy bucksawing and splitting wood, stocking the monsters and feeding the fireplaces. Such an overhead, plus a staff of twelve inside and twenty outside help, even in those days, was rather formidable so apparently the year-round routine was dropped.

A real estate brochure prepared by Clinton J. Ayres of Saranac Lake contains this summary of accommodations and equipment of Indian Carry Camp:

Living Room	6 Master Bedrooms	Maid's Dining Room
Library	6 Master Baths	Maid's Sitting Room
Dining Room	Butler's Pantry	6 Maid's Rooms
Office or Powder Room	Kitchen	2 Maid's Baths
	Laundry	Wine and Liquor Vault

Guide House (10 rooms and bath); Guide House (11 rooms and bath); 2 Garages (space for 8 cars); barn with stanchions and horse-stalls; boathouse with two boat slips; complete domestic and fire protection water system.

The Indian Carry Club

The Indian Carry Camp, seasonally occupied during intervening years by Roderick Swenson and others in the family, went on the market in 1945 but was eventually sold to partners Gregory Nowakoski, ex-foreign service officer and Bernard Nemeroff, a New York City lawyer, in October 1966, following a complicated negotiation period involving the combined estates of two of E. P. Swenson's sons.

Among the first priorities was the switch-over from wood to oil which, even at the outset, proved to be both expensive and impractical in such a large, high-ceilinged, spread-out building where hot air heat is notoriously ineffective.

The partnership lasted for two years at which time Nowakoski took over with the very sound — at the time — concept of well-conceived and not inexpensive development of the 500 acre property. However, before the plans could be appreciably put into effect, the A.P.A. and its highly restrictive regulations put a virtual damper/kibosh on the project.

The mixture of colors on the Park Agency map — part orange, which allows about 3.2 buildings per acre and yellow, which apparently permits 8 or 9 structures — resulted in a discouraging mishmash making developmental plans too expensive, too impractical and virtually impossible to carry out.

And that's the way it was at Corey's and Wardner's Rustic Lodge, during the Swenson era and as it is now at the Indian Carry Camp on Upper Saranac Lake.

Chapter 7

Prospect House, Later Saranac Inn

The three most popular and most luxurious Adirondack resort hotels — all in Franklin County — were the Loon Lake House, Paul Smith's and Saranac Inn. Having worked as a bellhop at Mrs. Chase's (The Loon Lake House) and having seen the other two during their heyday, I would say that the Inn, especially in the 1940's, was the poshest.*

Not only the largest but also the swankiest these three hotels, each starting on a very modest scale, eventually expanded and improved until each could accommodate nearly 1000 guests. Annexes and cottages along with the main and service buildings made small villages when filled with wealthy vacationers and staffed with four or five hundred employees. It is noteworthy that the whole economy of the region was almost entirely dependent upon the success of these resorts.

The Prospect House, so called by Daniel S. Hough, its builder in 1864, because of its superb view, had a rather inauspicious start. Hough, who had been one of Paul Smith's first patrons, somehow lost much of his sizable fortune and, having seen that Paul was prospering, decided that he could certainly do just as well. Therefore, he bought property on the north end of Upper Saranac Lake, where he had often hunted and fished, and soon had a small hotel up and open for business.

Hough, who knew little or nothing about the management of a hotel — even one that accommodated only fifteen people — soon found out that it takes more than mere desire to be successful. Even though he brought silver, costly cut glass, expensive china and linen from his New York home and furnished the place lavishly, he and his wife still couldn't make a go of it. Moreover, since at that time it was off the stagecoach routes, he hardly had a sporting chance; so, after nine uncertain and unprofitable years, he gave up.

About that time Christopher F. Norton of Plattsburgh bought several thousand acres of timberlands in that section and started extensive logging operations. There were lumber camps throughout the region from the Brandon line to the Upper and Lower Saranacs and also along the Saranac River. However, Norton — the "King of the Saranacs" — also got in over his financial head, and went broke too. He couldn't meet mortgage payments on $75,000 indebtedness so the Mutual Insurance Co. foreclosed. During his ownership Norton rented Hough's log hostel to E. R. Derby of Bloomingdale and the new manager and his wife, far more practical and competent than Hough, put the place on the road to solid success. Business improved enough to warrant the addition of a wing and another cabin; later more improvements increased its capacity to about fifty guests.

Although it is not clear just how Derby acquired the property, the best guesstimate is that he did so by paying the back taxes and making his squatter's rights stick. Anyhow, he ran the little hotel profitably until the Spring of 1884 when, while on a trip to New York

---

* This work has an interesting derivation: An acronym, it refers to the selection of the most comfortable staterooms (the sun factor) on ocean trips to the Orient. *P*ort side *o*utward; *s*tarboard side *h*omeward-bound.

Prospect House, Upper Saranac Lake (Stoddard)

Prospect House, Blagden's "Cabin" (Stoddard)

70

City to buy supplies, he suddenly died. His wife, with Edward L. Pearse as manager, tried to continue the business but the clientele started dropping off so, after two discouraging seasons she sold out.

The following article, which appeared in the June 5, 1882 issue of the New York *Weekly*, was undoubtedly the most exciting incident in the life of Ed. Derby:

A Struggle For Life

"E. R. Derby, the landlord of the Prospect House, Saranac Lake, was recently the hero of a very exciting exploit. While driving from the Prospect House to Bloomingdale, in passing through the woods he heard cries of help proceeding from a ravine a few rods distant from the road. Springing from his carriage and running hastily to the edge of the ravine, Mr. Derby saw an infuriated bear raging around the trunk of a small maple, eagerly trying to dislodge Gardner Maloney, a Saranac guide, who had taken refuge in the branches of the tree.

With genuine heroism Mr. Derby drew his revolver and rushed to the rescue. Skilled in woodcraft, he was enabled to creep unobserved by the bear to within a short range, when

North from Prospect House, Upper Saranac Lake (Stoddard)

he opened fire upon the brute. The first fire took effect in the shoulder and was quickly followed by a second that lodged in the bear's head.

The only effect of these was to distract the attention and increase the fury of the bear, who abandoned the siege of Maloney and directed his attention to Mr. Derby. He charged furiously upon that gentleman who coolly fired two more shots with wonderful precision at the head of the approaching brute, and turning beat a hasty retreat in the direction of the road.

The speed told rapidly upon Mr. Derby, who turns the scales at 230 pounds, but he made a tremendous effort to reach his team, a pair of spirited young horses, thinking if he could once gain his seat in the carriage, the team would afford safety. Unfortunately, the horses, excited by the firing, were on the alert, and, catching sight of the bear, ran furiously down the road, leaving Mr. Derby to settle with the bear.

Not a moment was to be lost. Mr. Derby discovered a tree near by. Springing into its lower branches he reached a point of safety half dead from exhaustion.

The bear, bleeding profusely from many wounds, was undaunted and aggressive, and did not leave his enemy long to arrange a new campaign, but began the ascent of the tree.

Mr. Derby drew a sheath-knife, and with that in his teeth, prepared for a desperate encounter. Discharging the three remaining shots of his revolver at the head of the bear, he seized the knife, and, holding by a limb with his left hand, struck desperately at the forefeet of the climber, nearly severing one claw and cutting enormous gashes in the animal's shoulders and head. While struggling for his life the limb by which Mr. Derby was holding broke, and he was precipitated to the ground ten feet, sustaining severe bruises and a badly-sprained shoulder.

In his eagerness to reach his foe the bear tumbled from the tree also, and rushed at Mr. Derby, who had recovered his feet and, unable to retreat, was awaiting the attack, his sheath-knife in hand.

The bear arose on his haunches, and by a dextrous thrust, Mr. Derby's knife was driven straight through his heart, and the animal succumbed.

Mr. Derby suffered severe scratches and loss of considerable blood. His clothing was literally converted into strings by the claws of the bear. Exhausted and suffering from loss of blood, Mr. Derby was assisted by Maloney, who had witnessed the last of the struggle, to the house of John Howe, where he remained. Maloney recovered the runaway team, and Derby drove to Bloomingdale, where his wounds were dressed by Dr. William. . . ."

Derby got a great deal of pleasure telling about his experience with the two city sports who had stayed overnight and were ready to continue their boat trip the next morning. Before departing they happened to compare bills:

"I paid $12.00," said the first fellow.

"$12.00! Why my bill was $20.00!" exclaimed the other. Inasmuch as each had had the same service they thought that the proprietor had made a mistake, so they hurried back and looked up Derby.

"How's this?" asked one, "you charged my friend here $20.00 for the same thing for which you billed me only $12.00!"

"Lets see your bill," requested Ed., who took the statement, looked at it closely and remarked, "Oh, I see where the trouble is. My wife made a mistake in addition. Your bill should have been $20.00 also. $8.00 more will straighten matters out!"

The puzzled pigeon blinked a couple times, reluctantly shelled out the balance and the party moved on.

Mrs. Derby sold the Prospect House in 1886 to a group which later incorporated as the

Saranac Inn in 1903 (Stoddard)

Stage Departing from Saranac Inn

Daniel W. Riddle, Supt. at Saranac Inn

73

Saranac Inn Guidehouse (middle) and Annex right 1903

Saranac Inn Store with Cooler in Background 1903

*Saranac Inn: L to R Carpenter Shop, Blacksmith Shop,
Paint Shop 1903*

Saranac Inn Laundry and Windmill 1903

Saranac Inn Woodyard, Forest Home Road 1900

Saranac Inn Sawmill, Forest Home Road 1903

(Firth photos)

"Upper Saranac Association." At the same time they secured control over the entire Township 20 of Great Tract 1 Macomb's Purchase, which contained about 26,880 acres with no less than fifty bodies of water of varying size and shape. Although logged over in 1860-1, twenty-five years previously, there was now a saleable second growth, so the new company put a dam across the Big Clear Pond outlet, erected a sawmill and thereby obtained lumber not only for their own use but also for sale.

At Derby's Daniel W. Riddle, who had cured at Saranac Lake, became acquainted and later formed friendships with several of the people who organized the "Association." Besides Dr. Samuel Ward of Albany and brother Quincy Riddle, a New York lawyer, Daniel R. must have favorably impressed Dr. Dunton, Mrs. Peabody and Mrs. Chandler because he was offered the position of manager of the new Saranac Inn. He promptly agreed and stayed with the organization until his death in 1913. During the years just preceding his demise, when his health deteriorated appreciably, he accepted a decrease in his work load and functioned as nominal superintendent.

An old Saranac Inn brochure, put out in 1888, provides proof that that hotel, capacity 100 at the time, was becoming increasingly popular in spite of the transportation difficulties: "Boats, supplies, camp outfits and livery may be had at the Inn, kept for the accommodation of guests and travelers. Sites for camping out are abundant about the Lake and many fine camps now line the shores of Upper Saranac. Saranac Inn is now easily accessible by the new route from Plattsburgh, over the Chateaugay Railroad to Saranac Lake, thence by regular daily stagecoach to the Inn, distance of about 15 miles. The old routes via Plattsburgh, Port Kent and Westport on Lake Champlain, Malone and Moira on the Ogdensburgh Railroad and by boat conveyance through the lakes are still open and present their old and attractive features of travel.

"The quickest passage from New York is by sleeper over Hudson River Railroad to Plattsburgh, thence by rail in the morning to Saranac Lake and by regular stage through to Saranac Inn, making a passage of about 18 hours from New York. Through fare — about $13.00."

The logistics problem was conveniently solved when Dr. W. Seward Webb completed his Mohawk and Malone (M&M) "Golden Chariot Route" through the mountains from Utica/Remsen to Montreal in 1892. This of course eliminated the necessity for the roundabout route by way of Plattsburgh and the Chateaugay Railroad (later the D.&H.) and cut the travel time by more than at least a third. . . .

Prices were more modest back in 1888. "The terms at the Inn are $3.50 a day," Manager Riddle noted. "Special rates made by the week or season. Guides with boats are obtainable at $3.00 per day. A mail is received daily at the Inn postoffice and there is a telegraph station in the house. Also a telephone." Civilization had most emphatically come to that scenic neck of the North Woods!

Saranac Inn and the vicinity of which it was the social center was the vacation mecca for many of the nation's most affluent and influential people, among them governors of the Empire State and others as well. Roswell P. Flower, after whom the little lake formed by damming the Saranac River was named, although a Jefferson county man, was a frequent visitor at the Inn. Vice-President Levi P. Morton, who later (1894-5) was governor of this state, demonstrated his attachment to the region by building camps at Pine Brook and on Eagle Island. Governor Frank S. Black liked to hunt and fish along the Saranac waterways. Theodore Roosevelt, as a young man stayed at the Inn while collecting material for his widely acclaimed *Wild Life Bulletins,* and often came back while governor.

Charles Evans Hughes, of Glens Falls, as governor and later chief justice of the

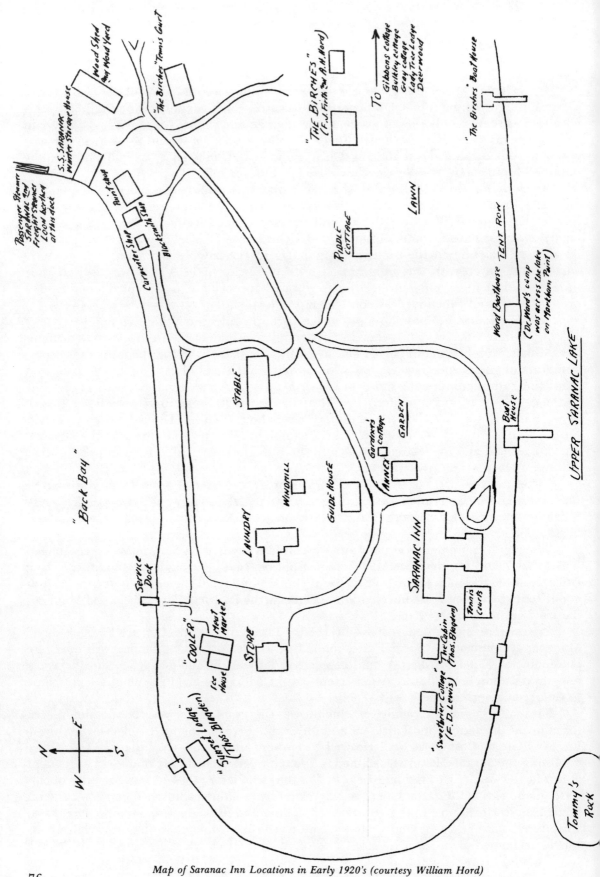

Map of Saranac Inn Locations in Early 1920's (courtesy William Hord)

Aerial View of Saranac Inn in its Heyday — 1920's

Supreme Court, leased one of the larger Inn cottages and for two Summers used the place as the gubernatorial headquarters. Later in life he and his family seldom missed his cherished Adirondack vacation.

Other notables were Governors Earle of Pennsylvania and Stephen Merritt of Connecticut — the former near what is now Donaldson's Trading Post and the latter at Bartlett's and the "Saranac Club."

Unquestionably, the most publicized seasonal visitor was Governor, later President Grover Cleveland, who spent the honeymoon with Frances Folsom, his second wife, in 1888. At first the couple were quartered in a suite at the Inn but later Thomas Blagden's Camp Alpha, the picturesque log cabin close by the hotel, was made available. Still standing, although considerably remodeled, this attractive place was occupied for many years by Mrs. William G. Rockefeller and members of her family and, still more recently, has been owned by her daughter — Mrs. Frederick C. Lincoln.

The Clevelands were frequent guests not only at Saranac Inn but, since he was a far better than average fisherman and author of *Fishing and Shooting Sketches* (1907), he became well acquainted and informed about the northern Adirondacks. His speeches and public papers indicate his affinity with and concern for the problems relative to the establishment of the Adirondack Park in 1892. The legendary Martin Moody of Tupper Lake was very likely his favorite guide.

When D. W. Riddle retired he was succeeded by M. D. Marshall, who managed the Inn for fourteen years before the property passed into the control of Harrington Mills, by far the best-known of its proprietors and without a question among the most successful — if not the most after Paul Smith and Mrs. Mary H. Chase — hotel owners in Adirondack history. Starting his career as the concessionaire in the old Shoreham Hotel in New York, he rose rapidly in the hotel business. Among the first which he managed was the Grafton in Washington, a residential house patronized principally by diplomats and legislators. In 1915 he built the Harrington, a commercial house in the capital city. A manager of White-face Inn at Lake Placid he attracted the favorable attention of directors of the Upper Saranac Inn.

In 1920 he bought out the interest of Dr. Samuel Ward, president of the organization.

Among his most successful resort hotels were the Coquena and the Clarendon at Daytona Beach, Florida.

Those who knew him considered Mills to be a farsighted business executive whose wide experience prepared him for profitable hotel management. Moreover, he was a genial and considerable host who gained the affection and esteem of his associates and clientele. As the result of his long experience in Washington, he knew many of the most prominent lawmakers of the nation and most of the foreign diplomats. Laurence A. Slaughter, a son-in-law, was manager until 1946.

After his death on March 5, 1935 another Mills son-in-law, Frederick E. Altemus, who had also been associated with the operation of the Inn for many years, was appointed manager by A. S. Kirkeby, president of Kirkeby Hotels, and his associates, who had purchased the hotel in August, 1946.

The Kirkeby hotel chain also operated such prestigious hotels as The Warwick in New York City; the Blackstone in Chicago; Beverly — Wilshire and Sunset Towers in Beverly Hills, California and Hotel Nacional de Cuba in Havana.

By 1946 Saranac Inn had been expanded and modernized so that it could accommodate more than 1,000 guests and was rated as the most resplendent such establishment in the mountains — with one noteworthy exception: even at its peak some of the guests in the less expensive rooms never did cotton to the communal bathrooms.

By the end of World War II all the surviving large Adirondack resort hotels — and there weren't that many still standing and as yet untorched — were in deep financial trouble. Paul Smith's main building had burned in September 1930, a result of faulty wiring according to the ensuing investigation, and the famous Loon Lake House followed in September 1956, the casualty of a not-too-accidental conflagration.

The Automobile Age was well on its way so people who used to pass the entire Summer in one vacation spot succumbed to the yen for travel — pack as much touring pleasure as possible into the allotted period. The traditional, leisurely re-creational and recreational pattern changed rapidly as the nation shook off the trauma of the war and sought entertainment release and relief in as many ways and as many places as possible.

The victims of this frenetic pursuit of highway happiness were the owners of the formerly profitable huge hotel complexes which rapidly became vacation white elephants. How to adjust to the changing tempo, moods and demands of the times called for some high-octane thinking and planning.

One of the most sensible and logical solutions, and the method pursued at Saranac Inn during several fairly rapid ownership changes, was catering to the convention business — which proved a real Godsend to resorts such as the Lake Placid Club, the smaller Whiteface Inn — and Saranac Inn. Before the Summers started and well into October, usually doldrum days at the resorts, the spacious hostelries were able to extend their seasons and thereby better weather the ever-increasing tax burdens and the steadily declining regular season patronage.

In 1957 the Inn became the property of the Sharpe Hotel organization.

Mr. and Mrs. Willard Boyce, Harrington Mills, Judge Paddock at Boyce Retirement Party 9/29/28

Altemus — Mills Wedding Party at the Inn

Dining Room of Saranac Inn in 1930's

Drawing Room of Saranac Inn in 1930's

Mrs. Evelyn Sharpe spent $300,000 in 1958 in a massive redecoration project which still could not produce the desired effect — the generation of increased business for the Inn — so it too experienced the chanciness of weather conditions and the lack of a guaranteed income. After several spotty seasons and light convention bookings the Sharpe interests lost interest and sold the Inn to the Fields Hotel Corporation which, as expected, was confronted by the same unfavorable factors plus increased competition from the more popular Lake Placid establishments.

During that period the sale of several of the cottages eased somewhat the insurance overhead, but the outlook was definitely bleak for the owners and the area economy in general. Incidentally, the Inn paid ten per cent of the Santa Clara property taxes and a similar amount to the Saranac Lake Central School District. Many persons — as many as 400 in fact — found employment there in various capacities; an estimated three-quarters of a million dollars was pumped into the area's cash registers and bank accounts every Summer by the guests and personnel at the hotel. . .

All that Spring of 1962 there were strong and repeated hints that the Inn was about to close down forever and even though the convention schedule was full the Fields Saranac Company of New York City nevertheless threw in the sponge and confirmed the persistent rumors. Only the golf course stayed open that season. Then on August 1 the hotel again changed hands — for the last time this time to Charles and David Vosburgh, auctioneers of Cortland, New York and De Land, Florida. Although Brener and Lewis Co., New York brokers who handled the sale said the selling price was confidential, the actual figure, however, was later found to be $400,000. This transaction marked the end of the line for the storied Saranac Inn and the start of the Vosburgh era on the Upper Lake and its environs.

Saranac Inn from the Lake

Buffet at Inn in 1960's

Lounge at Inn in 1960's

The Worrisome Years

The hard-pressed owners of the large outdated hotel complexes in the Adirondacks as well as elsewhere were eventually confronted by an unpleasant and inescapable decision — what to do about and with their white elephants. Rather than pour ever-larger sums of money down the proverbial rat-holes, some of the proprietors — such as the worried owners of the Prospect House (Blue Mt. Lake), the Sagamore (at Long Lake), the Stevens House (Lake Placid), the Algonquin (Lower Saranac Lake) and the Wawbeek (Upper Saranac Lake) — gave the orders that put the demolition crews to work.

Others, intentionally or otherwise, paid their homage to Prometheus, the god of fire, and consigned their problems to the flames. The Loon Lake House, the Ruisseaumont (at Lake Placid), the Ampersand and Miller's (Lower Saranac Lake) are prime examples of the incendiary solution. And of course there were many other such structures that met the same fiery fate — some of them torch jobs (arson) and others traceable to plain tough luck. Whatever, the landscape was rid of another passé eye-sore and constant source of apprehension.

Immediately after the sale of the huge old had-been, Saranac Inn, the buyers of the satellite cottages started sweating it out. They, however, wasted no time putting their concerns on record and continued to do so for the ensuing sixteen years right up until the final, fiery curtain.

By 1968 the members of the Saranac Inn Lakefront Association, supported by Grant Simmons, president of the Association of Residents on Upper Saranac Lake, dispatched a strong letter of complaint to the Franklin County Board of Supervisors demanding action on the dismantling of the Inn and warning of the consequences if no action was taken. Besides Simmons the signers of the manifesto were Frank Goldman, president of the Owners

Association; Saul Wexler, vice president; Daniel Mahoney, Carroll Treacy, J. W. Lang, M.S. Shatluck and James Woolsey, Jr.

The letter stated that the signers had purchased their properties in September 1962 and that the Inn had deteriorated so badly that it constituted a definite fire hazard. They also wrote that they had appealed to the ostensible owners, Charles Vosburgh and Robert Duley, an owner of record, but all to no avail. They also asserted that Supervisor Vanderwalker had been notified on several occasions but that he had ignored them.

The document revealed, moreover, that there had been two near misses in the sense that two of the large buildings had burned. Furthermore, they warned that the entire peninsula would be imperiled if the Inn, which they termed "an attractive nuisance," ever caught fire.

The letter of protest — with the words Please Take Notice underlined — then gave three warnings:

(1) That there exists a condition at the Saranac Inn Peninsula fraught with fire, health and safety hazards.

(2) That nothing has been done to rectify the situation although many warnings have been given.

(3) That therefore if there is any damage or injury resulting from fire or property damage from the sufferance and allowance of this nuisance the County of Franklin will be charged and held liable for said damages or injuries!!

Except for routine contacting of Vosburgh and Duley no actually effective action was ever taken by the supervisors.

The Adirondack Daily Enterprise, in an article dated November 1975, commented about the snail's pace dismantling of the abandoned Inn in these well-selected words: "Perhaps the most monumental on-going one-man extravaganza [hereabouts] is the razing of Saranac Inn. Unfortunately for the news media the man doing the work is publicity [and camera] shy.

"And why not, when you think of the possible pressures from the Adirondack Park Agency, from legal firms and others interested in the process of demolition other than the owner himself, Robert Duley of Plattsburgh?

"What problems face the stocky, well-muscled Gary Garrow in his daily assault on the monstrous 276 room former showplace of the early century can only be imagined.

"And yet he faces the task with a modicum of anxiety and seems to have a well-ordered plan in the back of his mind. He did say that he wished some help and that his boss is not seriously considering adding a crew to expedite the job.

"Since the Inn has been under the salvage phase hundreds of Summer travelers stop by and, if not warned, will often go prowling through the dim interior endangering their lives even though the property is posted.

"A casual observer might say that the work, which started over a year ago is 20% completed but the exterior portions have hardly been ripped away except at the West end.

"It is a startling and even heart-breaking sight to see the fine old Inn in its present condition and one also wonders how it has been spared from fire and acts of vandalism." Very valid and perceptively prophetic words because the vandalism factor could certainly have been a contributory cause. However, there is still another distinct possibility that someone besides vagrants could quite conceivably have set the fire — if indeed that's the way it happened. Not to be overlooked is the admittedly outside chance that children could have been up to the age-old playing with matches game with spectacular results." Whatever the actual cause, the effect was an inferno.

The Dread Becomes A Reality

Less than three years later, in the early afternoon of June 17, 1978, the nemesis of so many other rambling old wooden firetraps took its toll during a wind-swept seven-hour conflagration which threatened not only the Inn and its former satellite cottages but also everything within a three-mile radius as well. The strong winds scattered large embers which ignited hundreds of smaller fires on camp roofs, boats, cars, fields and timberland and caused great concern even in Lake Clear, three miles away, some of whose residents also had more than their wanted share of worried moments.

Especially vulnerable were the six large cottages lined up downwind of the inferno and, since the Inn itself was obviously doomed, the hundred-plus firemen from Tupper Lake, Saranac Lake, Bloomingdale and Paul Smith's-Gabriels concentrated on saving the camps. Many stayed all night drenching the debris and dousing the many minor blazes. Before the ordeal was over more than three hundred volunteer firemen were involved in the frantic effort to save the structures.

In the meantime Rangers from Encon (Department of Environmental Conservation) were kept very busy putting out the numerous small fires in the wooded area between the Inn and Route 30 and along that road toward Lake Clear's nearest houses and outbuildings.

During the most critical stages of the desperate situation the fire-fighters were badly handicapped by the burning of two lengths of four-inch hose fed by the pumpers operating from the lake. This resulted in lost pressure when it was most needed and undoubtedly hastened the doom of the Inn.

In an all-out attempt to save the close-by cottages the firemen used back-packed Indian pumps and the owners their own equipment to put out the roof fires. Fortunately, since many of the camp-owners were there for the weekend, they were able to do all they could to save their property. Moreover, the fire broke out during daylight, which made the challenge somewhat less difficult.

At the peak of the inferno the wind-fed feasting flames poked long probing fingers forty to fifty feet into the sky and the central pillar of fire soared almost a hundred feet upward in a solid lurid shaft.

Strangely enough the Mahoney camp, the one farthest away from the Inn and their vacation home for seventeen years, caught fire while the other five escaped the fiery fate.

Fortunately, too, even though nearly three hundred firemen and many fascinated on-lookers were on the scene, there were very few injuries. Besides the few superficial cuts and bruises that were reported, only two more serious injuries occurred. While trying to save the Mahoney camp two Saranac Lake firemen — Kim Duso and Dick Ohmann — were knocked from ladders when a cornice collapsed and toppled them the two-story distance to the ground.

Men from the Saranac Lake Fire Department stayed at the site Saturday night and well into Sunday evening drenching the still-smoking ashes and charred timbers until three bulldozers arrived and pushed the rubble into three separate steaming heaps.

By Sunday noon only a tall chimney and a lone fireplace were all that was left as forlorn reminders of the far-famed and fabulous Saranac Inn. But, as an aftermath and a sort of grim consolation, the remaining cottagers soon realized that their recurrent, somewhat psychedelic nightmare was over at long last. [The information on which this segment is based came from issues of the *Adirondack Daily Enterprise*. The graphic articles were written by its publisher Bill Doolittle; the top flight photos were taken by Susan Doolittle. Many thanks to each for their permission to use such first-rate sources.]

Fire Photos June 17, 1978. Courtesy of Susan Doolittle and the Adirondack Daily Enterprise.

The Vosburgh Era at the Inn

Whenever people discuss the comparative importance of the contributions made by the various individuals who have had a pronounced affect on the course of Adirondack history, the names that come easily are those of Seneca Ray Stoddard, the photographer; Verplanck Colvin, the surveyor — author, and the renowned William H. H. Murray, the writer and lecturer. Although all three had many other arrows in their quivers, those assets are frequently overlooked. But the fact remains that each of these men in his own media unquestionably rates the most credit for popularizing our entire Adirondack region.

However, when it comes down to selecting the person who has done the most to publicize the Saranac Lake area, especially in recent years, it would be difficult to bypass the late Charlie Vosburgh, who departed the land of the living on December 30, 1978, and his impact upon that very special area — the Saranac Inn environs.

Granted, he was controversial because he got things done and in the process antagonized many people of the type that strenuously and vociferously resist anything that rocks their own particular boat or threatens their special sphere of interest. The local real estate agents in particular were envious of his free-wheeling style, flair and financial success. Others among the disenchanted were those involved in disputes over boundary lines and related misunderstandings. Whether or not their gripes and grievances were valid is a matter unknown except to the principals themselves — and one of them is no longer with us. Nevertheless, the consensus of those familiar with the general situation is that nobody else has generated so much interest and acrimony, conversation and entertainment and thereby put so much more property on the Santa Clara assessment rolls. For those who watched him in action on the auction block he displayed the spell-binding style and guile of P. T. Barnum, enhanced by the Yankee shrewdness and persuasiveness of the fictional David Harum who, incidentally ruled the roost in Homeville (Homer) N.Y. not far from Cortland, N.Y., Charlie's former hometown.

Although he started his career as a Southern Tier farm and livestock auctioneer, working strictly on a commission basis, Vosburgh soon saw the light and realized that someone — such as himself — with gambling instinct could make far more moola by buying a sizeable shebang and selling it piecemeal. Acting on that hunch he headed North into tall timber country, lined up his prospects with discretion and imagination and with the help of his son and well-trained staff — some of them acting as shills — he eventually officiated at the demise and disposition of more than fifty impressive real estate and personal property deals.

Among these were outmoded, down-at-the-heel hotels, defunct country clubs, cottage colonies and the seasonal playpens of the very rich. Examples included Hollywood enclave near Old Forge; the Lake Clear Inn; the Club Farm and Signal Hill properties, both in Lake Placid; the entire hamlet of McKeever, a logged-out ghost town; Seligman's luxurious Fish Rock or Sekon Lodge camp on Upper Saranac Lake — and of course Saranac Inn, the pride and prize of them all. . . .

On July 31, 1962 and for a reported $400,000 — one-fourth down — Vosburgh bought the 3,000 acre spread on Upper Saranac. Included were the completely furnished 276 room Saranac Inn, the yacht club, over 400 furnished cottages and lodges of varying sizes, 3,000 feet of Upper Lake shoreline, 40,000 feet of frontage on smaller satellite ponds, several islands and a championship caliber 18 hole golf course. Without doubt the purchase was one of — if not the most important varied business transactions in Adirondack history. With no apparent loss of momentum Charlie put the promotional program into high gear and, using saturation advertising, set the stage for the Big Affair.

The Buyer — Ralph Bowles; the Seller — Charles Vosburgh

On September 18, 1962, just six weeks later and in the Stanhope Room of the Inn, Vosburgh started the ball arolling by remarking that the estimated value of the property about to be knocked down was, according to a recent Insurance appraisal $1,078,250. He also commented that the Inn had grossed a cool $1,200,000 ($38,000 in a single day) the previous and final year of its operation. He further explained that even if the buildings were torn down, the new buyer would be getting very desirable and saleable shorefront frontage for a piddling $15.00 per foot [now worth from $200-250 and up depending upon location].

The warm-up session concluded, the bidding started at $10,000 and rose rapidly in $5,000 jumps to $50,000 — but then decelerated perceptibly. Showman Vosburgh pulled out all the stops in his verbal repertoire and alternately coaxed, threatened, insulted, ribbed and ridiculed his audience for nearly an hour. Then at 12:35 p.m. he finally banged his gavel and closed out for $75,000. The startled buyer — Ralph Bowles, a Florida restauranteur — expressed amazement at his bargain while the auctioneer registered deep concern because, just before he rang down the curtain, he was heard to say, "This is the worst thing that has ever happened in this locality."

Early in the bidding Vosburgh speculated that, judging by the niggardly offers, most buyers seemed interested only in the salvage potential. Furthermore, the general feeling among the 400 people present was that the Inn would never again open its doors.

When asked, Bowles replied that he had come to the auction with no intention of buying the place, that he personally would never go into the hotel business and, moreover, hadn't had time yet to decide what to do about and with his unanticipated purchase. He, however, rejected a $50,000 offer for the personal property — furniture, lamps, drapes, beds, sprinkler systems, boilers and other fixtures.

Vosburgh's total take for the day was $189,250. Featured were later whirlwind sales of ten cottages which in twenty minutes flat brought in sums ranging from $5,000 to $10,000 for each furnished camp, depending of course on size and location.

The 200 acre golf course was sold to Harry Littman, a Washington lawyer, for $48,000. . . .

Predictably enough, nearly a year after the auction Bowles apparently gave up on his efforts to unload the property and notified Vosburgh that he had changed his mind and wanted out. No one knows just what he had to pay for the switcheroo but it is a matter of record that in early June of 1963 Charlie and his talented crew put on an encore. In Act 1 of the repeat performance Robert Duley, owner of Ellenburg Creamery and resident of Platts- burgh bought the empty Inn and adjacent property for $16,500; another $17,000 got him several smaller cottages including "The Wigwam."

In separate sales lakefront lots without buildings brought $3,500 to $5,400. Contents of the Inn and Yacht Club sold for varying prices; e.g. a 12' x 15' Oriental rug for $60.00, wicker chairs for $11.00 each, 5 card tables for $20.00, lots of blankets — $25.00 and 2 garbage pails for $15.00 each, hardly recognizable as bargains.

The Kelly House and lot brought $10,750 and the large general store — $2,300.

For me and the other 400-500 fascinated people who sat out the second auction, undeniably one of the highlights of that Summer was the virtuosity of Vosburgh and son, the skillful exercise of applied psychology, the antics of the shills, the spite bidding, the spectator and participant (bidders) action and reaction were entertainment at its human best.

In late August 1964 or 65 Charlie put on another of his virtuoso performances, with excellent supporting staff assistance, at Seligman's former sumptuous Sekon Lodge (also known originally as Fish Rock Camp). On that memorable day nearly a thousand active participants and curious non-bidders watched and listened intently as real estate, furnish- ings — much of it handcrafted furniture made by the resident or area guides — paintings by Charles Bull and other topflight artists, and other valuable personal possessions were sold for far more than customary prices to an obviously affluent set of customers. Proof again that auctions and auctioneering have become one of the world's most popular indoor and outdoor pastimes. . . .

In an *Adirondack Daily Enterprise Weekender* article, dated October 22, 1979, Harold Bishop reported an interview with Charlie and Georgina Vosburgh. Although he featured the former he nevertheless credited her for her obvious and effective supporting role in these carefully selected words: "She is his strength and he is her reason for being strong. They complement each other." Having grown up in a family of active auctioneers in the Champlain Valley her help was of prime and recognized importance.

Commenting on Charlie's reticence the observant Bishop aptly concluded: "His story can't be had from him. His whole story will never be had unless someone has five or ten years to search it out."

I'll certainly buy that because on several well-remembered occasions I personally tried to extract his story from him but even though he talked volubly, animatedly and informa- tively about his early years and his profession (calling), he neverthelesss stubbornly refused to allow me to tape record the several sessions for future use in a projected book on auctions and auctioneering. Too bad because it would have made a great book!

One final comment: Fortunately for Vosburgh all of his wheeling and dealing in sub- division of real estate took place in the 1960's, years before the advent of the Adirondack Park Agency and its restrictive land-use regulations. Understandably, had he appeared on the scene ten years later he would have been stopped dead in his tracks, exasperated and completely stymied. However, knowing Charlie, I'm sure that he would have proven a foeman worthy of their best steel.

Chapter 8

The Wawbeek

The derivation of place names on the Saranacs made frequent reference to one of the area's natural features — its huge rock formations. The late William Rockefeller called his luxurious "camp" Wonundra or Big Rock; Isaac Seligman dubbed his place Fish Rock and the hotel that dominated the southern end of the Upper Lake also adopted an Algonquin term — Wawbeek.

This superb location has always had more than mere scenic importance because it controlled the Lake end of the historic and preferred Sweeney Carry, the three-mile portage [a term not used on this side of the Canadian border] connecting the large lake with the Raquette, the main river route through the region. Because of its strategic position it became the bone of contention between competing logging interests from the earliest days of that once-thriving and most important industry. For that reason it became, in 1878, the arena for a bitter, prolonged feud between two strong-minded and determined men — Capt. James H. Pierce of Bloomingdale and Col. Christopher F. Norton of Plattsburgh, the aggressive "King of the Saranacs." This power struggle constituted an important phase in the history of the Upper Lake and the Wawbeek area in particular.

These two men were foemen eminently worthy of each other's steel. Pierce, who was born in New Sweden, Clinton Co. on August 27, 1826, eventually became one of Essex County's foremost men. Starting as a clerk in Keeseville in 1843 he was transferred in 1845

Hon. C.F. Norton,

Christopher F. Norton

Captain James H. Pierce

to Fredericksburgh, Va., then to Milwaukee and Neenah, Wisc. in fairly rapid succession. In 1852, in company with James B. Dickinson, he erected mills and forges besides doing business in lumbering and merchandising in Bloomingdale's largest emporium. Married to Miss C. O. Dennin in August, 1856 he served in the Union army with distinction from 1862 to 1864.

After the War he was a farmer in the Town of Franklin, then entered politics as supervisor for four years and, subsequently, was elected member of the Assembly and served three terms — 1869-71, thus becoming the first member to be returned to Albany from the county (Franklin). In 1877 he went back to Essex County and practiced law. He was supervisor for the Town of St. Armand for seven years before the War Between the States and ten years after returning to Essex Co., he was considered to be a very generous, public-spirited and congenial leader who, like his close friend, Paul Smith, delighted in anecdotes and social affairs.* Obviously a man with such sterling qualities was well-qualified to take on the formidable competition from Plattsburgh — C. F. Norton, who also had a home in Saranac Lake for a time. [Bloomingdale Ave.]

Born in Fredonia, N.Y. in 1821 Norton, whose father was a wool merchant, went into the lumber business in Erie, Pa. in 1845 and amassed a small fortune before moving to Plattsburgh in 1866. A man of impressive physique and appearance, dynamic and ingratiating, with a phenomenal memory and formidable talent for administrative details and handling men, he was a big man in every respect and the possessor of a giant-like matching ambition. He was always as well-dressed as his lumber; moreover, his rise to dominance was fast and his subsequent financial collapse was equally rapid — too many irons in the proverbial fire. The precipitating factor in his downfall was not lumber but sour investments in real estate and iron in 1877 cost him more than $100,000.

It was believed that had he been able to raise sufficient capital to tide him over a six-month period he might conceivably have been able to recoup his money, because both the iron market and the real estate situations staged a fast switcheroo about that time — but unfortunately too late to benefit him.

Like many other successful industrialists Norton was keenly aware that most of the critical action affecting his varied interests was taking place in Albany so, when asked to consider a nomination as state senator on the Democratic ticket in a notoriously Republican district, he readily consented and was elected in 1869 by the voters of Warren, Essex and Clinton counties.

Also like too many other aggressively greedy politicians, Norton got himself entangled in a very obvious personal power-play in which he flagrantly put his own self-interest above that of his constituency. The following letter to the editor of the Plattsburgh *Sentinel* dated Feb. 23, 1871 and signed C. Cob tells the whole sordid story. "Mr. Editor; My attention has been called to a bill introduced in the Senate by Senator C. F. Norton which, if passed, will place practically the entire Saranac River watershed in the hands of a corporation (C. F. Norton and Co.) and will deprive others of its use, subjecting them to that corporation's dedication and preventing their using the River if the Norton Co. so chooses. . . .

"Among its provisions the Norton Co. would be given the privilege of driving other owners' logs — whether they wish to employ the company or not — for one-half cent a log per mile. This would deny other individuals the right to do their own driving. Now this may seem like a small price to pay but I have been informed by a man who had charge of the finances of drivers that the average cost per standard (single log) for driving logs the whole

---

* John Titus   *Adirondack Pioneers* Troy Art Press, 1899

Sweeney — Daniels Cabin

distance from Saranac Lake to Plattsburgh was only $.17 apiece. By the terms of this pending bill it would cost nearly three times as much.

"Another stipulation in the Norton Bill is the hydraulic clause which would enable him and his three associates (John Merrill, L. L. Smith and J. K. McKillip) to build more dams and reservoirs to impound water, and in doing so to take over other people's property whether or not they are willing to sell. Also included is the privilege of withholding water when wanted for other uses by other people, and then releasing it in such quantities as they wish for driving the logs — and then shutting it off completely without giving downstream business a sufficient flow of water for any use whatsoever.

"Forge and mill-owners, how does that suit you?

"These are just some of the provisions of the Senator's bill which require looking into by everyone with riverbank property. It has been generally assumed that the 1847 law making the Saranac "public" highway was very liberal in its coverage and permitted everyone concerned to enjoy its benefits.

"The question now is simply this: Was Christopher F. Norton elected to represent the best interests of his constituency or is he there to subvert their interests to his own?"

Incredibly enough, that outrageous bill passed the Senate but a fairly thorough research was indicated that if it ever became law — which it possibly did — it never produced effective results for Norton. . . .

Col. Norton subsequently moved to Perry's Park, Colo., where he was active in the lumbering business until his death there in 1890. His wife, Charlotte Moore, a member of one of the oldest Platsburgh families, studied medicine after her husband's death and practised in the West.*

---

* Maitland C. De Sormo *Heydays of the Adirondacks* Saranac Lake: Adirondack Yesteryears Inc. 1974

Wawbeek End of Sweeney Carry (Stoddard)

The foregoing biographic sketches provide the necessary background and frame of reference required to understand the personal and economic rivalry represented by these two worthy and resourceful opponents. However, to eliminate the non-essential details in the interest of space saving, just the most significant move in the ensuing showdown need be given.

Recognizing the strategy implied in the time-tested truism that possession is nine points of the law, Norton hired Oatman C. Coville, a well-known Saranac guide, to settle at the Lake end of the Sweeney Carry, probably in the old Sweeney-Daniels cabin. At the Raquette River end of the overland route he ensconced Oliver Tromblee. This ploy beat Pierce to the draw and thereby ended the lively contest of wits and personalities. The positioning of just those two pawns ended the prolonged chess game and Pierce was forced out.

It didn't take long for Coville and his wife — like the Martins, Bartletts and Coreys — to realize that they occupied a very desirable and potentially profitable location, so they bought forty acres from Norton and built a rough half-way house to accommodate the steadily increasing flow of seasonal visitors — and there they stayed until Coville's death while on a visit to a Boston suburb thirteen years later.*

Tromblee also took an understandable fancy to his ménage — eight-person capacity — on the Raquette River and stayed on there until his demise. Old maps still pinpoint the place, long-since departed, as Tromblee's.

In 1891 the peripatetic T. Edmund Krumholz* and a man named Smith bought out Mrs. Coville and built the Wawbeek Hotel, in its day one of the finest in the mountains. Here is what E. R. Wallace's *Descriptive Guide to the Adirondacks*, 1894 edition, has to say about the picturesque place. "From Bartlett's Landing we cross the Upper Lake to Hotel Wawbeek, 2 miles above Rustic Lodge on the west shore, and land at Sweeney's place (formerly Forest House). From there we pass over the 3 mile Sweeney Carry to the Raquette River (Tromblee's). From there to Big Tupper Lake it is 11 miles. Hence the distance saved in comparison with the Indian Carry — Stony Creek route is about 12 miles.

"The Sweeney Carry is a pleasant forest road traversing for most of the distance

---

* Coville, who was deaf, was apparently deeply involved in a conversation with his young grandson when a train struck and killed him.

---

* Krumholz really got around: Before becoming co-owner of the Wawbeek he previously worked at Martin's; later in his career he managed The Ruisseaumont at Lake Placid, The Sagamore at Lake George and several Southern hotels.

through an immense sugar-bush. Both the proprietor of the Wawbeek and Oliver Tromblee, who keeps a small hotel at the river end of the portage, provide transportation. Price $1.50 per load; passengers $.75 each; party of several — $.50 each. At Tromblee's good meals are obtained for $.75 cents. . . .

"A lovelier picture is rarely seen than that beheld from the commanding eminence on which the Wawbeek is seated. Beautiful green islands frequently fringed with beaches of white sand stud the waters of the Lake in front, and on the right and left. Old Whiteface, with the light spot [slide] on his brow ever conspicuous hovers grandly into the sky, asserting his supremacy over many other ambitious peaks that rise and face him, dim and shadowy in the distance. Far, far beyond the vision's utmost grasp, the unbroken forest stretches away. It is a scene to be viewed for hours with increasing delight.

"The Wawbeek is a pre-eminently attractive and fashionable summer resort. In architecture it is very picturesque, and with its shapely towers and grand proportions forms an imposing feature in a landscape that claims the admiration of every beholder. Broad verandas nearly encircle the building, offering shaded promenades and views of scenery full of varied beauty and grandeur. It has nearly all the modern appointments including public and private baths. Open fireplaces enliven the office and many of the apartments.

"From nearly every room (each high, spacious and well-equipped) may be witnessed an animated water-scene, a virgin forest [sic] and numerous mountains. It has thorough sanitary improvements approved by experts. Pure water from a distant spring, mountain-born, is conducted through the house in iron pipes. Wall tents (carpeted) and handsome cottages suitably furnished and especially desirable to those seeking perfect quiet and better air are dispersed amid the leaf-fringed grounds.

"The table is liberal, perhaps unexcelled. Boating, fishing, rambling through the

Wawbeek Hotel in 1895 (Stoddard)

"The Loon" Freight Boat on Upper Lake

Some Upper Saranac Lakers (Stoddard)

woods, games of billiards, croquet and lawn tennis are among the amusements enjoyed.

"Every possible arrangement has been made to promote the health, comfort and enjoyment of 200 guests. Camp outfits are procurable here. Telegraph and post office (Wawbeek, N.Y.) are in the house. Steamers "Saranac" and "Loon" touch at the landing daily and convey passengers to the different camps and hotels on the Lake. Fare to Saranac Inn via stage and boat — $1.25.

"A stage runs daily from the Wawbeek over a good road through the forest 9 miles to Tupper Lake village, there connecting with trains on the Northern Adirondack R.R. (stage fare $1.50) and with steamer to Big Tupper Lake (3 miles)."

Wallace certainly trotted out his full arsenal of praise in this exercise in poetic prose and practically outdid himself in the process. Nevertheless, many other discerning visitors also pulled all stops in praising the place. Among them were Caroline Rockwood, whose *An Adirondack Romance* (c. 1897) uses it as the setting; Margaret Sidney's *Adirondack Cabin* (c. 1890) has several long chapters featuring the Wawbeek; Helen Bridgman's *Conquering*

The Second Wawbeek

the World (c. 1925) also devoted several segments to the fascinating place.

Artist A. B. Frost produced a number of sketches, the best of which featured an animated scene on the Carry.

In spite of its obvious assets and its popularity the Wawbeek's success was temporary and it met the same obstacles that spelled the doom of so many Summer hotels — short seasons, unfavorable weather, and uncertain patronage. Although it had top-flight management even they could not avert the inevitable course of events.

A clipping from the Tupper Lake *Herald* in its "Old Days" column for August 14, 1914 describes the rise and fall of the splendid hotel in the following manner:

"The old Wawbeek Hotel, a famed landmark on Upper Saranac Lake, was slated to go under the hammer. With the exception of State lands the shores of Upper Saranac are owned by wealthy men who have elaborate camps, but there are four points of public entry that must remain public in perpetuity," the Herald reported. "The Wawbeek stands at one of those points. Behind the clerk's desk in the lobby hangs a painting of the original Wawbeek, a log building of early Adirondack type, built before the first timber was sawed in this region. The cracks between the logs were chinked with plaster and the roof covered with shingles hand-hewn in the area. . . . Rough though it was it prospered. On the site of this building was erected a new Wawbeek,* a splendid summer hotel said to cost $100,000. . . . but was no financial success. It was sold under the hammer [auction] several times and recently was bought by a company of wealthy camp owners. They installed a manager to run it, but owning a summer hotel proved too much of a luxury even for them, and two years ago (1912) it was closed. Last season W. H. Reardon, who had been a successful hotelman at Long Lake, reopened the hotel and had a fairly good season, but some kind of hoodoo seems to hang over the Wawbeek. This time it was in the form of an inspector from the State fire marshal's office, who ruled that the structure did not meet modern fire-protection requirements. As compliance with these regulations would require costly remodeling, the Wawbeek did not reopen this season and now it has been sold to A. J. Ginsberg of Tupper Lake. The hotel will be torn down for salvage, the furnishings will be sold and the land will go for campsites or a cottage colony."

Another article from the same paper dated July 31, 1914 stated: "A. J. Ginsberg of Tupper Lake, who had bought the Wawbeek Hotel and cottages, announced that week than an auction would be held on August 7 and 8, 1914 at which time the entire contents of the Hotel property would be sold at the site." The unsold items were hauled to Tupper, stored in the McNeely block, formerly the Family Theater, and finally disposed of at subsequent sales and auctions. . . .

According to knowledgeable information sources the present Wawbeek Hotel, a considerably smaller structure, was built by Ferris Meigs in the early 1920's. Clarence Petty told me that he had spent several of the best summers of his life working there. His duties were principally that of boatman — taking passengers to their camps on the Lake or on errands to Saranac Inn, the hub of the Upper Lake. The craft had no name but it did have one of the greatest marine engines of all time and was a Fay Bowen. Its treatment was unworthy of such a fine craft for it was practically abandoned, allowed to sink at its boathouse slip but fortunately was finally raised, refurbished and given to the Adirondack Museum, where it is now on display along with other representative survivors of Adirondack transportation history.

---

* As Stoddard photos show, the original structure — the so-called Sweeney-Daniels cabin or Forest Home — was not torn down as this article would indicate. For years it served as a guidehouse but was eventually demolished when its deteriorated condition made it an eyesore [Editor]

The Second Wawbeek. Painting by Iskat c. 1970

Meigs hired one of the most experienced hotelmen in the East — Roy Baker, who had previously managed inns in Lake Placid, Maine and Florida. Incidentally, Baker also designed the new Wawbeek, using as his model the Chrysler estate main house on Sea Island, Georgia. The more than competent manager stayed on for fifteen years.

Another of the owners-managers, according to Harry Purchase, was Raymond Charest, an experienced Massachusetts hotelkeeper, whose tenure was 1947-52.

The next owner was Harry Purchase, head of the hotel management department at Paul Smith's College. During his thirteen-year operation (1952-65) the Wawbeek enjoyed many reasonably prosperous summers and benefited considerably by accommodating overflow guests and conventioneers from Saranac Inn, besides their own seasonal clientele.

My own introduction to this outstanding hostelry came in 1966 when my wife and I spent a memorable three-week vacation there, and I can well understand why the location has evoked so many enthusiastic responses over the years.

One of my lingering recollections has to do with the fabulous lake trout fishing which has traditionally featured that end of the Upper Lake and directly across from the Wawbeek. Early on that particular morning, awakened by the sun in my eyes, I ambled over to the window, looked out and saw a fascinating scene being enacted over near Doctor's Island, or Grey Rocks as it is now known, and so named by the late Sherwood Marvin. There were several boats at anchor and, as I watched intently, first one and then another figure would stand up in their respective craft and reel in busily. The light on that side of the Lake was still too dim and the distance was too far for me to be able to distinguish the size of the trout being extracted from the water and maneuvered into the nets, but I knew that they weren't dealing with minnows.

That location and near Church Island and Fish Rock, formerly Seligman's palatial

Fire Photos 3/1/80 by Ed Hale

camp, have produced some real lunkers over the years. The late Mollie Fribance, Charles Wardner's daughter, told me that during her girlhood days at Rustic Lodge there were many plaques on the walls and porch. These had tracings of the trophy trout and the vital statistics of each — weight, length, name of catcher, date of same. Mollie recalled that there was one sketch of a small leviathan and so-called supporting evidence that gave its weight at forty-seven pounds; there were very few records of lakers under forty. Undoubtedly their brothers and sisters and descendants of that ilk are still lurking in the chilly depths, but to my knowledge haven't made the fatal mistake of opening their capacious jaws to ingest assorted hardware items whose terminals are tempting crawlers or six-inch chubs. . . .

Harry and Terry (Therese) Purchase ran the Wawbeek until 1965, when they sold it to Mrs. Van Voorhis, who has been in residence during alternate seasons at "Bircholm," the camp on Deer Island, since 1917. With her usual thoroughness and insistence upon quality the new owner, with the Purchases as managers for two years, steadily built up the business until she decided to deed it over to St. Lawrence University, which already had a conference center on Back Bay, near the deserted Inn.

In September, 1968 Wawbeek Inc. bought the adjoining seventy-acre Camp De Baun, a boy's camp run by retired Lt. Col. H. B. Edwards and his wife. This choice property, containing a half-mile of lakefront, had originally been owned by the Walters family, who built their large camp enclave in 1907. In 1937 it was purchased by Henry Gaisman of New York, chairman of the board of the Gillette Safety Razor Co. Mr. Gaisman invested a considerable amount of money improving the property before giving it, about in 1950, along with the neighboring Goldman (previously Otto Kahn) Bull Point holdings to Mt. Sinai Hospital in N.Y.C. That institution sold the property to Edwards.

Wawbeek Fire — photo by Ed Hale

Wawbeek Fire — photo by Ed Hale

Such not infrequent turn-overs have made this coverage as well as that of most owner-ship successions rather difficult to follow but, since there is considerable interest in these transactions they are included. Anyhow, they help round out the history of the Wawbeek, the replacement for the only one left of the six large hotels that once stood proudly on the shores of the storied Saranacs. . . .

Less than two years after Saranac Inn went up in flames the second Wawbeek suffered the same fiery fate. About 7:20 on Saturday, March 1, only a few days after the *Sports Il-lustrated* contingent had checked out and the Wawbeek staff had held their own celebra-tion prior to closing the place until the start of the Summer season — disaster struck.

The blaze started in the kitchen when Guy O'Connor, the asst. manager, was using the deep fryer, whose thermostat apparently was not working properly and as a result the coil caught fire. Attempts to smother the flames were unsuccessful because the burning grease kept re-igniting. Compounding the problem was the malfunctioning of an overhead chemical spray system.

Upon arrival the Tupper Lake Fire Department crew soon had the fryer fire under control, but they soon discovered that the flames had spread through a flue to the attic area and were swiftly traveling the entire length of the three-story building. In less than a half hour the whole structure was ablaze.

By then the Saranac Lake fire-fighters, later joined by the Paul Smiths — Gabriels squad, were on the scene and working against great odds because, as often happens in such emergencies during the cold season, sufficient water was unavailable. Even though five fire trucks brought water from the Tupper Lake hydrants, the delays gave the flames too much headway. In the meantime a small portable pump, operating through a hole cut into the thirty-inch ice cover of Upper Saranac Lake, 200 feet away, did little to check the steady progress of the inferno.

At the height of the conflagration, readily seen from Tupper Lake, eleven miles away, the flames were probing more than 100 feet into the night sky and casting lurid shadows on the snow. By then the decision was made to give up on the obviously doomed structure and to concentrate on saving the several nearby buildings. By early morning all that remained of the sixty-year-old popular entertainment center were smoldering embers and the still-standing chimneys.

Luckily, there were no injuries and the staff were able to rescue pictures, antiques and some valuable small machinery items before the ceilings fell and the salvaging had to cease.

Ironically, the Wawbeek had only recently undergone an extensive $150,000 renova-tion and winterizing process in preparation not only for occupancy by the *Sports Illustrated* personnel but also to convert the pleasant old place into a year-round resort.

Clarence B. Randall, v.p. for business affairs at St. Lawrence University, the owners of the Wawbeek, stated on the day after the fire that although it was highly unlikely that rebuilding would be considered, nevertheless the University would continue to use the re-maining property — ten cottages and a smaller annex lodge — for seasonal commercial purposes.

The loss of the comfortable, pleasant and picturesque Wawbeek — the scene of many "happy hours" — will be keenly felt by the thousands of people who have been entertained there over the years. Like its larger counterpart on the Upper Lake — Saranac Inn — the Wawbeek now exists only in memory and history.

Chapter 9

Evidence of Indian Occupation of Saranacs Region

Most recognized historical authorities seem to agree that there never were permanent Indian settlements in the northern Adirondacks. There was of course seasonal occupation for hunting and fishing purposes and, while there, the red-skinned visitors planted corn or maize and very likely other crops as well — those that would mature rapidly in good soil during the notoriously short growing season.

Although some of them, like the Sabattis family, came up the Raquette River from the St. Regis Mohawk reservation, and settled at Long Lake, most of the transients came from farther east in the St. Lawrence Valley. These were the Adirondack or Abenakis whose raids, according to Arthur Parker in his *Archeological History of New York,* "along with the hostility of the southern Iroquois, at length compelled the Laurentian Iroquois — the Mohawk, Onondaga and Oneida tribes — to form a compact which later took in the Cayugas and then the Senecas."

This is an interesting statement because it sheds an entirely different light on the fighting skills of the maligned "bark-eaters." Therefore, it would indicate that the down-graded Adirondacks were not always on the run to avoid extermination by their fierce enemies from the Mohawk Valley.

Also noteworthy in that connection is the derivation furnished by William Beauchamp in *Aboriginal Place Names of New York:* "The Adirondack mountains perpetuate the common name of an important part of the Algonquin family, though they did not choose it for themselves. The Adirondacks, or Tree-Eaters, were so termed in derision by their enemies, as though they had no better food, and the Onondaga still use the word Ha-te-en-tox with the same [and almost the same sound] meaning. Roger Williams gave the Algonquin name Mid-tukme-chakick, Tree Eaters, a people so called (living between three and four hundred miles west into the land) from their eating only Michtee' chquash, that is, Trees! "They are tree-eaters, they set no corne, but live on the bark of chestnut and walnut and other fine trees." He confused these with the Mohawks. To live thus implied poverty or lack of skill and hence the Iroquois use of the name, Cadwallader Colden considered them the Algonquins proper, "those who treacherously killed their Mohawk friends at Montreal. In the war that followed the latter were shrewd and well disciplined. The Adirondacks, by this means wasted away, and their boldest soldiers were almost entirely destroyed."

To further explain — or confuse — the name derivation issue I inject or introduce the following item from *High Spots* October, 1933 issue. This was written by J. N. B. Hewitt, Smithsonian Institute ethnologist:

"The idea that the Adirondack Mountains derived their name from a tree-eating tribe of Indians is erroneous.

"The origin of the name is found in the Rock Clan group of Indians which lived on the lower St. Lawrence river in the early sixteenth century.

"The word originally was "Arendahronon," the Huron language meaning "they of the great rocks" or "they who are great rocks."

"When the Mohawks' southern neighbors of the Hurons tried to fit the word to their tongue it became "Tatirontaks." The Mohawk lexicon lacked a stem meaning "a rock of stone and they confused it with the stem of their noun meaning "a tree" or "a log of wood."

"The final syllable "a" in the Huron language meant "to have size, to be so large." The comparable final syllable in Mohawk was "ak" and meant "to eat." So, instead of the name being passed on from the Huron to the Mohawk people in its true form of "the rock clan" it became distorted into "they who eat trees" and the legend grew up that the Algonkin tribe, once dwellers on the Ottawa river, were often driven to eat bark.

"The first record in the written word in history appears in an instructive vocabulary of Mohawk words," says Hewitt, "compiled in 1634 by a party of Dutch traders who had visited the Mohawk and Oneida tribes. They recorded the name as "Aderondacke" and startlingly observed that it meant "Frenchmen and Englishmen." Until other better evidence is discovered — which is quite unlikely — the statements of two other eminent historians will stand. The first of these is J. M. B. Hewitt of the Bureau of American Ethnology and a leading expert on the Indian tribes of N. Y. State. "So far as I am aware the wilderness and the mountainous region now commonly called the Adirondacks was never occupied [permanently] by any Indian tribe or tribes during the historical period, if ever before. The second authority — David Cusick, the respected Indian historian of the Six Nations wrote: "This country was never inhabited by any kind of people in the winter season.

Rev. John Todd in his *Summer Gleanings* mentioned that in 1840 on his way to Long Lake via the Saranacs he noticed indications of Indian cornfields especially at the confluence of Ramshorn Creek (the outlet of Stony Creek Ponds) and the Raquette River.

As for cemeteries, it is only logical to assume that a number of Indians might have died during their annual sojourns in the area. But since there never were a large number of these transients — probably only several families fairly well spread out for lebensraum (living space), there were undoubtedly scattered burials but no concentration of graves.

As in all cases there are exceptions which test — not necessarily prove — the rule. One example is a remark made by Clarence Petty, who was born and lived for many years at Corey's, on the Indian Carry. He recalled his father's saying that a cousin of his father (Clarence's grandfather that is), a man named Carlos Whitney, who was also a frequent visitor if not permanent settler, had several times seen small groups of Indians fishing through the ice of the Upper Lake. However, that does not prove that those people were year-round residents. It only shows that they knew a good source of food and traveled a considerable distance, in adverse weather conditions, to obtain it.

In all likelihood the largest collection of Indian relics ever assembled was that of James Wardner of Rainbow Lake. Over a period of many years he gathered specimens around his place and on his wide-ranging hunting and fishing trips. Sometime after the Civil War someone from Albany saw the collection and persuaded him to send it to Albany, where it was exhibited to raise money for the returning soldiers. After the display the bureaucrats in charge sold the items and vamoosed with the moola.

Fay Welch, who has operated Tanager Lodge, a popular summer camp for boys on Upper Chateaugay Lake for over 50 years, told me that he and the campers had found numerous Indian artifacts, mostly on the big sandbar which juts out at the head of the Narrows. Moreover, these included more important objects than the usual common arrowheads.

Jesse Corey put together a small but varied collection from his property, from the

Stony Creek Ponds and the Axton landing on the Raquette River. These were handed out to interested guests until the trove was exhausted.

In his highly controversial *Saranac Exiles*, privately published in 1880, Rev. John P. Lundy made these remarks about the Indian artifacts to be found on that famous Carry: "If young Borlase had gone with me to Corey's from the foot of the Upper Saranac he might have found stone implements and fragments of ancient pottery ornamented with zig-zag lines and swaticas (sic) to his heart's content, but which there attract no attention whatever, except from some collector. They are ploughed out every year and cast aside as worthless. A bottle of whiskey is of far more account. There is a log hut not far away fifty years old, which is of greater interest and pointed out with more pride and enthusiasm than this old Indian encampment and graveyard. And this half century of intrusion and settlement in this part of the wilderness has produced sad havoc and destruction of the forest, and wrought as frightful a desolation almost as that of Sahara itself."

The late Charles Bryan of Chicago, former president of the Pullman Co. and chairman of the board of the Inland Steel Co., owned Raquette Falls Lodge for many years. He told me that while most of his finds were logging days relics, he also had picked up quite a few Indian items along the Carry.

The one seasonal occupant that required no guesswork or conjecture was a real live and lively Abenaki named Daniel J. Emmett, better known as Indian Dan, whose home was near Sorel, Quebec. A powerful 220 pound half-breed who walked with a limp, Dan was a staunch friend of Noah John Rondeau, Adirondack hermit, who first mentioned him in Noey's 1932 diary after watching him build a birchbark canoe. In July, 1947 Rondeau recorded this tribute to Emmett: "At Corey's we stopped for a brief visit with Mr. Dan Emmett. Dan is of French and Indian descent, is 77 years old and for 37 years he has had a canvas set-up at Coreys, where he makes baskets, balsam pillows and many other useful and ornamental things from ash splints, birchbark and sweetgrass [there was also a wife and several children who helped make the merchandise]. He has limited English and splendid French vocabulary. He is courteous, honest and modest; and he has unique refinement of his own style.

"For 37 years he had enjoyed the utmost respect and confidence of natives and tourists about Upper Saranac Lake and wherever he goes. His friendship and esteem of others is 100 per cent loyal.

"Many have followed him to his remote hunting grounds in the wilds of Canada — and in turn they had taken him to their ranches in southern states and entertained him all Winter. And whatever the depth or height, like Madam Curie he never loses his head. He is 99 per cent worthy and without office or price. He has unchangeable perfect quality." How's that for a testimonial?

Chapter 10

The Indian Carry Chapel

Another feature of the Indian Carry was the chapel, built in 1888 by the Champlain Presbytery to serve the religious needs of the region but originally intended as part of the local mission outreach program for the loggers. This incidentally also accounted for the construction of the Island Chapel. Rev. Aaron Maddox, undoubtedly the best known of the several lumberjack skypilots, has been credited with its founding and personal ministry.

Eventually, it like the Island Church, became interdenominational, but more recently — from the 1920's on — it was maintained and sponsored by the Episcopal Church.

Two of its better-known if not prominent members and its frequent ushers were Noah J. Rondeau and Indian Dan Emmett. Much more about that in *Noah John Rondeau, Adirondack Hermit,* which I compiled.

The summer residents who preferred the high church form of Episcopal worship attended the Sabbath services at Saranac Inn's Church of the Ascension.

Still standing, although no longer used for religious purposes, the venerable old Chapel is now the vacation home of Dr. Don Ely, professor of communications at Syracuse University.

Indian Carry Chapel

Chapter 11

The Ampersand Golf and Country Club

By the end of the last century golf had become quite popular in the northern Adirondacks. There were rather rough nine-hole courses at Bartlett's, the Indian Carry (Corey's), McCollom's, St. Regis Golf Club (Paul Smith's), Loon Lake — and the layout built by the Ampersand Hotel in 1897 on property originally part of the Martin's (later Miller's) on Ampersand Bay of Lower Saranac.

Although most of the players were guests at the hotel, built in 1888 and structurally one of the finest in the mountains, many of the wealthier "camp" owners on the Lower Lake, their friends and the more prominent Saranac village professional class also enjoyed the game and its incidental social attractions, which included a spacious clubhouse and two tennis courts. From the beginning it served as a well-patronized entertainment center and convenient oasis.

According to Seaver Rice, who as an area teen-ager worked one summer as the boatman for an oversized craft with a carrying capacity of ten or twelve, the hotel bartender came across the Bay on the first trip, at 8 A.M., to prepare the libations and otherwise start the day off properly.

Seaver's brother, Herman, was caddymaster for several seasons and many local lads were able to earn their pocket-money by lugging single bags for $.25 a round and double duty for $.50 — considerable and welcome cash in those not-too-distant days, and not too-tiring work either because the course was nearly level and the bags were not overstocked with clubs. The usual contents were only six or seven — a driver, spoon, midiron, mashie, niblick, cleek and a rake, which was a sandwedge type of weapon designed to scoop the pellet (gutta percha originally) out of the shallow and not very formidable traps, bunkers and infrequent water hazards.

During that exciting historic era that featured World War I and the start of the turbulent, intemperate (a classic understatement!) Twenties, I spent several summer vacations caddying at Loon Lake Hotel's nine- later eighteen-hole course, a much hillier spread so I can readily sympathize with Seaver, Abbie Homburger (who also shagged tennis balls betimes) and Willie Mace (more about him later!). Other bag-toters who learned their golf and earned their spending money at the now extinct Ampersand Club — stout fellows who later became much more than merely local celebrities — were Earl Hazelton, Nels Davis, and surveyors Ives Turner and Bill Davis.

The course itself could hardly be classified as of championship caliber but like all except the relatively few famous layouts it was considered a fairly good test of golfing skills — and luck. Judged by today's criteria the holes were too short, the greens too small and bumpy, the rough too rough and rocky and the natural hazards — such as stumps, boulders and trees — too plentiful. Nevertheless, the Club's clientele found it convenient, pleasant and usually uncrowded.

Besides the day-by-day action the Ampersand Hotel staged a well-publicized end-of-

View from Ampersand Clubhouse after three Harvey Wallbangers (cocktails)

the-season tournament. This annual affair attracted many competitors from the general area as well as from Placid and Paul Smith's. One such event has lingered long in the memory of Seaver Rice, a spry 87-year-old youngster in heart who caddied in 1905 for Willie Mace, a former caddy himself but at that time a local post-office employee. Somehow Mace had wangled an invitation to play in this prestigious, customarily "gentlemen only" wingding but, in true Horatio Alger fashion, he triumphed and here's how it all happened.

On longer, better managed and manicured courses the more experienced and better-equipped contestants would have fared far better, but their lack of familiarity with the idiocyncrasies of the Ampersand Club's nine understandably constituted a handicap for nearly everyone but Mace, who of course knew the course like his own backyard.

From the Clubhouse the first two holes were on opposite sides — left and then right up Lake St. and then across the Old State Road, where the next six zigzagged back and forth behind Dickert's Taxidermy Shop and Tom Peacock's home, mostly open country then but now — three-quarters of a century later — thickly overgrown. The finishing holes were along the west side of Rte. 3 and on back toward the Lower Lake.

The opening rounds had taken their toll and narrowed down the field until there were only two survivors — Willie Mace and a big, handsome player named Cameron, whose father — Simeon Cameron — had served for a year as Lincoln's first secretary of war. Although a long-ball hitter and one of the Chevy Chase (Md.) Country Club's better golfers, his greater experience and ability were virtually offset by Mace's intimate knowledge of the terrain.

The match was nip and tuck all the way with neither player able to build up a comfortable lead. The sixth, seventh and eighth greens found them even-Stephen so the suspense accelerated for both men and the by-then fascinated gallery, composed mainly of Cameron's clique. On the final hole both their second shots reached the green with Cameron away and therefore the first to putt. He lined it up carefully and watched his ten-footer bounce along over the bumpy surface — and trickle past the cup!

Mace's turn now: but, as he surveyed his six-footer and was finally ready to stroke the ball, a Model T — probably the area's first such contraption — rattled by noisily. This of course broke Willie's concentration so he straightened up, collected his cool while restudying his project — and wished it into the hole!

105

"God!" recalled Rice, the caddy, "you should have seen their faces!"

For the fifty or sixty onlookers this was a real shocker and many vented their amazement and disappointment in a predictable but anything but sportsman-like fashion. Against the background of grumbling and mumbling one "lady," probably Mrs. Cameron, who was practically in tears, made no effort to be gracious in defeat. Her remarks still ring in Seaver's ears: "Why, it's not right! It's just not fair! To think that they'd let a person like that enter and play in this tournament! Who is he anyway?"

According to Art Hoffer, who heard various versions of this legendary match during the years that followed, there was an interesting and predictable sidelight. Apparently there was some lively betting totaling at least $1000.00 on the outcome of the match. Mace had also bet rather heavily on himself even though he would have had a hard time covering had he lost. When one of the betters asked him if he was prepared to pay off, he brazenly replied, "Sure, but you don't suppose I'd carry that much around with me on a golf course!"

When the time came to settle up, some of Willie's friends soon became mere acquaintances in a hurry because they had bet against him, and he insisted that they produce the moola right away.

But getting back to the remarks from the gallery, the obvious interpretation of those snide but characteristic comments is simply this: in those days and in fact until quite recently golf was very definitely a monopoly of the leisure class and no outsider was welcomed or permitted inside the charmed circle or clubhouse.

Incidentally, Mace rewarded Rice that memorable day with four $1.00 bills, a serendipitous sum to a thirteen-year-older in 1905.

Seaver also recalled that no caddy was ever allowed inside the Clubhouse; they whiled away the time while waiting to be called in a rough shelter near the brook behind the main building.

After the Ampersand Hotel was torched (it took the owners seven years to collect the

Tennis at Ampersand Clubhouse 1900

$100,000 claim!) on September 23, 1907, the property, including the Club, was sold by its owner, Charles Eaton, to S. D. Matthews, president of Filmart Laboratories, a motion picture firm. The golf course became a private club which functioned until the end of World War I.

Some of the former Ampersand guests had bought property and built "camps" on the Lower Lake so they and some prominent village residents formed the nucleus of the new club's membership. Among them were Mark Hanna, Pittsburgh industrialist; the Williamses of Mennen-Williams; the Stanleys of the Stanley Tool Co.; the Swains; the Hanes of the Winston-Salem textile firm; the Cluetts of Cluett-Peabody, Troy, N.Y.; the Fishers and Clarks of Rockledge (Saranac Lake); the C. M. Palmers, with newspaper control connections; Doctors Nichols and Marvin of Dr. Trudeau's staff at the Adirondack Cottage Sanitarium, et al.

Dr. E. L. Trudeau, Stephen Chalmer's "Beloved Physician," while apparently not a member, came often and on at least one occasion was the guest of honor.

Other local members were the McKees, Thurstons and Hewitts.

Luddy (Ludwig) Keller's father Toni (Anton) was steward at the Ampersand Club from 1912-1917. The son remembers another special occasion when Ruth Evans hosted a party honoring friends and associates of her brother Larry, who was the author of several best-sellers and therefore the object of considerable attention by well-known publishing firms who often sent top echelon representatives to meet Evans and other successful writers curing here in Saranac Lake.

By the end of World War I many of the members had lost interest and developed other priorities so the comfortable place was declared available for other purposes — and soon it was. The Volstead Act, unquestionably the nation's most unpopular, unfortunate and unenforceable piece of legislation ever enacted, became the law of the land — and the staid Clubhouse opened under new auspices and management as George Brown's Ritz. Shortly thereafter it attracted attention as one of the region's liveliest nightspots. Like the Bear Cub near Lake Placid it made up in merriment for its relatively small size. Dispensing readily available but very expensive firewater and superior danceband music it raised the weekend welkin, which reverberated from the Bay's low hills all the way up to Dickert's on Summer evenings when the wind was from the west.

Whenever the Prohis and T men (Prohibition Officers and Treasury Department law-enforcers) showed up — which was seldom in those days of widespread payoffs, tipoffs and kindred graft — the incriminating booze was lowered through a trapdoor cut into the living room floor and concealed by a bearskin rug. Judging by the reports of various satisfied customers and veteran topers, the accommodating place served as a veritable water hole until Roosevelt's Repeal in 1933.

Subsequently, the Clubhouse became a cure cottage for several Summers in the late 1930's. After that it saw a succession of owners including the Bakers, the Hoffmans and Ernie Stautner, ex-tackle for the Pittsburgh Steelers and more recently line coach for the Dallas Cowboys.

Since the clubhouse of this long defunct country club is our present home, its history has never lost its fascination for me. Although I was not aware of its intriguing and somewhat checkered past at the time my wife and I bought it, I nevertheless felt a strong affinity for the run-down place which eight or ten other potential buyers had looked at briefly and then, for a variety of obvious reasons, had passed up.

Lord knows, at the time — June 1972 — the place offered very few pluses offset by many more minuses. Moreover, for inexperienced buyers such as ourselves (incidentally my wife was emphatically unenthusiastic about the whole deal), very often the tendency is to allow the forest to obscure the trees. And that was almost literally the case because the well-wooded, two-acre mini-estate had not much more than that going for it! Actually the real estate itself — the land that is — and its choice location just across the road from Amper-sand Bay of Lower Saranac Lake were its major assets. As an extra element of serendipity the backyard brook also helped counteract the deteriorated condition of the three buildings.

Anyone who has ever optimistically undertaken the seemingly endless ordeal of renovating an attractive but ramshackle summer occupancy structure will readily under-stand and appreciate the situation facing a pair of definitely non-do-it-yourselfers. Such essentially major details as new roofs, new heating system, modern electric wiring and its incidentals, replacement of antiquated plumbing and bathroom facilities, acres of insula-tion in all the old familiar places, rebuilding the garage, etc., etc., etc., confronted us. All told it was positively frightening just to review the lengthy list of urgently needed im-provements and repairs. But one by one they got done and the house gradually took on charm and comfort.

Unquestionably, the most serious problem that required immediate attention was the discovery that we were the unintentional hosts for hordes of carpenter ants, which soon made their presence both audible and visible in the kitchen and dining room. Their ap-petites must have been insatiable and their food supply plentiful, judging by the incessant sound of their chomping jaws ingesting the wall and ceiling woodwork.

Such round-the-clock activity also aroused the intense curiosity of our two Persian cats, who weren't quite sure how to cope with the destructive little pests that appeared on floors and walls with ever-increasing numbers and frequency. Ginger and Parfy, the frisky sister felines, at first stalked the repulsive black nuisances with their noses only a fraction of an inch from the pursued, but they soon desisted when their would-be quarry took to climbing aboard the cats' noses and legs. By pawing frantically and shaking their heads and feet furiously the cats usually managed to dislodge the pesky black devils. While definitely not amusing to the Persians these encounters nevertheless were mildly hilarious to us humans, and the incidents have lingered long in our memories. Replacement lumber and new ceilings and the services of the local exterminator soon took care of that unpleasant situation.

Another emergency which had to be met was the inadequate water supply. Rusted pipes and puny pressure could not be overlooked indefinitely so something had to be done — and pronto. Since hooking onto the village system, several rough and rocky blocks away, would have cost the proverbial arm and a leg, we decided to drill a well instead. The driller, a dowser of sorts, assured us that water was both plentiful and readily available, but as the work progressed he cautiously qualified his comments and guesses.

Day after day the lofty drill clattered and shuddered as it bore through the bedrock. 100 feet, 150, 175, 200 — and no water yet! Nothing at 225 either so we did some fast think-ing and calculating. The driller was told to stop at 250. If no results by then we would seriously consider calling it quits! 250 and still nothing! What then??

Just about then we started hearing horror stories such as Walt Emmon's predicament. His lake's edge marina had yielded only six gallons a minute at 475 ft.! More comforting, however, was the report that an old geological survey map indicated a vast glacial lake at approximately 275 ft. Go ahead orders were given to the driller, who happily announced the arrival of a hard hunch that we were on the very verge of bringing in a gusher. Still grinding away grimly through Grenville granite the chattering machine reached 275, then

280 and then at 290 the first symptoms of the long-awaited water. Yet another 5 feet and the well came in with a rush — a young geyser producing nearly 10 gallons a minute!

Not so incidentally I am thoroughly convinced that we had much more than human help with that particular project because during most of the exasperating drilling operation my wife Sue sat, Bible in lap and prayers on her lips, at a window overlooking the ordeal. Later on she informed me that on that final day she had sent her entreaties heavenward especially intently and intensely. Just another testimonial and proof that the Good Lord really listens and delivers. Moreover, it implies that it takes much more than mere wishing to make it so regardless of what Judy Garland warbled so consolingly in "The Wizard of Oz."

Now that most of the seemingly endless and open-ended projects have been taken care of, we have been able to relish our accomplishments, renovations and improvements and settle down to enjoy our so-called golden years in our home that has seen so much action and provided so much varied entertainment for so many people over the span of so many years.

Moreover, on occasional balmy Summer nights, if I relax sufficiently and turn on the memory machine coded with the conversations of the people who knew the charming place away back when; and if I really concentrate, I can vaguely catch the echoes of sudden laughter and animated pleasantries — what Christopher Morley called the "subtle discharge of social static." Very apt indeed!

These verbal memorabilia — trivia to some people who prefer not to wallow in nostalgia — are often enhanced by the poignant vestiges of eerie dance tunes such as "Marcheta," "Mountain Greenery," "Smile Awhile," "Blue Moon," "Mood Indigo," etc. Or to change the mood, "Yes, We Have No Bananas," the "Music Goes Down and Around," "Mares Eat Oats," "Who Takes Care of The Caretaker's Daughter," etc. and ad infinitum.

Of course at the end of each reverie there's always "Good Night, Ladies" to break the spell and close the gates to the past.

Understandably all these ingredients and evocative elements have now become proverbial parts and parcels of this place's — the Clubhouse of the old Ampersand — peculiar attractiveness and varied vibrant history.

Ampersand Golf and Country Clubhouse 1978

Chapter 12

The Guideboat Builders: Willie Martin

The earliest sojourners in the Adirondack wilds, after the Indians, were white trappers and market hunters. Because there were no roads a light boat of some kind was a prime necessity. Everywhere an interlacing network of lakes and streams presented a formidable barrier to foot travel but provided a convenient and more or less continuous waterway for those travelers who had a craft light enough to be lugged easily across the numerous carries, or portages north of the Border. Although the Indian dugout and birchbark canoe were the traditional conveyances, by 1830 or so they had been replaced or supplanted by planked boats and skiffs of varied types.

In those days nearly everybody had to be a do-it-yourselfer so, understandably, many of the hardier, more resourceful men produced their own versions of a boat that met all five criteria of craftsmanship: sturdiness, cargo-carrying capability, lightness, speed and ease of handling. It could do everything a canoe could — and do it better. It also had the advantage of oars for the long hard pull across the broad expanses of windy lakes, silence for night hunting and speed to head off a swimming deer.

During those early primitive days the woodsman's boat was far more than a pleasure craft; it was a very important piece of equipment. In fact it very often made the difference between life and death, between "gittin' or not gittin' to where you're goin.'"

The evolution of a light, sturdy carry boat gathered momentum in the late 1840's

Aerial View of Lower Saranac Lake, Looking South

A Difficult Carry

when the first big wave of tourists and sports invaded the region. Quick to recognize as a good thing in the making the hunters exploited the situation and built up a prosperous business as guides and boatmen. Some of the money was used to improve the boats and thus provided keen competition among the resident craftsmen.

According to the late Kenneth Durant, author of *Guideboat Days and Ways* and the most thorough researcher of guideboat history, the true craft, sharp at both ends, did not show up until about 1875, approximately the same time when the term came into common use. Before that time the square or transom stern, similar to that of a wherry or dory, was the usual shape. The obvious superiority of the sharp-sterned version — not the true double-ender at first but eventually to become such — forced the phasing-out of the square-stern model. Active experimentation and improvement continued until well into the '80's.

Strangely enough the guideboat was not built at all like the canoe but like the North Atlantic Coast small fishing boats. Its ribs or knees were natural root-crooks of light, tough spruce but in matched pairs from carefully selected stumps. These knees gave the craft its shape and principal strength.

Betterments [fine old word!] devised by successive and observant craftsmen finally culminated in a number that had "the finish of a violin and the delicacy of a Swiss watch."

Sturdiness and lightness were the two prime goals of a boat-builder for the Adirondack scene. In the heat of Summer, over slippery, rocky, root-infested, up-hill and down-dale carries — and looking for all the world like a transient turtle — the traveler was very aware that every pound and even every ounce counted and was taken into account by the innovative builders. "By shaving off a bit here and another judicious shaving there they finally whittled the scantlings down to an almost incredible fineness. The result was a work

A Carry — The Start

A Carry — The End

and pleasure product of nearly racing shell quality and delicacy," commented Durant.

Properly cared for, the well-made "light truck of the waterways" was good for at least twenty years of hard work and heavy loads. Fragile on land, true, but in its element the classic craft could carry incredible cargoes. For years much of all the freight that went into the Adirondack woods went in by guideboat — packing cases, cook stoves, barrels of kerosene and all the accoutrements and implements essential to camp-life. On the remoter lakes, during construction of camps and outbuildings guideboats were lashed together catamaran-style and loaded with lumber.

They could easily carry a human cargo of three men and their gear, a couple of hounds and a deer carcass or two; "In an emergency they have been known to carry four or even six men across a mountain lake in an Autumn storm, pulled along by one pair of broad oars," reported William C. White in his outstanding *Adirondack Country.* "The boats had to be stormworthy because, like old-time sailors, few guides ever bothered to learn how to swim. 'Don't worry none in this boat,' one of the guides used to say, 'You're as safe in it as you would be in the Lord's pocket.'"

While there is uncertainty — even controversy — about who deserves the laurels for turning out the first really representative guideboat, the Adirondacks' gift to the world along with the packbasket, Donaldson credits Mitchell Sabattis, the celebrated Indian guide on the testimony of the Rev. John Todd, who supposedly saw Sabattis in action or had inspected a sample of his skill. Caleb Chase of Newcomb, Cyrus Palmer and his

A Complicated Passage

brother; Charlie Hanmer, Reuben Cary, the Stantons, Warren Cole, Merlin Austin, Wallace Emerson and George Smith — all of Long Lake; Frank Blanchard of Raquette Lake; the Parsons brothers of Old Forge; the Grants — father and son of Boonville, Ted Vassar and son and Ricketson of Bloomingdale; Kerst of Indian Lake; Luther Owen and son of Tupper Lake; Henry Hanmer and Albert Billings of Lake Placid; McCaffery of Saranac Lake — the list is long. Over Canton way J. Henry Rushton, noted for canoes, also made guideboats fashioned after the "Saranac" boat of Willie Martin.

The remarkable fact about all those craftsmen is that they were all more than merely competent. While some makers were lauded extravagantly perhaps for their superior workmanship and their products were publicized by widely-read authors nevertheless, in most cases there was very little difference in actual quality among the boats themselves. Carl Hathaway, a connoisseur and superior tool handler and guideboat builder himself maintains that out of the hundreds of repair jobs that he had done over the years only two or three could be classified as clumsily constructed. . . .

Most of the actual construction of the boats had to be done during the off-season because in Summer the boatshops had to concentrate on repair work. Apparently, most builders averaged five or six a year; Grant's in Boonville, for instance made only 378 boats in their 55 years in business. Caleb Chase reckoned that it took him a month of long days to complete a solo job. . . .

The classic guideboats varied in length from Nessmuk's "Sairy Gamp," built to order by Rushton* and all of 7 feet long, weight the same — a pound a foot — to 9 footers and on up to 22 foot "church boats." The standard dimension, however, was 15 or 16 feet. The weight, which was of course determined by the length, was gradually cut down by use of lighter materials and the paring-down process practiced by Willie Martin in fashioning his "egg shells" from over 120 pounds — for the longest job — to considerably less than half that, not counting the accessories.

Since it usually required twenty-one man days to create a boat back in the 1880's and with the prevailing wages $2.00 per day, these figures account for labor cost alone of $42.00 per boat which sold for $65.00. By the 1900's even a second-hand specimen brought $100.00; a new one about $150.00.

Taking into account the scarcity of the naturally and suitably shaped spruce stumps, the time factor and work definitely entailed in locating them and cutting them out, it is easy to understand that these basic components — plus the labor and time required to assemble the craft — plus a reasonable profit for the boss, it is small wonder that today the final price tag would discourage all but the better-heeled customers. And they are many!

If you noticed that the really big names among the Saranac boatbuilders were not included, there was a real reason for the omission. They were being saved for more adequate coverage. While McCaffery of Bloomingdale, whose shop incidentally was on the third floor of the Stark's hardware building, now Aubuchon's, was certainly no slouch. The traditionally notable local names were those of Willie Martin and his associates — Fred Rice, Sr. and Theodore Hanmer.

---

*Either because he would not or could not Rushton did not make guideboats until 1888, when he decided to add the "Adirondack" or "Saranac Lake" to his line of racing and pleasure canoes.

   Here's what he had to say about the two best-known types of such craft: "If I had a long distance to go and couldn't have dinner until I got there, I'd pick the Long Laker, to me the fastest rowboat in the world. She pulls easy and is not cranky. . . . The "Saranac Laker" is lighter and extremely fast; not recommended for women and children but very popular with guides."

   "Nessmuk" (George W. Sears) commented. "Yes, the Long Lakers are fast but cranky and uncomfortable to ride in." Take your pick of the opinions of recognized experts.

Some of Willie Martin's "Eggshells"

Willie Martin (1849-1907)

Although Caleb Chase, the resourceful Newcomb craftsman, is generally credited with the pointed stern product as well as other less conspicuous refinements after he set up shop in 1850, most so-called authorities and aficionados agree that there was one feature that he did not originate. And that improvement was the decrease in weight which made Martin's "eggshells" so popular among weight-watcher guides in particular.

Willie's father, as has already been noted in the chapter on his hotel, later Miller's Saranac Lake House, built it in 1850 or so. Since much of his clientele consisted of sportsmen, he hired all the available guides — about 40 — whom he furnished with boats. Willie went to work for his father in the shop on Lake St. and began to turn out jim-dandies to meet the brisk demand by guides and campers.

William Allen Martin, obvious nickname Willie, was born in Saranac Lake on October 7, 1849 and grew up in his father's brand-new hotel on the Lower Saranac, the first approximation of a vacation resort in the region. A naturally gifted machinist and carpenter, he went to work for his father in his early teens. A skilled boatbuilder from North Elba spent the Winters prior to the outbreak of the War Between the States, making and repairing boats so the youngster watched and occasionally assisted the older man. When he was sixteen he seemingly felt that he would like to see what he could do on his own, so he requested and received somewhat reluctant permission to test his skill. The result was so surprisingly good that both his father and McLenathan were amazed. From then on he was on his way to becoming an independent entrepreneur.[*1]

This happened after his father had lost his first hotel by mortgage foreclosure and had built the Edgewood near the intersection of the road by that name and Lake St. Among the first guests at the second hotel was a consumptive named T. Edmund Krumholz who, when

---

[1*]The strongest objection to the very light Martin boats (40 lbs. or so) was that they didn't ride deep enough in heavy water and thus bobbed about and were more difficult to handle.

his health dramatically improved, wanted something to do for occupational therapy purposes. He and Willie went into partnership as Adirondack guideboat builders, erected a workshop across the road and went into business. After 11 months Krumholz, an example of one of the most celebrated cures on record — from desperately sick in 1882 to strenuous activity as noted hotelman a few years later and co-partner in the Wawbeek management in 1888.*²

After several years of flourishing business the workshop, in the Spring of 1886, was totally destroyed by fire with accompanying loss of records and materials and equipment. Although he replaced it as soon as possible and opened for business the following Summer, the fire and failing health forced his retirement and early death at age of 58 on Feb. 24, 1907.

In addition to his boat carpentry ability the reticent introvert, who apparently lacked the drive and aggressiveness which could easily have made him prosperous and famous, was also an expert telegrapher and accomplished, self-taught pianist.

Willie was also involved, along with his father, in a well-devised scheme to expedite the traffic and tourists between Martin's Hotel and Bartlett's on the Saranac River source of Middle Saranac (Round Lake). Between Lower and Middle Saranacs, there is a small island which separates the River and creates two sets of rock-bound minor rapids. These necessitated unloading and reloading the freight scow and guideboats. The elder Martin decided, in 1877, to blast out a channel wide and deep enough to accommodate a small steamboat by diverting river water.

Mission accomplished they were all set to launch the "Water Lily," built that Winter by Willie and Fred Rice, Sr., and featuring cabins of high gloss cherry and carefully selected bird's eye maple. The big day came on July 4, 1878, according to Alfred R. Donaldson in his landmark, two-volume *History of the Adirondacks.* "She had on board Sousa's Band — which was playing at Martin's that Summer — and people flocked from miles around to see and ride on the new wonder. Most of them were gazing for the first time on the first steamboat which ever plied any inland Adirondack water."

Incidentally, the fate of the dam at the Middle Falls, now occupied by the Second Locks, was not unexpected. Guides complained bitterly that it wrecked their business, some hotel-keepers claimed that it was scaring away the trout and deer and ugly letters threatening destruction of the little steamer kept pouring in. Not long afterward on a conveniently dark and stormy night the disgruntled opponents blew the barrier to well-known smithereens.

Never rebuilt but replaced by a dock at the foot of the rapids, the "Water Lily" and Capt. Clough's large freightboat stayed in business for several years before discontinuance. The elegant little "Water Lily" was sold to George Billings of Lake Placid in 1881, moved over there but later on sank at her slip and was consigned to an inelegant watery fate.

Nevertheless, even though that fine example of workmanship is no longer visible, there are still extant a goodly number of his other creations — his guideboats.

Nowadays, a Martin name-plate is a hallmark and guarantee of superb craftsmanship.

---

²*He later ran the Ruisseaumont in Lake Placid, the Sagamore in Lake George and a hotel in Camden, S.C. In short, he really got around.

Probably the "Water Lily" (Stoddard)

Chapter 13

The Guideboat Builders: Fred W. Rice

There were two Fred Rices who made Adirondack history and it is imperative that each be known for his importance. The older Fred, who had a W as in William for his middle initial, was one of the first as well as best local photographers but that wasn't the only arrow in his quiver — he was also right up there in the upper ranks as a guideboat builder in particular but a boatbuilder in general as well. Probably deserves just as much credit as any other builder of the true guideboat — both ends pointed.

His son, Fred M. Rice, also a boatbuilder — heavier boats adaptable to inboard and outboard motor use but few if any guideboats as such. His most representative product was "The Gull," which is now in the Adirondack Museum.

Fred Jr.'s real claim to fame was his many years of experience and service as a woodsman and guide — especially his association with Martha Reben (neé Marta Reben-tisch), undoubtedly the best nature writer the region ever had and demonstrably among the nation's most popular outdoors authors. Her books — *The Healing Woods, The Way of the Wilderness* and *A Sharing of Joy* — published in this country and in England, are still being widely read. Moreover, their locale — Weller Pond for the most part, that picturesque bay adjunct of Middle Saranac which has become almost as much of a literary sanctuary and tourist attraction as the more renowned Stevenson Cottage. Much more about that and them — Fred M. Rice and Martha Reben in the separate chapter.

Fred W. Rice, the father, while deservedly well-known in his own era, nevertheless was somewhat over-shadowed by his more publicized contemporary guideboat craftsman, Willie Martin, with whom he was closely associated in his early years in Saranac Lake. Donaldson, for instance, devoted an entire article on Martin's guideboat achievements while merely mentioning Rice in passing. Possibly he lacked the information needed for a rounded treatment. However, he does credit Rice with an important assist — in the building of the "Water Lily" in 1877 and launched with great fanfare, featuring Sousa's Band the following July. The launch stopped at Rice's dock and serenaded him in honor of his part in its building.

But before coming to Saranac in 1876 Rice had already become established as a sailboat builder at Essex on Lake Champlain. Next he went to Chestertown where he married Harriet Todd, after which he left for the supposedly greener pastures of the mountains. Much of the mule-drawn conveyance was loaded with tools and a knocked-down (disassembled) sailboat. Little room left for non-essentials such as family belongings, which were apparently not numerous.

The Rices, according to the accompanying version of their family background, had been prominent in county history. The first of them came to America in 1638, not too long after the arrival of the Pilgrims. In England the family progenitors rated a coat of arms — an arm, argent and a chevron between three ravens sable. Crest, a raven proper.

The elder Rice was born in Hartford, Conn. on March 27, 1852. At an early age he

Fred W. Rice and Family

Fred Rice's Boathouse (left) and Studio (right)

migrated to Essex, where he was employed as a civil engineer and foreman for the Whitehall and Plattsburgh railroad which was started in 1868, bought by the Delaware and Hudson Canal Co. in 1873 and completed in 1874.

Upon arrival here (Saranac Lake) in 1876 Rice either built or bought a log cabin at the corner of Algonquin Ave. and State St. while the larger home, boathouse and rental cabins were being built on the shore of the Lower Lake on what is still known as Rice's Point, not far from the present Trudeau Institute. Boatbuilding was his main activity for several years. It is noteworthy that one of Rice's guideboats was displayed at the Louisiana Purchase Exposition in St. Louis in 1904. Fred agreed if promoters would ship it express to Seattle, Rice's next port of call after his inheritance from the will of his brother, — William Marsh Rice, founder of Rice Institute, Houston, Texas.

The boat attracted a great deal of attention and was described in the Fair historical catalog as "the first boat seen of the design and a fine piece of craftsmanship." It was also featured at other such fairs and elsewhere.

Somewhere along the line the energetic Rice had developed an interest and pronounced skill in photography, so he added to his boathouse a studio and set up in business as an all-around (portrait and landscape) camera artist. The accompanying sample demonstrates his proficiency in his second calling.

In 1901, as narrated in considerable detail elsewhere in this book, Samuel Langhorne Clemens, far better known as Mark Twain, spent the summer of 1901 in the camp owned by his friends — the George V.W. Duryees. Since the Rice enclave was fairly nearby it was only natural for the two men to see each other at least occasionally. Since also any photographer worthy of his salt would be more than eager to put his distinguished neighbor on record, he asked permission to photograph the Clemens family.

Twain consented but with one important provision — that the resulting pictures would never be shown for any reason whatever until both Olivia (Livy) Clemens and her celebrated husband had departed from the land of the living, which happened in 1910. Promise made and photos taken and kept under wraps until recently when Fred's youngest daughter — Anna Rice Jacobsen — gave me permission to use them.

It is easy to understand why I feel that the only visual reminders of that particularly pleasant sojourn in the characteristically stormy life of America's greatest author have greatly enhanced that segment of the story.

The Rice family, besides the parents, consisted of eleven children — four boys and seven girls — the first of whom, Fred M., was born in 1876 and Anna, the youngest, in 1903. There's an intriguing story about one of the girls. It seems that Mrs. Nathan Straus, whose summer home was at Knollwood on Lower Saranac Lake, and her husband had recently lost a daughter (death) and the bereaved mother was having a hard time adjusting. One day she came over to the Rice home, saw one of the girls who may have reminded her of her recent trauma or possibly because she felt instant affection for the attractive blond-haired child. Whatever, she told Mrs. Rice that she would like to adopt her and would give the family $10,000. The mother politely refused the offer. Then Mrs. Straus said, "Well then, if I can't adopt her, will you let me name her?" "Of course," replied the relieved parent. "All right then, I'll name her Ernestine Straus Rice." That name was soon shortened to Erna and Erna it's been ever since.

Fred W. Rice's red letter day came sometime in 1902 after his brother William died. This member of the family had gone previously to Texas to work as a surveyor for a railroad being built through the Lone Star State. Providentially, he invested all his available money in land, little dreaming what lay underneath. In due time oil speculation and development

Dr. Charles Peabody's Cottage, Moss Rock Point, Upper Saranac Lake (Fred Rice photo)

began and his property was right in the middle of all the action. Consequently, he soon found that he was a multi-millionaire — about 65 million according to the *Encyclopedia Americana*.

Ten million of this the public-spirited fortunate one gave to endow a college in Houston that was logically named after him — Rice Institute.

Regrettably, this beneficent man was murdered by his valet and, since he was unmarried, the money was left to his brothers and their children. Before the disposition and division of the inheritance could take place his New York lawyers had to locate the heirs. This was done in the usual way — by advertising in the newspapers of the day, a rather ineffective method when those searched for don't read the city papers each day.

Serendipity entered the drama at this point: John Harding, the owner of the Algonquin Hotel, right next door to Rice's boatshop, did read the New York papers habitually and saw the search notice. He contacted Fred who forthwith headed for the meeting with the lawyers — and came back home a very rich man.

In 1904 the ever-restless Rice sold his business and headed west to Mercer Island, near Seattle, Washington but before he left there is evidence that he gave Theodore Hamner his guideboat plans and patterns. How much use the latter made of them is problematical.

Two years later Mrs. Rice, apparently homesick, and two of her daughters returned to Saranac Lake.

Rice himself moved once more — this time to Tracy, California where, full of years of enjoyable living he died in 1934, aged 82.

As the children came of age each received an inheritance. Five of the girls and one son eventually married and moved to the Sunset State. Fred M. used his bequest to build a boatshop at 65 Algonquin Ave.; his brother Herman had a dairy farm where the Armory is now on the State Road. Another son, William had a taxidermy business. Interesting family, the Rice's. More about Fred in the Martha Reben chapter.

Anna, another of the daughters, went to a New York City art school, stayed after completion of the courses and was employed by a firm of Finnish jewelers who taught her how to prepare clay and bake it — ceramics it's called now. Fifth Avenue jewelers considered it to be a new form of plastic but her products received several prestigious awards which brought her much recognition. She returned to the hometown in 1936, opened her own shop but for awhile retained a corner in a Rockefeller Center Shop. For years she was the ceramic arts teacher in the old Will Rogers Hospital. Quite a family — the Rices.

Theodore Hanmer at 83

Chapter 14

The Guideboat Builders: Theodore Hanmer

Wherever and whenever the subject of guideboats and their builders comes up — as it does more and more often in this rather special neck of the woods — invariably a discussion, friendly usually but sometimes heated when the discussers are connoisseurs of the choice craft, reaches its peak when the inevitable question is asked. Just who was the best builder — and then the names start coming out. Invariably and quite understandably local pride requires that Long Lakers extol the efforts of their champion — whether it be Palmer, Stanton, Cole, Cary, or Charlie Hanmer, the most recent craftsman.

Those most familiar with the boat-builders of the Saranacs insist just as vigorously that the best guideboats ever turned out were made by Martin, Fred Rice or one of the Hanmers — Theodore or son Willard. In a show of modesty the younger Hanmer once told Charlie Keough, who also knows his boats from long experience handling and repairing them, that the best boat he had ever seen was a Caleb Chase, from Newcomb. The truth is that all of the builders were surprisingly good but the earlier craftsmen, working with a minimum or no machinery at all deserve the lion's share of the kudos or credit.

Born in 1860 at Black Brook, a hamlet between Ausable Forks and Silver Lake over toward Lake Champlain, Theodore Hanmer went to the local school the prescribed number of years and then got his first job — driving a stagecoach. This didn't last long because he became more interested in watching village woodsmen putting together their hunting and fishing boats. About 1883-4 he departed for the greener pastures of Saranac Lake, then just starting to become famous as Dr. E. L. Trudeau's promising health resort. After working and learning for several years as Herbert Salisbury's assistant and also at Martin's, Hanmer went into business for himself. Within a short time the word got around that he could put out an exceptionally good product and soon he had all the work he could handle.

While a lesser craftsman might have yielded to the temptation to sacrifice quality in order to make more money, he steadfastly refused to produce inferior goods.

North Country Life: Spring 1957 edition, carries an interview recorded by Ed. Schutz of the Schenectady *Union-Star* which is probably not only one of the relatively few such conversations but almost certainly the last.

As the reporter wrote it, "Old Ted Hanmer, 97, cups his hand around your ear and says in a wavering, fading voice, 'Will's still the best boatbuilder in these parts.' Then he added, 'It takes a woodsman to build a woodsman's boat, you know!'"

Although the late Ted Hanmer didn't make the first Adirondack guideboat, the fact remains that the Hanmers, father and son Willard, have laid hands to and on more good ones than any other family with the exception of the Grants of Boonville — H. D. (1933-1911) and sons Lewis (1878-1960) and Floyd (?) who, with three and sometimes six helpers put out a total of 378 guideboats.

Riley and Ben Parsons of Old Forge also produced a large number of quality boats.

Theodore Hanmer (right), Willard (left)

Since there were never more than two working together — father and son — in the Hanmer shop it is not known just what their total output was. 200 is the best guestimate.

Until five or six years before his death, the elder Hanmer used to go over to the workshop in order to loosen up his stiffening fingers. The machines his son handled so dexterously very likely meant little to him so he continued to use hand-shavers and sharp penknife to fit the boards together. To him the whirring sanders, electric saws and drills might speed up the operation a bit but couldn't do it any better. In fact he insisted that they didn't do it as well, but for that matter he never thought too much of outboard motors either.

Will, the son, showed Schutz how each plank had to be shaped differently in order to fit exactly the boat's contour. "Here's the print I use," he remarked as he handed the visitor a very old blueprint. The figures were so faint that it was hard to make out each dimension, but for the younger man that wasn't necessary because he had long before memorized them.

"And under the smudged writing in the corner," the reporter commented, "I'll swear it said: from an advanced design of an Adirondack Guideboat, by Ted Hanmer, 1893."

Theodore Hanmer's last boat, built in 1945, was sold to a Dr. Herber of Twitchell Lake and, knowing its historical value, the delighted purchaser must have treated it with T.L.C. (tender loving care).

Incidentally, the senior Hanmer also made boats for each of the six daughters — Bessie, Belle, Jennie, Blanch, Addie and Kate. Bessie, a nurse at Stony Wold sanitarium, took care of her father the last seventeen years of his life. She recalls watching her father, then 83, working on the porch of their home at 123 Lake St. Willard had brought over the materials from the shop to make things as convenient as possible and Theodore still had enough digital dexterity to turn out a fine craft, the one later sold to Dr. Herber.

In the building process there were many shavings produced for which the old gentleman apologized but Bessie, far more interested in the end product than in the incidental débris, willingly assumed the extra housekeeping chore.

Truman Hanmer, the other boy in the family and also a gifted carpenter, helped his father for many years. For a time he was caretaker at the Bucknell camp on Upper Saranac. A keen hunter like his father and brother Willard, he had a camp at Boot Bay on the Lower Lake. Probably his greatest achievement was his planting black spruce seedlings, which he carried in by packbasket from the Lake Clear nursery, on the side of Boot Bay Mountain. Today this reforestation project is well grown and clearly visible from the Lake.

Truman later purchased a motel and restaurant at Lake Clear which he ran until 1943, when he sold out and went to Syracuse where he continued in the carpentry business. He came for his father's funeral in April, 1957 but two weeks later he died, aged 66, the aftermath of a heart attack.

Theodore, full of years and acclaimed as one of the Adirondack guideboat's foremost craftsmen died April 20, 1957, aged 97.

Truman Hanmer (left) and Friend

Chapter 15

The Guideboat Builders: Willard Hanmer

"Like father, like son." If ever that old saying applied to any parent — son relationship it certainly did to Theodore and Willard Hanmer. Although Hanmer, Sr. may have done some guiding in his early days on the Saranacs, he was much better known for his superior craftsmanship. Willard, on the other hand, was an active guide for several years probably because — especially in hunting season — it is almost impossible for any red-blooded Adirondacker to even think of doing anything else until that long-anticipated and seemingly far too short annual ritual is over.

As a prime example of Will's devotion to deer-hunting here's this story which his long-time friend, Charlie Keough, told me. Hanmer did much of the boat repair work for Harrington Mills, owner of Saranac Inn for many years — from 1912 until 1935. Somehow someone had collided with the Inn's thirty-foot launch and stove a twelve-foot gash in its side and thus making it inoperable. Although the season was over, Mr. Mills, an exceptionally efficient businessman who liked to have things done with speed and precision, contacted Hanmer and requested him to come over. The latter complied, sized up the job and proceeded to cut out the damaged section. However, he did not complete the repair job but just left the invalid at a dock in the Back Bay — and took off.

Mr. Mills happened to see the errant one in the area one day and asked him when he was going to finish the job. The answer was startling: "You know, Mr. Mills, I've just plain forgot how to put those boards back in!"

That may sound like effrontery or even insubordination but it wasn't. What the exasperated hotelman had overlooked was that hunting season was just starting and that nobody or nothing was going to deprive Hanmer of the pleasures of those precious first few days of the annual occasion.

Apparently, there wasn't much action in the woods for a week or so that year so Mills was really becoming concerned and quite impatient. Finally though, the provocative Nimrod showed up, looked up the Inn keeper and declared: "Mr. Mills, I just wanted you to know that I suddenly remembered how to put those boards in!" Not so incidentally, many other employers have long since learned that it's customary or even traditional for Adirondackers possessing any appreciable degree of hunting or fishing proficiency to pay seasonal homage to the Red Gods. Said employers may not exactly like it but have had to either overlook or tolerate the yearly absenteeism.

Another Hanmer guiding anecdote via Charley Keough dealt with a mishap at Herb Alvord's boathouse below the Algonquin Hotel on the Lower Lake. It seems that he and his sport were getting ready to leave for a day's fishing off Eagle Island. Having made ready to take off, the frisky young guide, wanting to demonstrate his boatmanship said, "Say Mr. — did you ever see an Adirondack guideboat launched?"

"No," came the answer, "can't say that I have."

"All right, here's how it's done!" — and with that he shoved the boat down the ramp,

Willard Hanmer at Ease

fully expecting to show his nimbleness by hopping into the craft at the last possible second.

However, this time things didn't turn out quite as planned because his feet slipped out from under him on the slimy incline of the ramp — and he took a noisy header into the water. Keeping his cool as best he could he clambered up the dockside, recovered the boat, helped his passenger aboard and rowed away as nonchalantly as he could but which wasn't too convincing. . . .

The younger Hanmer was a very observant and natural craftsman who readily replaced his father in the boatshop at the corner of Algonquin Ave. and Lake St. Although he used modern tools he also was well aware that it was a job that required meticulous care and attention to details. Men who refused to rush and who would rather not bother than build a bad one were the only workers who had any business being in the business.

"Everything has to fit perfectly," he told an interviewer, "and that isn't possible with power tools alone. Besides, the actual assembly is just a stage [or phase] in the art of building a guideboat."

"No machine can go out in a stand of white pine and pick the best one, or haul up giant spruce roots that will work as ribs. The roots are the strongest part of the tree so they are used in the strongest part of the boat — the rib structure." Then he produced several boat ribs out and sanded to various sizes, a disassembled skeleton of a guideboat.

"Nothing can be steambent; it won't work without any thwarts; steambent ribs would open up the tip of a guideboat until it looked like Tom Sawyer's raft. These ribs — 26 pair to a 16 foot boat — are cut out of the roots to the exact shape they will hold in the boat. They will give and take a buffeting in rough water but they won't warp out of shape.

"The planking is important too. It's all quarter-sawed timber, made that way so the grain edge faces the outside surface of the boat. There's a trick to cutting it and there's a lot of wasted wood but it's as strong as the back of an ox. It won't expand or contract in the water.

"Look at this," laying his hand on an inverted boat, "see how the planks are shaped

Nature provides a natural curve for the sturdy
ribs that give this light craft its strength

Planking for the bottom board is pine or cedar,
quartersawed to prevent splitting and checking

Inside stems are fastened to the bottom board,
as are the boat's 22 to 25 pairs of spruce ribs

Driving home one of the 3000 brass screws used
to join planking and ribs in a well-made boat

Marking the yokes for the spot where they will
rest on the yoke rails is an exacting operation

and beveled to a feather-edge. Each plank starting at the keel, overlaps the next one. I put some non-hardening glue between the boards and screw them down. It takes about 14 gross of brass screws for each boat. Then I run in the tacks, 3 to 4,000 of them, where the feathered lips join. The tacks are an inch apart, alternately driven from the inside and outside and bent over with a rivet.

"Also each plank is shaped differently to fit exactly the contour of the boat.

"The guideboat will shoot rapids [rowing facing forward, a trick in itself] as well as a canoe and is far more durable. It is light enough — 40 to 50 pounds depending on the length — for one man to carry, and on a still lake a good man can row it over a mile of water in four and a half minutes."

"I would rather build guide-boats than write about them, but will try to relate some early experiences that I can remember.

"It does not seem possible that fifty years have passed since I first set tacks in a guide-boat for my Dad and learned how to cane seats, and sandpaper boats and so on. It does not seem possible that I could be the last of the line of Adirondack guide-boat builders in the world.

"Those old time guide-boat builders were mostly all great craftsmen, members of a particular trade, and as I build boats each Winter I think back at the hard work and long hours that went into each boat and all the equipment that went with it.

"There were no light, high-speed woodworking machines in those days such as I have in my shop today, and even the hand tools, like ratchet screw drivers and better grade planes and chisels were not to be had. Even the sandpaper was of a poor quality.

"In spite of all this, most of the boats built by these old timers were so well built that I wonder when my last boat is completed, how well I will have qualified with those who have finished their boats and gone before me.

"I had to learn all the art of building by hand which meant sawing ribs, planking, stems, gunwales, and all the equipment — seats, oars, yokes and paddles — all by hand and then plane and finish the rough-sawed parts by hand.

"The machines which I have today certainly do a lot of the work and mostly the hard work, but I had to spend many hours and long evenings experimenting and learning how to apply these machines to do the work on a guide boat.

"I can remember one boat builder who claimed that before spiral screw drivers were made the screws were driven with a small bit brace, which was the quickest way possible to drive the fourteen gross of screws it takes in each guide boat.

"I know that there are so many tacks to stick in each boat that one could develop a sore thumb before the building season was over if he did not shift the tack heads to different parts of the thumb.

"I also remember when just a lad that I wove the cane in so many boat seats for so many consecutive days that I thought I was seeing double.

"One of the jobs most dreaded by the boat builders was the digging of spruce roots used for the stems and ribs. These roots used to be mostly chopped out of the stump, and there were usually stones and tap roots which would hamper the work and make it harder. Today, the chain saw is a boon to this part of the work, which not only saves time and hard work but saves in the root material as well.

"One of the most important factors in guide-boat building is to have the proper lumber for planking and bottom board or keel. And how to put it together. The lumber for this planking and keel has to be quarter-sawed so that there will be no shrinking or expanding, only in the thickness of the lumber. Boats built with quarter-sawed lumber stand the tests of time while boats that were built of flat-grained lumber were not worth the price of the lumber used in them.

"There was a time when some builders used iron screws in building. In repairing these boats in later years I got my fill of digging out iron screws and swore that when I started building boats I would never use anything but brass screws, a practice which I have always followed.

"When Spring comes, after working through the Winter months and building the several boats on order each year, I am usually glad when the last boat is completed, but then after repairing motor-boats and sailboats, or making paddles and oars and other equipment during the Summer and after the hunting season I always have an urge to start building boats again. There seems to be a feeling of confidence in one's ability, not to be afraid to tackle any kind of a job in wood-working once you have learned to build an Adirondack guide-boat.

"It seems too bad that time is running out of these fine boats, but the timber of which they are built is also vanishing. It could well be that over the next horizon there will be lots of time and all kinds of lumber so that the art of guide-boat building will not be a thing of the past."

For a short time Willard also included in his line a combination guide-boat for front four feet and the rest a rowboat especially built for outboards with square stern or transom. However, these were never as popular as his guideboat specialty so were gradually phased out of his operation.

Several years before his death the Adirondack Museum recorded on film the step by step process of fashioning a guideboat so the history of the art has been perpetuated. The boat building also has a display of the various parts and procedures entailed.

After his death in May 1962, six unfinished hulls were assembled with seats, cleats, rowlocks and other essential fittings by Pauline, his wife, who had been his chief helper for many years.

A Finished Hanmer Product

Chapter 16

The Guideboat Builders: Carl Hathaway and Others

Hanmer need not have worried about the guideboat's future because in the past decade there has been a resurgence of interest in the Steinways of the waterways. Apparently Willard felt at the time he made his pessimistic remarks that Carl Hathaway, who had been his helper for several years, would not continue the business on a full-time serious basis but, fortunately, things worked out otherwise.

Ed Hale, in his write-up of Hathaway in the Watertown *Times* 6/22/79, caught in well-chosen words the nature and character of this noteworthy successor to the Hanmers and all the countless other guide-boat builders over the years. Even though I have also interviewed Carl, Ed Hale's appraisal is far more perceptive and characteristic than I could ever produce; therefore, with friend Ed's permission and his Good Housekeeping stamp of approval the following delineation is basically a verbatim excerpt job: "Carl Hathaway stands like a tall spruce set for survival against the prevailing winds, roots deep and trunk spare to sustain his bent for taking care. The rhyme and reason of Adirondack caretaking puts wilderness freedom in cadence with the hired man's chores. Work for pay balances with Nature's rhythm.

"'It's a good life,' he says. 'I couldn't want anymore than I've had — close to my wife, family and Nature.' Carl Hathaway bustles with care. "His deep-set blue eyes see what others overlook — the curve of a boss root, the motives of a man."

"Mr. Hathaway carves his own place in Adirondack history in his own boat-shop (formerly the Hanmers) on his own land. He cuts two-foot thick clumps of winter ice on Upper Saranac's Gull Bay for his employer's summer use.

'Low pay buys peace and contentment,' he says simply. 'And you can't beat that.' His caretaker job at John L. Loeb's on the Upper Lake started in 1953 and carries on the tradition started by his father, who was Col. S. P. Witherill's superintendent at his big place on Gull Bay. Witherill was the son-in-law of Bucknell, principal benefactor of the college named after him.

"The Hathaway life has a natural order and sum total like the ledger that Mrs. Hathaway keeps. The husband, wife and two daughters — Patricia Ann and Judy Ann — all pull together. They all can shoot, cane seats and skin animals.

"On the back porch are guideboat seats to be caned. On the living room wall Mrs. Hathaway's eight-point buck is flanked by otter and fisher skins. The daughters were raised on deer drives where they learned to keep their powder dry.

"Judy Ann's husband, Tom Phillips, is also a caretaker, or more euphemistically termed, an outside superintendent at the Wawbeek, presently owned by St. Lawrence University and the gift of the Van Voorhis family.

"The shop smells of cedar, pine and spruce. Each piece of wood is treated with the respect of long acquaintance — perhaps eight or nine years. It comes the hard way.

"He's always looking for the boss root with grain curves in the arc of the boat's ribs,

Carl Hathaway (Ed Hale photos)

spruce for both the ribs and bow and stern stems. Pine or cedar for the planking and real cedar for centerboard.

'It's a continual search. Last winter for example I spent three days bringing nine native white cedar trees from deep in the woods for planking. By the time you get what you want from it you have a lot of damned expensive kindling!'

"Hathaway bought the shop from Hanmer's widow in 1965, shortly after Willard's death. Three years prior to the purchase he had worked Winters for the owner. 'The last year before his death he started to teach me. I liked wood-working and he needed help.'

'Everyone thought Willard was contrary but we got along.' "His daughter, who was listening to the conversation, interjected 'That's because you are too!'"

"Contrary is a word often heard in the Adirondacks where the weather, the village and the mountains deflect the prevailing currents of the times. It sometimes means an individual has a way that honors craftmanship, loyalty and self-sufficiency — a way that doesn't jibe with the uniformity and conformity of the blacktop culture.

'I'll probably never be the craftsman Willard was, but I stick as close as humanly possible to his methods — always allowing a little for a few tricks of the trade that I've picked up along the line!'

"A year's work means one or two Hathaway guideboats which now cost $3,500 for materials and 300 hours time on each one. He also repairs about 15 other boats. To date his total output has been fifteen new craft and over 200 repair jobs.

"Carl estimates that there are about 2,000 guideboats in the North Country. Judging from new orders received and the widespread interest in the boats themselves, he senses a rebirth in their popularity. Middle-aged sportsmen and couples like them — the people who admire and enjoy good living and fine workmanship. 'You know two people can slide a guideboat along like hell, and, besides its much easier and far more comfortable than paddling a canoe,' remarked Hathaway

"Hathaway is well aware of the tradition of the master craftsman. But he especially respects the guides who built their own boats over the long winters and to their own individual needs. 'Each built into his own boat exactly what he personally wanted. Each had to have skill and patience. Moreover, I've only seen one or two that were clumsily built,' he stated.

"That of course is part of the Adirondack tradition of taking care. Furthermore, it's a tradition that's now in very good hands — Hathaway's. . . ."

Willard Hanmer's regret over the very real possibility of guideboat-building becoming another of the steadily increasing numbers of so-called lost arts was more than a bit premature.

He would be delighted and relieved to know that at least five other men are actively engaged and deeply interested in perpetuating the tradition. Two of these are also Saranac Lakers — Ralph Morrow, who has already built eleven with still more ordered and George Outcalt, who although he has produced only two also plans to make more as time permits.

Interestingly enough, George has done a great service to the boatbuilding profession by fastidiously fabricating at least 50 beautiful miniatures which are complete in every detail. These have sold well in area outlets and at the Adirondack Museum which, of course, probably features the largest boat and guideboat display in the world.

In Long Lake, the generally accepted birthplace of the Brewster Buggies of the wilderness, Fred Burns has put out ten and Harold Austin three or four. With this upsurge of building activity and rising customer enthusiasm the future of the guideboat is most definitely rosy. And that's as it jolly well should be.

Caning the Seat

Octogenarian Fred Burns, the many-sided guideboat builder and oarsman, also turns out paintings that equal his boats in quality — and that's saying something significant. All his boats are crafted from the traditional local materials except that since either is hard to come by he has to settle for West Coast imports.

Still another craftsman who would like to produce nothing but wooden boats is Everett Smith of Parishville. Since guideboat building is such a time-consuming and unprofitable business on a full-time basis, he and his partners of necessity have to take on anything that he can get, which includes powerboat repairs and reconstruction.

It is noteworthy, however, that their one and only guideboat so far was exhibited several years ago at The Willard Hanmer Races in Saranac Lake and won the award for craftsmanship. The honored boat is now the proud possession of a Seattle, Washington aficionado.

Quite likely other names should have been given more space — names like Cross and Patnode who built boats for the Paul Smith's trade. And there were of course still other competent craftsmen almost too numerous to mention.

The noteworthy fact is that the Tiffany-quality well-kept guideboats are once again coming into their own and are worth at least part of their weight in gold — and you know what that yellow stuff is fetching (good old word that) on the international market these days.

Contrary to rumors there are still many of the 22 carat jobs around in club boathouses, on the racks of the private camps and elsewhere — but they are almost invariably considered as much-to-be-admired-but-mustn't-touch museum pieces and heirlooms. And who can blame the owners for that attitude!

Chapter 17

Fred M. Rice and Martha Reben

Many people who have become enamored with the Saranacs have heard about Martha Reben and sought out the section she made famous in much the same manner that Thoreau immortalized Walden Pond. Her favorite haunt was remote Weller Pond, which is actually a satellite of Middle Saranac Lake and accessible via a shallow lily-pad bordered slough or by trail from Saginaw Bay of Upper Saranac. *The Healing Woods,* her first book, was based largely on her experiences and observations during the ten-year period from 1931 to 1941.

After three bed-ridden years and two operations and after the doctors had recommended still more surgery, "I knew that I simply had to find some way to get out of that hospital room if ever I was to get any better," she wrote.

The means of escape came providentially in the form of this ad in the local paper: "Wanted: To get in touch with some invalid who is not improving and who would like to go into the woods for the Summer." She answered the ad and discovered that it had been placed by a robust, good-humored woodsman and boatbuilder named Fred Rice, who had hoped to locate a male patient who, like others had, could afford to pay him guide's wages.

Although he had misgivings about taking the very sick Martha into the woods and finding her without money, he nevertheless let her appeal soften his Yankee horse-sense. He agreed to take on the project for just what it would have cost her to stay in the village.

Mrs. Rice also strongly seconded the venture, helped with the preparations and became like a foster-mother to Martha, who walked out of the sanitarium that day and never went back.

Weller Pond, one of Rice's bailiwicks, was twelve miles by boat and far enough away to provide solitude. By degrees Fred took her on canoe trips, tempted her into long walks, generally introduced her to woodslife and watched her health improve appreciably.

By the second season the semi-invalid was spending weeks alone while Rice was away working at his guiding trade. Left to her own devices she soon developed an affinity for the wild animals and birds and started a journal recording their antics. These amiable and ingratiating creatures such as Mr. Dooley, the duck who was afraid of water and brought to Weller by packbasket from the village and Rufus, the rascally raccoon, one of the stars of her second book — *The Way of the Wilderness* (1955), are only two of her numerous memorable friends.

The Healing Woods (1952) represented a tremendous amount of work for a woman who wasn't fated to finally regain her health. There was a background of twenty years of collecting material, eight years went into the actual writing and the 250 pages were rewritten four times before she considered it ready for publication.

During that period, according to the author, "Mr. Rice taught me a lot. 'What does this mean?,' he'd ask. Or he'd say, 'This is nonsense! Make it accurate and clear!'"

Moreover, since the typing effort would have been an exhausting experience even if she had known how, Fred Rice taught himself and using the two-finger method produced her manuscripts.

As their health waned with the years Martha and Fred sought campsites closer to town on Hungry Bay of Middle Saranac, in a fisherman's shack a mile north of Bloomingdale on the Saranac River, and on Pope Bay of Lower Saranac.

The winters they spent in what is now the Carlin home, which was originally intended for summer occupancy only but was made habitable by the carpentry skill of Rice. This small house is located just outside Saranac Lake on the old State Road, now Route 3, on the road to Tupper.

The success of her two books attracted the attention of C. V. Whitney, who bought the movie rights. In 1956, Martha and Fred stayed in one of Whitney's camps on Fat Fish Pond so that she would be available for consultation. Although the movies were never made, her financial situation was made considerably better. But even though her books sold fairly well here and in England, she never did make a fortune in royalties.

A Sharing of Joy, her third and last book, was published in 1963, just a few weeks before her death, age 53, on January 7, 1964.

Fred Rice also had a genuine flair for descriptive writing and had a pamphlet published entitled *Fifty Years in a Health Resort.* Its main theme was that nature is a far better healer than doctors and that Trudeau's theories about treating tuberculosis were somehow neglected when the sanitariums became big business.

From 1947-1958 Rice also put out a mimeographed annual letter addressed to their camping neighbors. These chatty messages contained many interesting details which, since they were not all included in the Reben books, help round out their combined observations and recollections.

Fred Rice outlived Martha by only two years; he died, age 90, in 1966. Both were cremated and their ashes scattered over Weller Pond, where these words were carved on a hardwood slab: "Reben Point. May this spot be kept as a memorial to Martha Reben, whose life, and books on her life here, have inspired so many."

While this reminder is eminently fitting and proper, another person — Fred M. Rice, who made it all possible — also should be included and so given his fair share of recognition and praise.

Martha Reben and Fred M. Rice

Chapter 18

The Saranac Guides: Sam Dunning

The literature and unwritten lore of the Adirondacks is chock-full of references to the guides, whose logical and natural prototype was James F. Cooper's legendary Leatherstocking or Natty Bumppo, that paragon of vigor, virtue and omniscence. The process of virtual deification was perpetuated by Hoffman's, Lanman's and Headley's versions of John Cheney, Hammond's Tucker, Mather's Alvah Dunning, Murray's adulation of "Honest John" Plumley, Warner's pen portrait of Old Mt. Phelps etc., etc. The list can be expanded with little difficulty and the myth of the noble savage can be easily stretched to include his counterpart, the white-skinned Superman. In the eyes of the city dweller the ruggedly independent, semi-primitive life of the frontiersman — and the Adirondacks were for centuries a formidable barrier to civilization — was enviable and eminently praiseworthy.

However, the Leatherstocking legend did contain one substantial truth: the superior class of guides were indeed the lords of the forest and their clients either immediately recognized that fact or soon learned to do so. As Henry Van Dyke put it: "in the Adirondacks everything depends upon your guide."

But the conditions that once made guiding an essential and flourishing profession were of relatively short duration — from the first ascent of Marcy in 1833 roughly to the completion date of "Webb's Golden Chariot Route," The Mohawk and Malone (Adirondack Division of the N.Y. Central) R. R. in 1892 — say sixty years overall.

In the early pre-Colvin days large areas were still unsurveyed, the existing maps were often inaccurate, the roads were scarce and either impossible or impassable much of the year, and the trails were confined mainly to the carries. The highways were the waterways. By the late 1880's roads had been improved, several railways crossed the region, steamboat lines serviced the lakes — and the need for guides diminished in direct ratio to the course and speed of so-called progress.

The first solitary trappers and settlers in the North Woods, as elsewhere, needed no training to be guides; they either knew their woodcraft or they left their bones in the woods. Into their solitudes came the vanguard of the venturesome hunters and explorers who willingly paid the frontiersmen good money for what they did every day of their lives. As White eulogized them in his superb *Adirondack Country:* "Some of the early exponents seemed to tower over their successors as high peaks over hummocks." They were unique and extraordinary but their fame was due in large part to the various writers, artists and photographers who found in them a new type of American and put them vividly on paper, canvas or pictorial likeness.

Depending upon the woods experience of the writer and his general attitude toward his fellow human beings, the recorded descriptions and evaluations of guides run the gamut from enthusiastic praise to caustic sarcasm and all points between. Marc Cook in *The Wilderness Cure* (1879) delineated him with this short segment: "The Adirondack guide is born not made. He falls so to speak out of his log cradle into a pair of top boots, discards

Saranac Guides at Sportsmen's Show, N.Y.C. 1904

the bottle for a pipe, possesses himself of a boat and a jackknife and becomes forthwith a full-fledged experienced guide."

Pieter Fosburgh in his unsurpassed "Goyd" article from *The Natural Thing* regaled us with this clever appraisal: "Other backwoods parts of America attracted sportsmen, appealed to families of wealth as sites for summer homes, and became vacation areas. None ever produced that paragon of the woods lore or that shrewd rascal — according to who did the reporting — known as the Adirondack guide. He has been portrayed variously as a limitless font of stories and yarns, a tracker with the skill of a bloodhound, a better shot than Annie Oakley, a chef who could take baking powder, flour and salt and outcook Delmonico's and an all-knowing rustic philosopher in unchanging costume, his trousers hung from loose suspenders, a felt hat with trout flies on the hatband on his head and a watchchain dangling into a side pocket. His proudest boast was that he could take a city man into the woods, shoot his deer for him, cut it up — and knock down anyone who said that his patron hadn't shot it."

At the other extreme is this diatribe from Rev. John P. Lundy's *The Saranac Exiles:* "A more inpudent, lazy, extortionate and generally offensive class (with of course some exceptions) than these gentry would be hard to find. The angler or hunter subjected to their tender mercies has cause for congratulation if he escapes from the wilderness with a whole skin after surrendering to the sturdy beggars his choicest tackle and accoutrements, furnishing unlimited drink, tobacco and cigars, submitting to the outrageous over-charges, caprices and insults and listening to the lying boasts of these woodsy humbugs who guide their prey in the manner and direction which best suits their own convenience!" Now there's a downright disgruntled man speaking!

To counterbalance that vituperative explosion here's a more mellow and compassionate assessment by an anonymous contributor to *The American Angler* of Sept. 22, 1883: "The life of a guide, notwithstanding the gush that has been written about him, is a hard one, and there are few who would not abandon it to engage in a less arduous mode of livelihood. It is a fact too that the man who has followed that occupation becomes prematurely aged, and notwithstanding his life in the woods, with all the benefits supposed to be attached thereto, many a bronzed fellow presents the appearance of an old man before he has yet reached his prime. A guide may try to get the best of you in a bargain, but once enlisted in your service, he will serve you loyally. . . .

"Many come from distant sections, many from great cities for reasons best known only to themselves, and become lost to the world. Some are said to be men of education and prominence who through reverses lost caste and sought obscurity in the woods. The great majority, however, are just what they appear to be — men who have been born, spent their lives and expect to die in the wilderness." Well said indeed! . . .

In the so-called Golden Age of the Adirondacks every important hotel had its staff of guides waiting expectantly around the guidehouse or boathouse like hansom cab drivers in Central Park or on Mt. Royal in Montreal. These "hotel guides," who were low men on the totem pole, were paid by the hour to run errands or row an old lady around the lake. The "house guides," the next step up, were paid by the month as employees of an estate, and were on call and were ready to cater to the sporting whims of the owner, his guests and family. The top echelon, the aristocrats of the guild, were the "private guides," who had their own clientele who reserved them for a week or a month and paid and tipped well. Whatever his place in the pecking order, the guide's standard personal equipment in-

"Goyd' by Clayton Seagers

variably featured his hat, suspenders (galluses) pipe and conspicuous watch chain, usually anchored by a bulbous gold watch. Standard pay in 1890 was $3.00 per day — and they earned every cent of it. . . .

By the 1880's there were about 500 guides working the Adirondack region. The 1910 *Game Laws and Guide Directory* put out by the Remington Arms Co. listed 30 for Essex Co., 83 for Franklin County, 20 for Hamilton, 11 for Lewis and 5 for St. Lawrence. Undoubtedly, there were others but the point is that their heyday was definitely over by then — and few have taken their place. The best of them became caretakers for camps; some became game wardens. After 1908 all guides had to register with the Conservation Department. Although as of 1950 more than a thousand so-called guides registered, they were mostly men who were regularly employed but always willing to quit their jobs during fishing or hunting season. As White put it: "They follow a memory rather than a profession."

The 1979 list of N.Y. State registered guides contains 346 names — 3 of them women. 126 claim expertise in Franklin and Essex counties, 13 in the entire Adirondack Park region and 13 in both Adirondack and Catskill Parks. 10 announced themselves as qualified to be "guide, philosopher and friend" to anyone wishing to go afield in anywhere from 7 to 15 counties. Such modesty!

The amusing factor in all this is the ease with which anyone nowadays can become a full-fledged, duly licensed guide. Instead — as most people believe or are led to believe — of requiring multiple skills dealing with a wide range of woodsmanship techniques, the only actual feat is signing one's name on an application blank. That plus a two-dollar fee and a superficial check of a person's background in order to eliminate convicted criminals. No field tests — just a list of vital stats and tabulation of sporting interests — and so-called accomplishments therein.

However, that is due to change shortly and become a considerably more difficult course of sprouts. In order to acquire the panache in the future the applicant will have to actually demonstrate his first-aid knowledge, prove conclusively that he can read a map and handle a compass, operate a boat or canoe competently, know fish and wildlife regulations and be able to identify species thereof, swim well and successfully pass a reasonable wilderness survival ordeal. No piece of cake hereafter — which is as it should be of course. . . .

As you have already noticed this has been an admittedly long — overlong to some im-

Typical Guide's Cabin and Occupant

patient people no doubt — lead-in to the real meat of the upcoming chapters on Saranac guides. In an honest effort to provide a full treatment of the subject of guiding in general before getting down to particular guides, I have obviously overdone it but felt that in this case too much was far better than skimpy, right-on coverage.

At long last then, there soon follows a series of sketches dealing with six of the Saranac, region's most noteworthy guides. Three of these are sterling representatives of the earlier era — Sam Dunning, Henry Martin, and Pete O'Malley. Ellsworth Petty and Herb Clark were, according to those who should know, just about the finest examples of the latter day period. Bob Marshall, Clark's protegé, was an ecological guide, the scarcest kind of intelligent leadership.

It should be understood that there were undoubtedly others who deserved this belated recognition but the lack of adequate information and the shortage of space made that understandably impossible.

Charles Hallock in his very popular *Fishing Tourist* (1873) described most entertainingly the motley collection of guides which he encountered at "St. James of the Wilderness," alias Paul Smith's. To my knowledge no one has ever come up with a more complete inventory of male humanity. Here it is: "That evening the members of the Club sauntered down to the guide-house, where they were confronted by a delegation of those forest-rangers. Said rangers understood that the gentlemen were "going in" and wanted guides. Said rangers were hirsute, swarthy, raw-boned, iron-ribbed. . . . There were guides of all sizes, ages, nations and degrees; lazy guides, talkative guides, low-bred guides, bragging guides, silent guides, bad guides, good guides, independent guides, hotel guides, thirsty guides, gray-haired guides, carroty-hair guides, bald-headed guides, cross-grained guides, guides well-recommended, and guides without character — Frenchmen, Yankees, Irish and Indians.

"All offered their services and were ready to go anywhere, anyhow and at any time; they were ready to tramp it, to pack it, to boat it, to rough it, to take it easy, and to take it straight; they knew all the best camping, hunting and fishing grounds and had been there before; they knew their way into any part of the wilderness, and they knew their way back. . . . and each guide had his boat. Beautiful craft they are and drawing but three inches of water and weighing but sixty to eighty pounds."

Now, I don't know exactly what category Sam would fall into, because there is so little known and recorded about him. However, that little tells a lot about a crusty old character who enlivened considerably the wilderness experiences of two delighted authors — Joel T. Headley and Frederick S. Stallknecht. Headley, who wrote one of the earliest books on the region — *The Adirondacks* or *Life in the Woods*, 1858, told about seeing Sam at Martin's the previous Summer. Here's the impression the congenial but voluble old guide made on the outlander:

"Everything is democratic in the woods and several guides engaged to go out with parties dropped in to have a chat with the gentlemen. One of these whom they called Sam was an original. He was a capital guide, willing, cheerful, a good cook and strong as an ox. Standing full six feet two in his stockings he thought no more of putting his boat on his head, oars and all and carrying it for three miles over streams and logs and hills and through swamps than I would an empty basket. Sam has only one fault — his tongue never stops. He says a great many queer, laughable things and a great deal that is stale, flat and unprofitable. Still he's an honest, kind, capable and accommodating guide.

"Last year he went out with a party from Boston and Cambridge, and his democratic notions received a shock from which he will never recover. His harmless rattle was con-

Sportsman and Guide — A Friendly Chat

143

sidered disrespectful and Sam, who had never before seen anybody too good for him, was taken wholly aback by the distance at which he was kept. He was treated simply as a paid servant at home. Now this was a new revelation to him. In his long life in the woods he had seen nothing like it before, a rollicking free-and-easy set he had always been with hitherto and so much stateliness and dignity in camp-life quite bewildered him.

"He said, however, that he had his revenge on one of them. On a long and uneven carrying-place, over which he was floundering with his boat on his head, the gentleman began to grumble at the difficulty of the way and repeatedly asked Sam if there was no way to get across except by walking. 'Yes,' replied the guide, 'ketch a sucker and put him between your legs and scull over!' Sam said that ever after that the man regarded him as a strange animal whose company should be carefully avoided.

"His dislike of Bostonians and Cambridge men, as he calls them, has become chronic and he will run on for hours about them. He has a large tent, which my companions wish to take along with them. But I dislike tents; they are heavy to carry, in a rain they are damp, while you are afraid to build up those roaring fires near them which make a bark shanty so comfortable by serving the double purpose of driving off the mosquitoes and of keeping you warm.

"They were, however, determined to strike a bargain with Sam, and I, who had hitherto been a mere listener, asked him how many his tent would hold. 'Just two Boston men — I have tried it — they will fill it full, but it will hold six New Yorkers easy!'

"Why, Sam," I replied, "I didn't know the Boston men were so much larger than New Yorkers!"

A Swim for Life

'Well, they are,' said he; 'I've measured them with my tent. One takes up just as much room as three New Yorkers!'

"It seems to me," said I, "that you bear the Bostonians some malice. What's the matter — why don't you like them?

He drew himself up à la Webster and in a severe, grave tone replied. 'Sir, they've got more dignity than dollars!'

In Stallbrecht's account Sam is in fine fettle on their way to the Philosopher's Camp at Follensby Pond. Says Sam, 'That rub of the boat [on a rock] sorta reminds me of rubbin' agin a good-looking widder down in Essex County last winter. I spose she was a widder, anyhow she was in black, and she mighta bin a grass, for with all her black drygoods her eyes kinda glistened when I helped her outa the stage.

'Wall, it begun to rain and as she hadda couple miles to go the boys about the hotel were in a pucker to get up her trunk, which was one of those big square black shanties on wheels with yeller skylights all over. The horses were out ahead and it was three miles tuh the nearest cart, and as fer leavin' her bandbox and finery for a minute no woman in the world would be expected tuh do that, so I sez to myself, 'Darn it all, I'll break the rule,' for let me tell you, the moment I'm outa the woods for my winter tour down to old Essex, I hug the hotel stove for five or six weeks, and hear what's goin' on in the world, I'm a gentleman. . . . But, says I takin' a look at the widder in trouble, 'Marm,' says I, 'I'll see yuh over the Carry, so off goes my coat and in lessn' ten minutes I had her hunderd and fifty-pounder safely landed over tuh the house. Wa-a-all, there warn't nobody home except the old black cat so of course I sot down and had a little familiar. Says I, 'Sam's in clover for this ere day', but dang it all, I had her tuh myself for only three days when up comes a chap on the stage and walks off with my widder to the nearest minister — and off they went without sayin' as much as a good-bye! So sez I, 'I'll stick to Brave [his hound] and the woods; never will I find a woman so true to me as this here old dawg. When we two are off on a lay, I'd like to see the man what'll rob us of our game!'. . . "

That's about it for the story of the bumptious, garrulous Sam — except for the statement in Tertius Van Dyke's biography of his father, the Rev. Dr. Henry Van Dyke, that the author of *Little Rivers* etc., when young, yearned to be a Saranac guide like Sam Dunning! The good Dr. undoubtedly had not yet read Stallknecht's article.

Chapter 19

The Saranac Guides: Henry Martin

Although Martin was essentially a St. Regis guide and the brother-in-law of Oom Paul Smith, his career also featured his phenomenal skill and daring as a river-driver on the Saranac. Furthermore, he was the favorite guide of the young Theodore Roosevelt during his boyhood vacations at Saranac Inn, so he richly rates coverage in this opus.

Born in Franklin Falls in 1860 his entire life was spent in the woods. During his early manhood he was considered to be one of the finest — if not the very finest — riverman in the Adirondacks. He was credited with knowing every eddy and undercurrent of the streams which floated logs — knowledge based on close and frequent observation which often spelled the difference between life and death for the logger.

His fame attracted the attention of a New York sportsman who had a betting disposition. At a gathering in the Union League Club one evening, the sport remarked that he knew an Adirondack guide who could ride a log across the East River.

"I'll bet you a thousand dollars that there isn't an Adirondack guide or any other kind

Roughing It — Homer D. Martin

146

Trouting

A Successful Hunt

147

Lean-to Life in the Tall Timber

of guide who can be that!" proclaimed one of the company.

"I'll take that bet!" replied Martin's sponsor and the wager was posted.

Henry was notified and promptly accepted the challenge. Before leaving for the Big City, he selected a log that suited him, and took it with him in the express car. However, when the time came for the demonstration the man who was betting against Martin sized him up, agreed that he could pull off the stunt and the matter was settled to everybody's satisfaction.

An article in the *Plattsburgh Sentinel* on May 30, 1907 gave an eyewitness account of what had to be Henry Martin's most memorable river-driving experience. As E. C. Baker saw it: "One Spring we got caught in a jam on the Saranac River. A huge log had swung sidewise across the very brink of the last precipice at High Falls (Moffitsville) and soon over 40,000 pieces solidly lodged in the narrow gorge. Since we didn't use dynamite in those days, nothing could be done except cut out the key log [pull the cork].

"A volunteer was called for and Henry Martin was the only driver who stepped forward. A large rope was thrown across the River and held at each end by other men. Martin lashed himself to the rope and, with axe in hand, was hauled to the center of the gorge and then lowered to the pile-up. He chopped away for two hours while the rest of us were kept in terrible suspense. Finally the log snapped in two and immediately thousands of logs were released and pushed by the great accumulation of water, went tumbling, thundering and groaning like an avalanche over the precipice.

"As the key log snapped, Martin gave the signal and the rope was hauled taut by the watchful men on the riverbanks. The intrepid logger hung poised in midair momentarily and then was pulled safely ashore amid the welcome cheers of his comrades."*

Martin was very likely the first guide that Teddy Roosevelt ever had. As a boy he vacationed with H. D. Minot, his tutor, at Saranac Inn for three Summers. In order to regain his health he lived in a tent near the Inn and continued there his natural history studies started at Oyster Bay on Long Island and on the Hudson. "They soon became more than a boy's fun because some of the observations made when he was fifteen, sixteen and seventeen soon found their way into learned books. When the state of New York published, many years afterward, two big volumes about the birds of the State*[1] some of those early writings entitled *Summer Birds of the Adirondacks,* by Theodore Roosevelt Jr. and H. D. Minot, 97 different birds are listed."*[2]

During at least one of the three Summers — probably the first in 1873 — Martin was the guide, and it was said that the boy spent more time and had more fun with Henry than he did with the stuffy tutor.

Later on, Martin's woodcraft got him the position as chief guide with Hamilton Mc. K. Trombley, whose wife was a Vanderbilt. When the Trombleys built their luxurious "camp" on Pine Point, Upper St. Regis Lake and occupied it for many years, Martin was hired as superintendent. Later Frederick W. Vanderbilt bought the place and rebuilt it à la Japanese style of architecture. Henry stayed on as superintendent until after it was purchased by Mr. Pratt.

One of the strongest of the many powerful and able men in the woods Martin's health declined appreciably after the death of his daughter, Leah Martin Hickok, followed by the demise of his wife years later. The twin losses apparently undermined his health. His remaining years were spent with his other daughter Mrs. Hubert Dyer, in the Town of Brighton. He died age 75, on October 31, 1915.

---

* For more about river-driving read that chapter in Maitland C. De Sormo's [my] book: *Heydays of the Adirondacks* Saranac Lake: Adirondack Yesteryears Inc. 1975
*[1] Elon H. Eaton — *Birds of N.Y.* State 2 vols. Albany: Univ. of State of N.Y. 1910-14
*[2] Edmund D. Pearson — *Theodore Roosevelt, A Brief Biog.* New York: Book League

Chapter 20

The Saranac Guides: Pete O'Malley

Fred Hodges, my father-in-law, besides being a proficient photographer, was also very much at home in the woods — in fact far more at home there than at home. It is very understandable that during more than sixty years, as much as possible of which was spent in the woods, Hodges became closely associated with many other woodsmen and had plenty of opportunities to size up the 57 varieties of so-called guides while some of the real ones were still in circulation, especially in the Blue Mt. Lake — Fulton Chain region.

Based on those extensive contacts he was well qualified to rate the field and come up with these two general classifications. One kind of guide was chock-full of all sorts of remarkable stories and experiences — real ear-benders. He had seen the tallest trees, knew exactly where the juiciest berries grew, had craftily caught the biggest trout, had had frequent close encounters with ferocious panthers, vicious wildcats, cornered bears, enraged moose and wounded bucks. Strangely enough, he had of course always been more than a match for anything of four legs — or two. He and his formidable and equally legendary pals had cut the most and largest logs and predictably in the shortest time. Whenever he carried a boat he never had to take a rest, even on the longest, steepest trails. He knew by heart the names of all the trees, birds and flowers and whenever he didn't know pretended loudly that he did. A total and windy fraud.

The other sort of guide said little and got a lot of mileage out of that little. He was polite and capable. He didn't brag — didn't have to — about his skill and exploits with rod, gun, axe and guideboat. He always underestimated the number of deer and bear he had killed, or trout he had caught and their sizes. Whenever he didn't know the answer to a question, he readily admitted that he didn't — and didn't feel that he had lost face by doing so. Whenever these men talked you sat there and really listened.

Apparently Pete O'Malley was one of the second sort because Seneca Ray Stoddard, who had also been around extensively considered him to be his preferred Saranac guide. Moreover, he perpetuated his approval in one of his finest photos.

Praised by many discerning and recognized photograph critics as perhaps the most characteristically Adirondack scene ever taken, the print shows Pete at the oars and Charlie Oblenis, Stoddard's brother-in-law in the stern seat. The locale of the exceptional print is the little bay and point just south of the Wawbeek Hotel. . . .

The O'Malley forebears emigrated from Ireland during the Potato Famine of the 1840's and settled in the Colton-Potsdam section of the Adirondack foothills. Pete, one of three sons was the venturesome sort and disliked farming so he headed for the tall timbers at the earliest opportunity. As one of Martin's hotel guides he was assigned to Stoddard, who apparently liked him and his work so employed O'Malley whenever he was in the area taking pictures or gathering information for his maps and guidebook series.

According to Kate Dacey, Pete's niece, when his guiding days were over O'Malley assumed the management of the International Paper Company's small hotel at Piercefield.

Successful Hunters — Pete O'Malley, guide, and Charles Oblenis, sport — (Stoddard photo)

In Camp — A Sticky Wicket

This was an unusual place because following Company policy no liquor was sold on the premises — a smart move where lumberjacks are concerned. However, since Tupper Lake was not that far away, it is doubtful if any of those traditionally hard-drinkers ever died of thirst.

Five years of that type of relative inactivity probably proved to be about all a restless fellow like Pete could take, for he moved to a farm between Bloomingdale and Vermontville, near the present Pleasant View Inn. Still later he seemingly needed another change of scenery and bought a cure-cottage on Marshall St. in Saranac village. During the various changes he always maintained his escape hatch, a camp on the Upper Franklin Falls road, near the woods and waters that he missed from time to time.

How he met, wooed and married his wife makes a good story in itself. She — Belle Beatty — was a Canadian who worked for several Summers at Paul Smith's, where Pete met her. As often as possible O'Malley rode his horse over to date her. Belle, like any other clever female had a hard time making up her mind so played hard to get and kept him dangling. At the end of that special season she, still undecided, boarded the stagecoach and headed back home without letting him know her exact departure plans. Unaware that she had already gone, Pete showed up for his anticipated date to find that his heart-throb was among the missing.

Not easily discouraged and being familiar with the stagecoach route the dapper suitor remounted his trusty steed and raised considerable dust in pursuit of the slower-moving coach. Not long afterward he overtook that conveyance, plied her with his best brand of blarney and in general showed such ardent interest that she became convinced that he was the right man with whom to spend the rest of her life. . . .

Horses were seemingly his principal hang-up because at various times he owned fast trotters and thoroughly enjoyed racing them locally and at fairs in Malone and Ottawa. Also on the ice of Ampersand Bay. He died, aged 79, in the early 1930's leaving his wife, Belle, and a brother, James. Jack, an Albany lawyer had predeceased him.

If not one of the most publicized guides Pete, during his prime was nevertheless one of the best. Stoddard thought so and immortalized him in the unforgettable photograph which epitomized the most familiar Adirondack elements — a guideboat, guide (Pete O'Malley) at the oars, a sport (Charles Oblenis, Stoddard's brother-in-law), dogs and deer.

Frankly, that sort of lingering graphic acclaim is all that any guide — or anyone else for that matter — could ever ask for.

Chapter 21

The Saranac Guides: Tom Peacock

In his opening paragraph on Adirondack guides George Marshall quotes this amusing — typically Twain — passage from the latter's *A Tramp Abroad*. "Our troubles thickened about the middle of the afternoon and the seventeen guides called a halt and held a consultation. After consulting an hour they said that their first suspicion remained intact — that is to say, they believed they were lost. I asked if they did not know it. No, they replied, they couldn't absolutely know whether they were lost or not because none of them had ever been in that part of the country before. Therefore, although they had a strong instinct that they were lost they had no proof. . . . They had met no tourists for some time, and they considered that a suspicious sign."

Unlike the Austrian guides no Adirondack woodsman worth his salt would ever venture into any unknown section with a party because of the obvious potential danger to them and the damage to his reputation. If the good ones went astray they did it while on their own so there were no witnesses to their miscalculations. Moreover, they too were handicapped in the early guiding days because there were no tourists convocations in the woods then to serve as landmarks.

Verplanck Colvin's unvarnished description of guides and their duties is perhaps unexcelled: "The men employed during the season as guides and packmen in the labor of the different divisions numbered 51 all told. Being generally skillful hunters and trappers, their pursuits had led them along the streams and lakes where their game most abounded; and their natural skill as woodsmen made their assistance valuable, even in those sections with which they were unacquainted. Each carried upon his back a load of provisions, blankets and camp equipage weighing from fifty to sixty pounds. It was their duty also to build huts or shanties for the survey party, cut timber, build and keep up campfires during the night, act as cooks and perform such other labor as was necessary. It is not too much to say that almost all of them were faithful, intelligent and skilled men, ready to labor night and day for the success of the survey."

Besides all those chores and responsibilities many of the guides were superb storytellers too. An important part of their function was not only to keep their parties comfortable but also to keep up their morale. Furthermore, there was usually — especially among the veteran sportsmen employers — a reciprocal respect and sense of equality but with one added element — the guide, because of his greater knowledge and experience was the acknowledged leader.

Such men were as scarce in the Adirondacks so they were everywhere else in every other calling so, once their dominance had been established they achieved far more than merely local fame. Tom Peacock. Saranac guide, was definitely one of that top echelon of great guides.

Grace Hudowalski (editor) —
George Marshall — *The Adirondack High Peaks and the Forty-sixers* Albany: Peters Print 1971

Born into one of the pioneer families of North Elba he received a rural school educa-tion and helped his father, who was working shares on the nearby farm of John Brown, abolishionist, one of the most exciting figures in American history.

In an interview with the late W. H. Burger in the Winter of 1953 edition of *North Country Life* Peacock then 88, recalled that unforgettable evening, at that time only six, when Brown left for the ill-fated Harper's Ferry expedition and subsequent disaster.

He and his father, William, had been planting potatoes that day and were returning at sundown past the Brown home. Small groups of men were seen talking. About dusk the gaunt grey-bearded man rode up on horseback. More talk. Then he remembered that Brown bade them goodbye and he and his father went on home. He also recalled that he was particularly impressed by the horse, the first he had ever seen [oxen in those days did the hauling work] and the red bandana handkerchief Brown carried.

According to Donaldson the departure scene took place inside the Brown house. Young Peacock was supposedly told by his father to sit quietly in the corner of the room while the men talked in subdued tones. Shortly afterwards, the hoofbeats of a horse were heard and then, a few moments later, Brown entered the room, talked with the assembled men for ten or fifteen minutes, shook hands and said a solemn but not lingering farewell to each of them. Then one of the men followed him out of the house and helped him to unhitch the horse. The others stood silently in the doorway as their friend headed away from the mountain home for his rendezvous with death.

Peacock also recollected that John Brown looked very old that night — and although he was only fifty-eight he had already begun to stoop noticeably. However, he was still a commanding figure with powerful frame, upright bristling hair, square white beard and eyes that in the lamplight glittered wildly at times. [Donaldson description]

"When we heard about the raid on Harper's Ferry and that Brown had been hanged, my father was greatly upset and didn't eat or sleep well for several weeks. He again cau-tioned me to say nothing about what I had seen that evening at the Brown farm." Very likely he was afraid of their being arrested as accomplices.

When Brown returned it was in his coffin. It was a snowy Dec. 8, 1859 when the funeral took place at one o'clock. The services began with the singing of "Blow ye the Trumpet, Blow," an old tune familiar mostly to the Negroes, many of them fugitive slaves, who made up half the mourners. During this and another hymn, the prayer by Dr. Young and speech by Wendell Phillips, the coffin was so placed that everyone could see the dead man's face which was flushed instead of pallid. [Donaldson again]

Although these details were not part of young Peacock's reminiscences, they help round out the scene. However, he did recall that the surviving members of the unsuccessful Harper's Ferry insurrection furtively returned, dodging from house to house and barn to barn apprehensively to escape detection and possible capture. Several of them came to the Peacock house asking for food. For quite a while afterward he corresponded with Ruth Thompson, 84 year-old granddaughter of John Brown, then living in California. . . .

Tom killed his first deer at 13 with a flint-lock musket owned by Henry Thompson, Brown's son-in-law. At 17 he was already guiding parties through Indian Pass, down to the deserted village of Tahawus; he also made his first trip through the Saranacs at that age.

He was one of the guides for Pres. Grover Cleveland at the Prospect House (Saranac Inn) in 1878 and 1879 and was one of those who were with Colvin on his surveying projects in the Saranac region and very likely included in his commendation report to the N.Y.S. Legislature. He also guided Alexander Graham Bell, inventor of the telephone.

The old guide remembered that the Rev. William H. H. "Adirondack" Murray was very strong. Once when the parson and his friends were horsing around and testing each other's strength, someone promoted a "hefting" contest between Murray and Peacock and placed bets on the outcome. Each man was required to lift a heavy packbasket loaded with rocks from a sitting position on the ground. Murray tried but supposedly only half-heartedly because he was fully aware of the hernia possibility. Peacock, with a prodigious effort managed to lift it by rolling against a log and grasping a protruding stub. . . .

His father had a contract to supply the lumber camps at Big and Little Wolf Ponds, near Tupper Lake, in the late 1860's or early '70's, when Tom was still a youngster. They would load the lumber-sleds the night before and the next morning get ready to go. Just before leaving home they often put 25 to 30 bushels of potatoes and two or three quarters of beef in the hay and then started off from what is now the Bear Cub Road in North Elba.

The start was scheduled for 2:30 or 3 a.m. but Tom remembered distinctly driving through Saranac Lake — 11 miles away — as early as 3 a.m. They usually planned to get out on the Lower Saranac by daylight, which meant arrival at their destination about 9 in the morning to be enthusiastically greeted by the lumberjacks. The reason for the rousing welcome was that in addition to food for man and beast they also brought mail. In those days there was no official mail service as letters and messages were entrusted to just about every reasonably trustworthy Tom, Dick and Harry.

Although no braggard Peacock must have been quite a man and he proved it on many occasions. One of these happened one evening when he was sitting in the Guide Room at Martin's, the owner of the hotel came in and asked for a volunteer to take a message through to Big Tupper Lake. Nobody offered but after a long silence Peacock spoke up, "I'll take it," — even though he wasn't exactly overjoyed at the prospect of going through the Seven Pole Rapids* [sic] at night. Word had come in that the dam at that spot had raised the water level in the Raquette River fifteen feet in places.

Anyhow he started out and made it to Bartlett's while the lights were still on, crossed over to the Upper Saranac, rowed across to the Sweeney Carry and over that, across the Oxbow and into Big Tupper just at daybreak. Forty-three and a half miles in one night — not bad for one man and his guideboat in comparative darkness much of the way and almost total obscurity in many places.

Unlike most Adirondack guides, Peacock traveled widely and guided in other regions too. He hunted moose in northern Quebec and Ontario for fifty years and made several trips "out West" and to Texas and Arizona. During one of these treks he visited the Theodore Roosevelt Elkhorn Ranch on the Little Missouri near Medora, North Dakota. One Winter he supplied a Denver and Rio Grande railroad construction gang in Colorado with elk and deer meat, as many as nine elk in an afternoon.

He once estimated that he had shot at least 89 deer, numerous elk, bear (one huge cinnamon in Colorado) as well as lynx, wolves and a mountain lion. He could also remember when the now-extinct passenger pigeons darkened the Adirondack skies.

In 1939 when Harry Von Zell invited him to be on the famed "We the People" radio program, the renowned old guide insisted that his grandson be on with him. It was agreed and the two made an exciting experience for the national audience. While waiting to go on Tom Stainback was overheard practicing his part. He made a strong enough impression on

---

* Bill Burger must have misunderstood Peacock because the Seven Pole — actually the *Sitting* Pole Rapids are downriver from Tupper Lake, just above Piercefield, miles to the north of the regular guideboat route through the Saranacs to Big Tupper. Very likely Peacock referred to the rapids on the Saranac River where it leaves Round Lake (Middle Saranac) and where he would carry his boat — not try to run up through the boulder-strewn fast water.

Close-up of T. R. and Trophy Moose

Von Zell(?) that the latter suggested that the teenager go into radio seriously — which he did on the local Saranac Lake station.

Also evergreen were several anecdotes about T. R. One of the stories was based on an experience late one summer. Tom and another feller had just swum their horses across the river and got smeared with clayey mud; as they rode on up toward the ranch-house they saw Roosevelt coming up a hill, leading his horse. The setting sun was shining on his glasses and his buck teeth stuck out. He was carrying a string of sagehens which he had just shot. The jovial future president hobnobbed with Tom and his friend and told them stories — and as Tom recalled, "What stories! . . ."

Probably Tom's favorite anecdote was his "Ike Tale." "Back in 1903 and '04 I had a camp on Long Pond in the Narrows. One day right after I had returned from camp to my house, at 192 Lake St. a badly scared boy came in and said that he had just seen the "awfullest" animal back at Long Pond.

"We went right up by train and when we got there we found a moose moseying around. I went up to him, he reached out his nose and I patted it. You know, that con-sarned moose stayed around all that summer! He seemed very tame and I called him Ike after our game protector [Ike Stearns]. He would always come when I called him even when he was way up in the woods. But he didn't like women! His eyes would turn green if he saw one, then he'd start for her [a male chauvinist no doubt who hated floppy skirts].

"One day some boys saw him on a ridge at Slang Pond. He started toward them — they ran to their boat and he swam right after them — they carried their boat across into Long and he still followed them — right up to the porch of the cabin they had run into. Then he looked in at them through the windows and glass door.

"Finally I was down home in Saranac Lake one day. Old Mr. and Mrs. Turner were in camp. The boys came down and told me that the moose had noosed up the swing, which was hung on a 1½" rope. His horns got caught and hung up in the rope as he struggled to get free. Gilbert Turner tried to cut the rope. He lunged at Turner, his horns broke off and he went wild [became enraged] so old man Turner shot him, and that was the end of Ike. . . .

Prior to Bill Burger's interview with Tom Peacock he had already talked with another Tom — Tom Stainback, his grandson, then working for the local radio station. The young man told Burger about his grandfather and described him in such glowing terms that the writer felt that he just had to meet the man who could generate so much affection. Five days later he did and had the pleasant, productive meeting already covered.

However, in order to round out that report, I felt that no biographical sketch of (Uncle) Tom, as everyone called him, would be complete without the recollections and reactions of young Tom, who has had a very distinguished career himself as president of chambers of commerce in New York and Cincinnati and at present the effective president of Paul Smith's College, from which he was graduated in its very first class — 1941.

The grandson's memories are still vivid and warm even though he saw him last in Nov. 1942. Apparently Old Tom was tall, very powerful, tender and determined, an active church-goer and officer, and a person who, unlike most men who had led the rough and tough life of a guide and logger, never drank, smoked or swore. When his daughter and her husband — the Stainbacks — died, leaving three young children — Tom, Florence and Virginia — a great deal of pressure was exerted to have them put up for adoption, but the grandfather would have none of it and reared them himself.

Peacock, besides guiding at Martin's also worked at his calling at Saranac Inn and Paul Smith's, whose owner and Dr. E. L. Trudeau became close friends of Old Tom; he

Tom Peacock and Friends

also was with Vice Pres. Teddy Roosevelt in Sept. 1901 when T. R. was notified by messenger at Tear-of-the-Clouds that McKinley's condition had deteriorated.

Besides guiding and logging activities Peacock also cleared and developed the Helen Hill section of Church St. in Saranac Lake and built three cure cottages on land now occupied by DeChantal and the Telephone Co. buildings. . . .

The hunting parties at Slang and Long Ponds have also lingered long in Tom Stainback's mind. Over the years he and other companions including Jim and Jack Shea, Dick Ely, Charlie Ladd and Bill Green would converge on Tom's camps and spend unforgettable days hunting and evenings of poker, whose ground rules changed according to the contents of Peacock's hands. The flood of stories that he told still ring — albeit hazily — in the minds of the younger men.

On one memorable hunting trip at Turtle Pond, near Hoel, the party became befuddled and started a heated argument over their location and return directions. Since old Tom was well up into the 80's at the time, they felt that they were better woodsmen in spite of his insistence that he knew the exact whereabouts of the correct trail. Nevertheless, he was overruled volubly — time was lost floundering around in the tall shrubbery and they ran out of daylight. That long night they burned a complete tree as a campfire and sweated out the dark hours until daybreak. They decided to take Peacock's advice — and found that he was absolutely right. In spite of that reassurance he felt greatly humiliated that such a thing would happen. Bill Green, another frequent member of the hunting expeditions, recalled that even in his 80's the old guide could walk the legs off his juniors for half a day; in the afternoon he rested. Green has remembered a truly red-letter day — when the rest of the party made sure that their incomparable old companion got his last buck. With him ensconced in a chair they drove his target directly in front of him — and the bullet did its deadly work. Understandedly, it was a deeply moving experience for all concerned.

Green also bought Peacock's guideboat, a Martin, and still has it.

Nearly up to the year of his death Peacock stayed active, even doing heavy work such as bucksawing firewood. His failing eyesight slowed him down considerably, especially the eye with the cataract, which was a story in itself. As he was chopping branches from a tree one day, one of the twigs struck his bad eye — but in the process obliterated the cataract film. Ever afterward he called it his "self operation!"

The end of the earthly trail for the great old guide came in Nov. 1942 in the Saranac Lake General Hospital. Burial was in the Pine Ridge Cemetery.

Thomas H. Peacock, Veteran Guide, Dies

THOMAS H. PEACOCK

nac Lake Man Saw John
rown Leave for Har-
pers Ferry

11/1942
(Special To The Times)

"Tom" received an elementary education at North Elba and then took up guiding. He had killed his first deer at the age of 13 and still in his 'teens when he guided his first party.

In those days, the guide had

Last Photo of Peacock

159

Chapter 22

The Saranac Guides: Herb Clark and Bob Marshall

This article, from *High Spots* issue of October 1933, published by the Adirondack Mountain Club,is a heart-felt and heart-warming tribute to the memory of a great Saranac guide and mountaineer. Bob Marshall, (1901-1939) the writer of this sterling piece was an explorer, forester, conservationist and author of the classic *Arctic Village*.

"Herbert Clark was born near Keeseville, New York, on July 10, 1870, in the days when life was mysterious, wild, and harsh.

"Herb's grandmother, while driving the produce of her farm to market one night, suddenly found her horses stopping in horrible fright. While close at hand she heard chains rattling. Being a very pious woman, she said her prayers and got out to look at what had happened. She found the horses in a lather and all the tugs in the harness loose, and concluded that the Devil must have been after her. A few weeks later she got news that her mother had died. Similarly, Herb's father was walking home from the forge at Clintonville one night when he saw an empty ore car whiz past him down the center of the road at a terrific speed as if the Devil were in it. A few days later he too got news of his mother's death. When Herb was two years old his parents bought a farm along the road from Clintonville to Augur Pond. The people from whom they bought it had been very poor for many years, but suddenly became exceedingly rich. At the same time the peddler who customarily visited the neighborhood disappeared. Whatever the relationship between these events, the fact remains that throughout Herb's childhood the kettles on the stove would commence to rattle all at once, people would be heard talking upstairs when the whole family was in the kitchen, and one night Herb woke up to find a woman dressed in white standing by his bed. . . .

"Of wilderness there was also plenty in those days. Augur Pond lay just outside the true Adirondack wilderness, but it was in sight of the high mountains and still had in its vicinity many large blocks of unmarred timber. Such roads as existed were full of holes, and a journey by buggy of 40 miles was considered a big day. Wild animals were common. From their house the Clarks often heard panthers screaming. One night when Herb was about twelve, while he was walking home from Clintonville, he had to pass through a dark piece of woods. Suddenly he heard an animal following him. As soon as Herb emerged into the fields beyond the forest, he broke into a run. As he approached the house his mother heard him coming and opened the door. The light flooded into the darkness outside, and simultaneously a panther emitted a most terrible screech. 'My scalp was sore for three days after that,' says Herb after half a century. 'I guess that's when my hair started to turn gray.'

"Herb was born just before the great depression of 1873. His father, who had served three years with the Army of the Potomac, commenced to get an $8.00 a month pension in 1880, but from 1873 until 1880 the family was very much pinched for finances. There were eleven children, nine of whom survived infancy, and their support put a terrific strain on the diminutive income which the family got from the sale of its produce and from the odd

Herb Clark

jobs which the father and the older boys could pick up. Once the whole family went two or three days without anything to eat until someone gave them some potatoes. They had salt in the house, and that with the potatoes tasted to Herb the best of any meal he has ever eaten.

"In spite of the austerity which this background may suggest, Herb from his childhood was a jocular and dashing young blade. His fondness for poking the keenest sort of satire at hypocrisy and sham, for twisting up blusterers in their own boastful stories, was something which friends who knew Herb in his youth tell me he possessed while he was in the early teens. He apparently was a very handsome young man in those days and a great favorite with the girls whom he rushed by the wholesale.

"In spite of his lightheartedness and his fondness for gay times, Herb was also a terribly hard worker, and he had a tremendous sense of loyalty to his family. He contributed materially to its income from the time he was twelve. For about five years he worked on the farm and in such odd jobs as he could pick up around Clintonville. In those days they paid 50 cents for a 12-hour day at loading pulp wood. 'They gave you a drink of water and that was all in the line of food.'

"Herb's first job away from home came in the summer of 1887 when he went up to Hank Allen's farm at North Elba to cut hay. After his father died in 1889 Herb went away to work every summer, but returned to his mother in the winters. Most of his jobs required 12 hours work in the day, but he was always fresh enough to spend a good half of the night in jollity. His wanderings took him to Miller's old hotel on Lower Saranac, to Vermont, to New Hampshire, and to Saranac Village. In 1896 he commenced ten years of work at the old Club House at Bartlett's Carry between Upper Saranac and Round Lake. After his first winter there his mother died and thereafter he made his home around the Saranacs.

"He acted as night watchman at Bartlett's for two years, then for five summers rowed the freight boat 24 miles between Bartlett's and the Ampersand in the morning and guided in the afternoon, and finally for three years devoted himself exclusively to guiding. The freight boat was a huge Adirondack guideboat, nearly twice the length of the normal crafts of that design, and Herb sometimes rowed as high as 2200 pounds in one load. While at

Bartlett's he made the record of having rowed about 65 miles in one day, 24 of them with this freight boat.

"Perhaps it was such training which enabled Herb in those days to become undisputed champion among the rowers on the Saranac waters. In 1908 they held an All-Adirondack rowing race on Lower Saranac. This was won by a Blanchard of Long Lake, but Herb, although then 38 years old, came in a close second, only a half a boat length behind in a field of eight or ten of the best rowers in the entire Adirondacks. The next year, with Blanchard out, everybody expected Herb to be champion, but the race was cancelled. Herb continued as leading oarsman of the Saranacs through 1919, after which he retired from competition, as he always said he would do when he became fifty.

"In the spring of 1906 Ed Cagle, who had guided for our family at Lower Saranac for six years, decided to open a livery stable, and by an almost impossible combination of circumstances it just chanced that Herb came to work for Father. At this time my brothers, my sister, and I were all under ten years of age. I can not speak authoritatively of what Herb meant to the others, although I have strong suspicions. I do know positively that to me Herb has been not only the greatest teacher that I have ever had, but also the most kindly and considerate friend a person could even dream about, a constantly refreshing and stimulating companion with whom to discuss both passing events and the more permanent philosophical relationships, and to top it all, the happy possessor of the keenest of humor I have known.

"I remember one night as children when we were camping on an island in Round Lake. A couple of greenhorns from Schenectady were also on the island, and discerning in Herb an old-time guide, they asked him if there were any dangerous wild animals left in the Adirondacks. With a perfect seriousness, Herb regaled them for two hours on panthers, on wild boars, on rugarues, and on horrible snakes of many species. They became so frightened that they were going to leave right away, until Herb kindly assured them that none of these animals could swim, and so they retired to their tent on this oasis in a wilderness of bristling fury.

"For my brothers and myself Herb would make up the most amazing fables. A rock on Lower Saranac with a peculiar dent was where Captain Kidd had bumped his head. The Ausable River below the present Olympic ski jump was where the Monitor and Merrimac had fought their famous battle, and an old lady who came limping along as he told us this tale was used as a circumstantial evidence, for her shinbone had been taken off by a stray shell at the time of this great conflict. There were those great heroes of our youth: Sliny Stott, a sort of a reverse Paul Bunyan, who did everything inconceivably poorer than you would imagine it could be done; Jacob Whistletricker, a man with many marvelous drugs; Joe McGinnis, who got the fantod, a disease in which one shrinks to the size of a baseball; Susie Soothingsyrup, a gay young lass of many virtues; and of course the grandfather pickerel, which we would some day catch, with gold teeth and spectacles.

"Herb is full of songs. Almost every year he adds to his repertoire, which consists either of garbled versions of ancient popular ditties, fitted to suit his needs, or of jingles which he makes up expressly for the occasion. I recall once, while we were battling our way through the clumps of mountain balsam on Colden, hearing Herb's cheerful voice from far above us booming out:
'Don't let the golden moments go,
    Like the sunbeams passing by,
You'll never miss the cripple brush
    'Till ten years after you die.'

"Cripple brush" was the name which Herb gave to mountain balsam, and anyone who has had his shins and arms battered by half an hour's tussle with it will appreciate the appropriateness of the nomenclature.

"An ancient song, suddenly revised as a commentary on a prevalent viewpoint toward unemployment relief, ran:

"Say, old man, will you give me a chew?"
  "No, sir, says he, "I'll be damned if I do.
If you saved up your money, been as cunning as a fox
  You'd always have tobacco in your old tobacco box."

"In 1903 Herb married Mary Dowdell, a waitress at the Club House, and they are still happily wedded. They have had six children who have gone through High School, they have a splendid house, a large and excellent garden, and a garage for the cars of two of Herb's sons. But it has required very hard work to get these things. I remember that Herb would often row the two miles to his home when the day's work at our place was over, labor in his garden until dark, and then get up before daylight to work until about six in the morning. When there was no work to be done in his garden he would be out early, catching small frogs for which bass fishermen used to pay 60 cents a dozen. Even at 63 he is unable to loaf, and always finds something for his spare moments if it is only rubbing an extra coat of oil into a pair of shoes or putting an especially fine edge on an axe.

"One of Herb's greatest joys is fishing. 'I was born fishing, I guess,' he says. 'At least as early as I can remember I used to like to go off to Augur Pond and fish.' It seems to make no difference to him what the fish is, for he sets out with equal enthusiasm after pickerel, bass, brook trout, whitefish or lake trout and, with all, his success is abnormal. For a number of years his 18½ pound pickerel held the record for the Saranac waters. As a hunter Herb was even more enthusiastic, though less successful.

"Although Herb's greatest fame has come as a mountain climber, strangely enough he had never scaled a peak in the 4000-foot class until he, George Marshall, Carl Poser, and I ascended Whiteface in 1918. Thereafter, for the next six years, Herb, George, and I found Adirondack mountain climbing our greatest joy in life. We spent from 20 to 30 days during each of these summers on the woodland trails, and in the later years, even more delightfully, where there was no sign of pathway.

"When we first commenced our climbing there were few signboards and no trail markers at all. Neither was there the present heavy travel which really makes markers superfluous. It took some skill in those days to find your way about, particularly with the numerous fresh lumber roads which forked off from the similar lumber roads which constituted many of the trails. It was often quite a problem to decide which fork would bring you to your destination and which might end at some loading deck in a jungle of second growth. In solving these problems we all took a part, but Herb's interpretations showed the greatest frequency of correctness.

"In our later adventures on trailless peaks — and back in 1921 only 12 of the 46 peaks had trails to their summits — Herb was really a marvel. At the age of 51 he was the fastest man I have ever known in the pathless woods. Furthermore, he could take one glance at a mountain from some distant point, then not be able to see anything 200 feet from where he was walking for several hours, and emerge on the summit by what would almost always be the fastest and easiest route. Just as examples, I recall how perfectly he hit the dike which leads to the top of Calamity, travelling from Adams; how he found just the right slide which cut off a long battle with aspen and cherry thickets on Cascade; how he led the way straight to the top of Panther Peak which we didn't see for nearly five hours after we left the dam on Cold River. . . .

"I spent the early part of this summer [1933] at our home [Knollwood] on Lower Saranac, living alone with Herb. Every morning he would wake me up with some different song or quotation. On July 10th he came in shouting: '63 years ago this morning there was wild rejoicing in the Clark household. Let's celebrate by taking that trip into the Wallface Ponds!' So it was arranged that to celebrate Herb's 63rd birthday we would take the jaunt which he had been urging on me for several weeks.

"We started from Adirondack Lodge and followed the Indian Pass trail for eight miles, past the stupendous grandeur of the rock mass of Wallface. We left the trail to follow up the Wallface Pond outlet, a turbulent brook which tumbles over great boulders and smooth, granite slides to meet the stream from Indian Pass. About half way up to the pond there were bad beaver slashings, and beyond a steep climb over the slippery rocks of the creekbed. Soon, however, we stood at the outlet of Lower Wallface, which we had not seen for eight years, and though it had been seriously marred by beavers, its remoteness from the paths of men was a cause of genuine exultation. Around the Wallface Ponds we delighted in the shade freshness of one of the most beautiful virgin spruce forests on the continent. Leaving the Upper Pond we dropped steeply through another splendid stand of virgin spruce to that glorious series of cascades which is known as Roaring Brook. This seldom-visited stream cut its way through canyons, tumbled over waterfalls, brushed by thickets of lush, green herbage, and reflected the primeval forest of spruce and birch and hemlock. We followed along in silence and elation until we came to where the creek took a sharp bend to the left. Then we realized that we must cut across a narrow range of hills which separated us from the Moose Pond trail. Once this was reached, when the spell of the primeval was lost, Herb suddenly became his most jocular self. He invented gay songs to tease me and reminisced pleasantly on the days before the trails were so heavily marked, travelled, and covered with orange peels. On the last lap into Averyville Herb set a jaunty four-mile-an-hour pace, and when we emerged on the meadows after 25 miles, 10 of them without a trail, he was virtually as fresh as when he had started.

"This makes as appropriate an ending as I can conceive for the autobiography of this clear-headed, strenuous, exultant climber of mountains, this kindly, humorous, sensitive lover of the wilderness, Herb Clark."

Robert Marshall, Eminent Conservationist (1901-1939)

Herb Clark died in 1940, aged 70. By strange irony Bob Marshall, his vigorous and intense young friend predeceased his mentor by a year. At 39, he died of thrombosis on a Pullman car bound from Washington to New York, where he was looking forward eagerly to a family reunion. But into those brief years he packed an extraordinary amount of living and public service. After graduation in 1923 from Syracuse University School of Forestry and another degree from Harvard he moved to the Pacific Northwest and entered the U.S. Forest Service in Montana and Idaho. Here roaming through the serrated splendors of some of this nation's most spectacular primitive areas, he became convinced of the importance of wilderness to American traditions and ideals.

After four years of this work he returned to the East, got his doctorate in plant physiology at Johns Hopkins and then went to Alaska, where he wrote his widely-acclaimed *Arctic Village*. His next book — *The People's Forests* — aroused a storm of controversy. From 1933 to 1936 he was chief forester for the U.S. Indian Bureau and, in 1937, was appointed in charge of recreation and lands of the Forest Service.

Many times Marshall hiked 40 miles between sunrise and dusk and one trek he covered

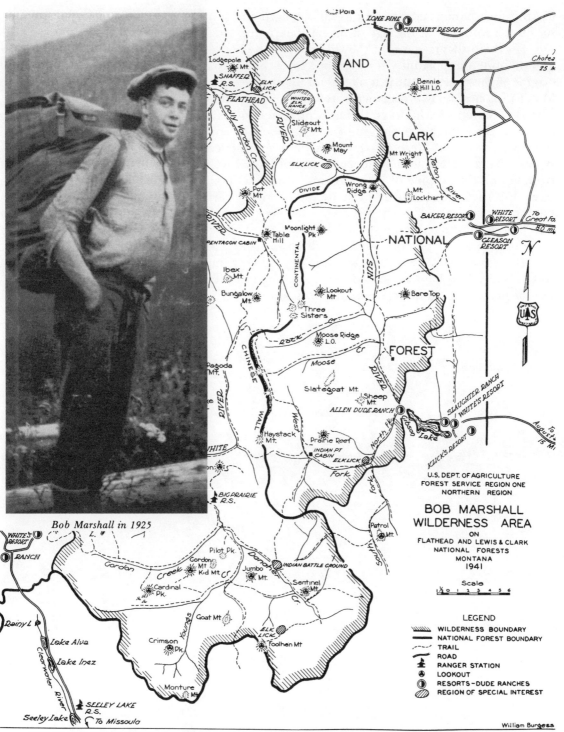

Bob Marshall in 1925

U.S. DEPT. OF AGRICULTURE
FOREST SERVICE REGION ONE
NORTHERN REGION

BOB MARSHALL
WILDERNESS AREA
ON
FLATHEAD AND LEWIS & CLARK
NATIONAL FORESTS
MONTANA
1941

Scale

LEGEND

WILDERNESS BOUNDARY
NATIONAL FOREST BOUNDARY
TRAIL
ROAD
RANGER STATION
LOOKOUT
RESORTS—DUDE RANCHES
REGION OF SPECIAL INTEREST

William Burgess

MAP OF THE BOB MARSHALL WILDERNESS AREA IN MONTANA, A MEMORIAL BY THE UNITED STATES FOREST
SERVICE TO THE LATE ROBERT MARSHALL IN RECOGNITION OF HIS DISTINGUSHED WORK
IN DEVELOPMENT OF ITS SYSTEM OF WILDERNESS AREAS.

65. But such numerous expenditures of strength and stamina eventually took their toll and so, on the Pullman at the age of 39, his heart stopped beating.

His main theme was that the wild country he knew and loved so well presented a vast and unlimited opportunity for everyone to become acquainted with the backgrounds and origins of the nation. But it is as the foremost advocate of wilderness protection that Bob Marshall is best known. Furthermore, in his will he left his fortune to its protection.

He also left as a heritage this moving statement of what the wilderness and far places meant to him, whether in the Adirondacks, where he spent his boyhood summers under the benign influence of Herb Clark, or in the remotest sections of the Rockies and Alaska's Brooks Range. Here it is: wilderness to him was — "The song of the hermit thrush at twilight and the lapping of waves against the shoreline, and the melody of the wind in the trees. It is the unique odor of balsams and of freshly turned humus and of mist rising from mountain meadows. It is the feel of spruce needles underfoot, and sunshine on your face and breezes flowing through your hair. It is all of these at the same time, blended into a unity that can only be appreciated with leisure and which is ruined by artificiality."

If that doesn't constitute *guiding* at its very highest natural, philosophical and spiritual level, I'll have to do a lot more reading in order to locate a more eloquent profession of perception, appreciation and dedication.

[Editor's note: Most of the material on Bob Marshall's brief but extraordinarily productive career came from his friend Senator Richard Neuberger's tribute in the Oregonian of March 1, 1942. It was entitled "He Was a Millionaire Who Walked Himself to death."]

Chapter 23

The Saranac Guides: Ellsworth Petty

As a preface to this chapter on an exceptional guide and man there are several passages from a speech made by the ill-fated Harry Radford* which aptly apply to Ellsworth Petty as well as to other such outstanding individuals who dignified their calling, themselves and the Adirondack scene.

At the annual banquet of the Brown's Tract Guide Assn. at Old Forge on Jan. 8, 1903 Radford made the following pertinent and heart-felt remarks about woods mentors whom he had personally known: "The sportsman's relation to his guide is scarcely less close, scarcely less sacred than that of child to mother, for no matter how much experience we of the city and town may have had in the ways of the wilderness, when we leave the beaten paths and the settlements and head for the backwoods with our faithful guide as our sole companion, we cannot but feel, as we follow the unblazed trail at his side [or behind him] that compared with the trained, inborn woodcraft of this life-long woodsman, we are but children in our partial knowledge of the woods and how to live in them. . . .

"In the fourteen seasons which I have spent here in the Adirondacks it has been my good fortune to bivouac in the same camp with scores of trusty woodsmen on many a lonely lake, in many a gloomy mountain pass, and under stars that shone upon as wild, remote and beautiful regions as ever sun set over in the Empire State. And I can say — and it gives me pleasure to say it — that on every occasion I have found the hardy, keen-witted woodsmen whom we engage in the triple capacity of 'guide, philosopher and friend' to be fully worthy of this wide — enhancing designation. . . .

"I cannot adequately express to you the strength of this familiar fellowship which exists between the sportsman and his guide; this rooted friendship which years of separation cannot shake, this admiration in which the man of the city holds his brother man who has lived his life amid the ennobling environment of the forest; this strange, magnetic band which united the city-bred woods lover and his guide."

Obviously highfalutin' wordage which a reticent guide might discount somewhat and accept with the proverbial grain or shaker of salt, but nevertheless the honest sentiments of an enthusiastic twenty-three-year-older and ardent disciple of "Adirondack" Murray. . . .

Ellsworth Petty apparently made a similar and lasting impression upon many people such as Radford cited, during the sixty-five years he lived and worked in the Upper Saranac Lake general region. He went there in 1895, probably stimulated by the stories told him by his uncle, Carlos Whitney, who had hunted and fished in that section after the Civil War.

As a guide at Corey's Rustic Lodge and later at Bartlett's he acquired his own clientele and joined the select group of woodsmen classified as independents, who represented the cream of the craft. Among his clients were the most prominent summer residents — the

---

*Radford and companion Thomas Street were murdered by Eskimo guides following a tragic misunderstanding caused by language difficulties. In July, 1911 the two young adventurers/explorers had started to cross northern Canada's Barren Lands from the Mackenzie delta to Hundon's Bay.

Ellsworth Petty

Goodyears, Rockefellers and Guggenheims. These and others were his steady employers for their annual fishing and hunting expeditions.

Customarily, the best of the guides were rewarded by year-round jobs as caretakers or superintendents of the palatial camps on the Upper Lake and Petty was no exception. At Deer Island, where he first worked for the Alfred White family, starting in 1896, he was credited with building the first of the now nationally popular Adirondack open camps or lean-tos.

When the Whites sold their part of the Island to the Edmund Lyon family in 1917, Ellsworth stayed on as guide and caretaker until his death in 1956, aged 93.

Four years before his death — on September 2, 1952 — the still active Petty in full possession of all of his marbles was the guest of honor at a party celebrating his 90th birthday. The "remember when?" gala occasion was given by Judge and Mrs. John Van Voorhis of Rochester, joint owners of "Birchholm" with the Francis Remington family. In addition to Mrs. W. Ellsworth Petty, wife of the celebrant, were his three sons, their wives and seven grandchildren.

The sons, who have had distinguished careers in conservation administration, were Chief District Forester William Petty, Jr. (later Regional Director of Lands and Forests); Clarence Petty, District Forester of Canton, N.Y. and Archibald Petty, Aquatic Biologist, Norwich, N.Y.

Much of the shared recollections were tape-recorded by the Van Voorhis — unbeknownst [good old word!] to the featured guest — who reminisced at considerable length about his early years as a railroader in Crown Point, his wrestling match with a powerful female and other such mental memorabilia. That, according to the partners, was a real red-letter day and the absolute highlight of that season.

The old guide had very firm ideas — or notions the younger generation would call them — about many new-fangled, so-called improvements, and conveniences and customs. For example, even though he saw many launches and speedboats churning the water of Upper Saranac, he was by no means enthusiastic about them. He steadfastly refused rides to the dock near his home. In fact he was almost contemptuous of motor boats: "They're always breakin' down in the middle of the Lake and you have to row 'em back anyway." Anyone who has ever had that happen with a 20 ft. inboard will find it difficult to disagree.

Petty also was totally disenchanted with daylight savings time, "Don't they know that they can't change the sun?"

Clarence, his son, also remembers vividly his father's .38-.40, a heavy octagon-barreled weapon: "It was just like a smokescreen. After you'd fired it [black powder effect] you'd have to wait two or three minutes to see if you'd hit anything! . . .

Late one afternoon Ellsworth Petty left Deer Island and headed for home in his trusty old guideboat but when he didn't arrive at his usual time, Catherine — his wife, got worried and notified her son Bill who called Clarence, another son and with several others they started combing the Lake. A high wind and strong waves made the work difficult so it was almost midnight before his boat was located at the head of a small bay on the east shore. His body was slumped over in the bottom, the result of a heart attack.

As Carl Hathaway, the noted guideboat builder commented, "That's exactly the way it should have happened, like Bing Crosby on a golf course, fast and at the oars. When my time comes that's just the way I'd like to go out!"

Chapter 24

William Distin, Adirondack Architect

As far back as the early 1960's I met Bill at various social affairs and, even though I had done relatively little serious writing at the time, I suggested that it was high time that he or someone interested should do a decent biographical sketch of him while he was still (even then he was in his 80's) in the land of the living. To be called Adirondack architects and architecture it should have been a significant writing undertaking.

Since I was willing but available only during the summer vacation, I suggested that he get a good head start on the project by dictating the vital stats and career résumé to his secretary. Or the other option was a tape recorder if that were more convenient. I agreed to get him one so that way we would also have the voice element — very valuable and trendy today as an oral history device — as well as the required grist for a story. We settled for the recorder, which I got for him and showed him how to use it.

That would have done the job but the long and short of it was that, since his eyesight was also dimming, it became very difficult for him to manage the buttons on the gadget. However, while the going was good one day I did get a half-hour tape segment which, combined with short newspaper pieces and the eventual obit, constitutes the basic materials out of which this tribute will have to be fashioned.

Oh, yes, by great good fortune I was told by his very cooperative partner, Art Wareham, about the impressive collection of glass negatives and photo prints taken by his father — William L. Distin — a renowned local photographer. Some of these I had already seen and by arrangement with the trustees of the Saranac Lake Free Library was permitted to have copies made by their photographer, the proficient Barbara Parnass.

Moreover, since top-flight architects customarily record on film the successive construction stages of the buildings they design, Art Wareham placed at my disposal for copy purposes a fairly adequate visual collection of the numerous private homes, public buildings and elaborate camps which he, his predecessors and present associates have designed.

Here's a story that should have been told many moons ago — but it wasn't and that fact has been a source of considerable personal regret ever since. Not that I have had the proper qualifications let alone credentials — and there's a whale of a difference between the two frequently used words. To do the job the person can have all the academic assets in the book but still not have the actual savvy, the basic know-how and the acquired skills to do a required job.

In my case I not only know nothing about the technicalities of architecture but, to make it even more difficult, I didn't really know very much about the architect about whom I'm writing right now. And so very obviously and admittedly all I can even hope to do with this fascinating subject — take that to include the profession as well as the professor being written about — is to produce a superficial but nevertheless long overdue essay (which means an attempt) about Bill Distin, the preeminent Adirondack architect.

To flesh out the definition and to establish the problem and the goal of this attempt, or try, let's look at the literary meaning of the word essay. It's essentially a composition of moderate length on any particular subject or branch of a subject originally implying want of finish but now said of any composition more or less elaborate in style and thought but limited in range. Right on, because even though I earnestly wish it could be otherwise, I frankly have neither the command of the technical terms nor the requisite knowledge to do the degree of justice due to the subjects — architecture in itself or the outstanding man who pursued that calling with so much success and aplomb. Want of finish, incidentally, is right on the button in this endeavor.

What all these prefatory generalities are supposed to do is establish my parameters — good word that — and then do what I can, within the already stated restrictions, to perpetuate the memory of a truly memorable man and one with whom I had a regrettably short acquaintance.

The architectual firm of which he later became a senior partner was founded by William Coulter, whose masterpiece was unquestionably the Adolph Lewisohn Camp on Upper Saranac from 1902-04. This superb example of Adirondack rustic was originated by William West Durant while building his prototype — Pine Knot — on Long Point, Raquette Lake. This and his other "Camps Beautiful" such as Sagamore, Uncas and Kill-Kare provided the pattern and set the style for numerous other palatial shebangs all through the mountains.

When the business started to flourish Westhoff was taken on, then Westhoff alone until 1908 when Distin became an associate. Then Westhoff was bought out by Scopes and Fuerstman. Shortly afterward William Distin acquired the ownership of the firm. In the 1930's Alex B. Wilson, a competent young Scotsman, became a member. Early in the 1950's Art Wareham became a partner and, with Distin at the peak of his career, the two became recognized as the best in the business. After the demise of Distin, Ronald Delair was selected to replace him.

As will readily be seen from studying the following list of structures of various types and sizes which the firm has planned over the years, the range and variety of their architectual prowess is downright impressive. In the public building category are the 1932 Arena and the Adirondack Community Church, both in Lake Placid; Petrova School, the Presbyterian Church, the Pontiac Curling Rink and the Boyce and Roberson building — all in Saranac Lake — and the Northern New York Telephone Building in Ogdensburg.

A partial list of camps would include Last Chance Ranch, Pardee's, Kelly's, Dunlap's, Waddell's, Rodzinski's Riki Hill — all in Placid — and many of the Lake Placid Club structures. On Lower Saranac, at least one of the six Knollwood cottages; the present C. C. Harris and Floyd-Jones' camps.

Outside the area they designed lavish camps at Minnowbrook and Eagle Nest on Blue Mountain Lake; the Robert Merrill Camp at Big Moose Lake; one of the bigger buildings at Sagamore, Raquette Lake; the Hendell and Bowles summer places at Sunapee, N.H. and Otto Kahn's retreat at Elberon, New Jersey.

The private home run-down is equally impressive: the House that Jack Built, Lockwood's on Turtle Pond, R. D. Todd's in Glenwood Park, the Montgomery Cottage, Alta Vista, "The Pines," Dr. Nichol's home on Park Ave., W. D. Clark's, Frank Smith's, Dr. Jenks', Rumsey's, Dr. Woods' — and others in Saranac Lake.

According to the obituary, dated Monday, March 18, 1970 Bill Distin will be especially remembered for his role as long-time architect of the Saranac Lake Winter Carnival Ice Palaces, the annual symbol of seasonal festivities in the village. Distin's imag-

William G. Distin, Sr.

inative touches brought the palaces to the peak of their fame in the early part of the century when they were "professionally constructed, grandiose and ornate ornaments famous throughout the world" [those at St. Paul — Minneapolis were often bigger but seldom more spectacular]. . . .

The Distin family came to Saranac Lake from Montreal in 1898 and moved into the home, at 54 Main St., which had been built several years before by Alfred L. Donaldson, the banker and author of the two-volume landmark *History of the Adirondacks,* which he published in 1921.

William Distin Sr. became associated with the peripatetic George Baldwin in the photographic business and took over the studio when Baldwin moved away to Lake Placid, and later on to Keeseville. In a relatively short time Distin was recognized as one of the most successful camera-artists in the Northland and at a time when the competition was keen indeed.

In addition to his prowess as a photographer he also achieved considerable fame for his paintings, etchings and pastels. He died, aged 66, on Friday, July 25, 1930 at his home on Kiwassa Road, Saranac Lake.

Young Bill Distin was one of the first class — five in all — to be graduated from Saranac Lake High School, then located on the site of the Hotel Saranac, in 1901. Himself an accomplished photographer and draftsman he acquired most of his architectural training at Columbia University and then returned to the North Country in 1907.

During the first World War the office was closed while he served with the Construction Division of the Army as Assistant Expediter of Hospital Construction. His architectural firm resumed business in 1919.

Bill Distin, in his time, was also known as an outstanding sportsman and member of the Saranac Lake curling team which won the Gordon International Medal in Montreal in 1938. Furthermore, he was a mountaineer who climbed Marcy more than fifty times on skiis or snowshoes and recorded much of the Adirondack's grandeur on film. Truly a man for all seasons and lover of them all.

He died, aged 86, on Monday, March 23, 1970 — and left a great gap in the village and regional scene.

Home of William Distin, Glenwood Park, S. L.

Chapter 25

Playgrounds of the Very Rich:
Lewisohn's Prospect Point, Now Young Life Camp

Even though comparisons are odious, according to the incomparable William Shakespeare, they are nevertheless indulged in profusely and for a very understandable reason. The sizes and numbers of human possessions all too often are considered to be valid measures and acceptable criteria for evaluating the essential worth and social status of the possessors. It's the rubbing-off process, the enhancement of individual stature, the prestige that accompanies the ownership of the biggest — therefore the best of course — of anything of recognized value. Whether it be a superb painting, a Rolls Royce or, for the purpose of this chapter, a luxurious Adirondack hunting lodge it all narrows down to subtle or blatant competition for the status symbols — and the "camp" represented the most conspicuous measuring stick in the mountains as well as elsewhere.

A canny Adirondack old-timer once made some interesting observations on the subject of camps. "When you talk about camps, you always have to say just what kind of camp you mean. Camp can mean more things than a porcupine's got quills. Mine's a small huntin' shack back in the bush. Now, that's one kind of camp. Some people have a tent platform on

Camp Pine Knot on Raquette Lake

Dr. Thomas C. Durant

William West Durant at Camp UNCAS

state land that they use in summer. That's a camp too. And then there's some folks who can't live in the woods less'n they have a forty-room mansion with more servants than there are trees on the place. They also have boatmen, 'n guides, 'n dance teachers, 'n waiters, 'n waiters to wait on the waiters — and that's a camp too!" So camp really does mean many things to many people.

However, during the heyday of Adirondack history, its so-called golden years — from about 1890-1930, "camp" usually meant the palatial spreads of the very wealthy, the expensive and expansive layouts where the nation's richest could "rough it" in style. While Paul Smith could correctly comment in 1880 that there was no other spot on earth where millionaires played at keeping house in log cabins and tents, this simple style of private camp didn't last long for those who could afford the best. In that connection it is noteworthy that the impetus toward lavish living came from another neck of the woods — the central Adirondacks, or more specifically the Raquette Lake region. And, as most people know, the person responsible for the trend toward the costly structures was William West Durant (1850-1934).

Born in Brooklyn and educated abroad the younger Durant inherited the same intense drive and love of excitement and business activity that characterized his father — Thomas C. Durant, the railroad mogul, the enthusiastic promoter, vice president and general manager of the Union Pacific Railroad. That completed and after involvement in other railroad schemes and some questionable stock dealings, the elder Durant concentrated on the development of his Adirondack interests. Among these were the building of the Adirondack Railroad from Saratoga to North Creek, as the first phase of a projected but never completed trackage to Sackett's Harbor; highway and water transportation to Blue Mt. Lake; hotel construction (Prospect House) and in general a magnificent playground for himself and his very affluent friends.

The son, William, became totally immersed in the varied grandiose plans and for the next quarter century gained undisputed preeminence as the region's most ardent advocate and pioneer developer.

Among his many noteworthy accomplishments the most memorable historically was the building of Camp Pine Knot, the prototype of the scores of luxurious and artistic camps that soon dotted the entire Adirondack region. Originally just a rather unimposing single -story structure built for his mother, Durant added a second floor, then enlarged and embellished it; by doing so he combined the elongated features of the Swiss Chalets he had seen in that country with the more rustic aspects of the typical Adirondack log cabins. The result was so pleasingly distinctive that it became the model which was copied everywhere in the mountains and, for that matter, everywhere else in the nation. Unquestionably, it was the Camp Beautiful in every respect.

As Donaldson described it: "It became the showplace of the woods. Men took a circuitous route in order to gain a glimpse of it, and to have been a guest within its timbered walls and among its woodland fancies was to wear the hall-mark of the period. Before it was built there was nothing like it; since then . . . there has been nothing essentially different from it."

Another feature started by Durant and imitated everywhere was the use of separate buildings for different purposes — dining room, living room, guest cottages, library, game room, bedrooms, servants' quarters, laundry, ice house, boathouses — a small community in fact. By so doing the owner could not only reduce the fire hazard nemesis which might easily destroy the entire single structure but which also made it possible to close off areas not in use.

Adolph Lewisohn and Granddaughters

Prospect Point Boathouse

Stairway to Main House

177

Main House at Prospect Point

Dining Room at Prospect Point

Still another practical but innovative idea was the provision for covered walkways connecting the various parts of the enclave, thus making movement among them comparatively pleasant even during unfavorable weather. Besides Pine Knot Durant also had built those other similarly lavish camps — Uncas — on Mohegan Lake, (later sold to J. P. Morgan), Sagamore on Shedd Lake, (sold to Alfred G. Vanderbilt), and Kill Kare on Sumner Lake (Lake Kora) which was sold in 1896 to Lt. Gov. Timothy Woodruff.

Although Durant once estimated his Adirondack land holdings to be about a million acres and his overall wealth at over a million dollars, a costly divorce and financial disasters bankrupted him. His design and structural achievement, Camp Pine Knot, is now owned by Cortland College of the State Univ. of N.Y.

Designed by William Coulter of Saranac Lake and started in the Spring of 1903 the Lewisohn camp eventually became a compound of about forty structures ranging in size from four principal units — the Main House, Dining Room, East and West Cottages — to small buildings for specific service needs. Twelve of the buildings have typical architectural characteristics common to the many large camps of the region. These include extensive rustic decorative effects, log construction and/or birch bark sheathing.

Since the seven-mile road from Wawbeek Corners to Saranac Inn was not built until 1909, most of the construction materials had to be hauled in by barge. For each phase of the project craftsmen such as carpenters, plumbers, blacksmiths, bricklayers and stonemasons were hired to make the doors, hardware, light fixtures, 40 fireplaces and retaining walls. Many of the construction crew spent the winter of 1903-1904 on location.

Coulter, the architect who specialized in the design of Adirondack vacation retreats, made many additions and improvements over the years until 1930. In deference to Lewisohn's German background, according to T. Robins Brown, who did the architectural and historical survey for the Preservation League, he used elements of German vernacular style such as large gables with half-timbering effect and broad overhanging roofs extending

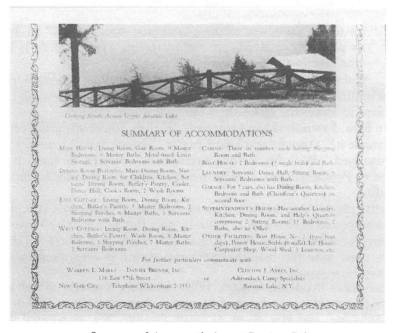

Summary of Accommodations at Prospect Point

over balconies and porches. This was done by using white birchbark sheathing and applied grids of spruce poles. Roof brackets and porch and balcony railings were "rustic work," roughly-dressed limbs and roots. Varying types of log construction were incorporated and there was frequent variation in wall treatment from story to story.

Most of the 4,000 — now 105 — acre estate is on an elevated peninsula which gives a superb view of the Upper Lake and its mountain background. The shore frontage is nearly a mile and a half in extent. Connected by a glass-enclosed walk and passageways and featuring many porches and verandas the buildings and their accessible yet secluded setting make this enclave one of the region's very finest.

Several of the main buildings were later winterized. The large garden helped make the estate somewhat self-sufficient and the recreational facilities were outstanding — two tennis courts, a miniature golf course, a six-stall stable, two boathouses with three 30 ft. inboard launches and numerous canoes, guideboats and sailboats. All in all a superior set-up as the accompanying summary of accommodations indicates. . . .

A personality sketch in *New York State's Prominent and Progressive Men* (1900) attributed Adolph Lewisohn's success largely to: "His wonderful judgment in selecting business associates, he having always been careful to surround himself with the very best material for whatever particular purpose there might be in point."

Stephen Birmingham in *Our Crowd* described him in this fashion: "Although he dreaded appearing ridiculous to the others in the closely-knit group of wealthy German Jewish families, nevertheless with his round little figure, his polished bald head, his near-sighted eyes peering through their comically thick spectacles, in his spotless white spats and vests aglitter with shining black buttons, he did at times seem the butt of all jokes. He was a Jewish Great Gatsby in a wrong decade and as a result seemed always a little inappropriate." Most of the time he didn't seem to care. "I wouldn't mind losing all my money," he once remarked. "I don't have to live the way I do — I could live very simply. But I'd hate to be thought a fool."

Lewisohn's quirksome personality seemed to have endeared him far more to the general public than to the members of the plutocratic "our crowd." In a tribute to his numerous generous philanthropies one of the recipients wrote: "Here is the key to his character: to give the best in the best manner."

When he died of a heart attack at his camp in August, 1938, his estate, once estimated at two hundred million dollars, had decreased — largely as the result of his charitable and personal devotion, to somewhat more than one and a half million.

Once when Sam, Lewisohn's son protested, "Father, you're spending your capital!" he replied, "Who made it?" Once he was heard to say. "I made as much money as I wanted to — and then I stopped." With his fortune successfully acquired he spent it freely — and much of it went to Prospect Point — well over two and a half million dollars, which was only the beginning.

What is particularly remarkable is that the owners of such costly complexes occupied them for so short a period each season — usually only the best month, August, but in some instances only several weeks or even days. Apparently, since they continued to come up year after year, they must have felt that the recreational and re-creational returns were well worth the financial investment.

Several years after his death Mladek Willy, banquet manager of one of New York's foremost hotels, bought the property and operated unsuccessfully as "Sekon in the Pines" until 1950. In 1951 Mr. and Mrs. Blum of South Orange, N.J. purchased it and ran it as "Camp Navarac," a summer camp for girls, until 1969.

SEKON LODGE

UPPER SARANAC LAKE, N. Y.   (PRINCIPAL CAMP)

Sekon Lodge or Fish Rock

Seligman Family Reunion at Fish Rock

181

The Game Room at Bache's Wenonah Lodge

Aerial View of Bache's Wenonah Lodge

The "Margaret". Launch Given by Seligman for Ambulance Use 7/3/17

At that time Young Life, a non-denominational Christian organization acquired the property. Each Summer since then over 2500 young people have spent a week at "Saranac Village." Although most of the original buildings still remain, three other major structures have been added but retain the original architectural style.

Careful maintenance has preserved much of the original splendor of the camp even though many elaborate touches have succumbed to the rigors of time and the harsh northern weather. Some specially designed furniture still remains as visual reminders of a more painstaking past and in the aggregate help preserve the aura and splendor created by Adolph Lewisohn, a man who was satisfied with nothing but the best. . . .

The term "great camp" used several times during these chapters requires additional definition and qualification because while many large structures were built in the Adirondacks only a comparative few — far less than fifty — have met the criteria that entitled them to be considered most outstanding and therefore great. In order to distinguish those worthy of such a rating the Preservation League of New York State, in collaboration with the state's Natural Heritage Trust and support from the National Trust for Historic Preservation, has become acutely aware of the urgent need to identify and when necessary, attempt to point the way toward the preservation of those on the verge of extinction by progressive deterioration.

The Preservation League's description of such noteworthy camps is as follows: "During the latter part of the nineteenth and the early years of this century wealthy persons constructed elaborate rustic camps in scenic locations in the Adirondacks. These Great Camps offered modern convenience and brought a gracious style of living to the wilds. They usually included a number of separate structures and often were located in splendid isolation

The Charles G. Harris Camp on Lower Saranac

on large tracts of land. These camps were essentially small communities incorporating a number of accessory services and structures — carpenter shops, icehouses, boathouses, woodsheds, smithies, water and electrical facilities, working farms — and necessitating the employment of large staffs. They were examples of a life-style and an era that have largely disappeared from the Adirondacks, but many of the structures remain as reminders of a different time and a different way of life. Some of the Great Camps are architectural, cultural and historic resources of substantial importance. Many persons have become interested in their preservation."

Obviously then, the majority of the large family vacation meccas fall short of meeting such exacting standards and very few along the Saranacs can possibly be considered for inclusion. Very likely, besides Lewisohn's original Prospect Point and Rockefeller's Wonundra only Bache's Wenonah Lodge and Seligman's Fish Rock could be so classified. Moreover, the last named has of course deteriorated considerably since the Vosburgh auction and subsequent acquisition by a considerable number of owners of the separate buildings which once formed the impressive enclave.

Although the Lower Lake has several large and attractive camps still privately owned, such as Mrs. Charles Harris' and the Floyd-Jones' Camp Massapequa, another place of distinction is the former Edmund Guggenheim spread, now owned by the Diocese of

184

Young Life 4 Views

Ogdensburgh. Not to be overlooked of course is the six-structure group of large log buildings known as the Knollwood Club.

Because of escalating taxes and constantly increasing maintenance costs the future of even the moderate-sized camps is clouded. That of the great camps is even more critical because state ownership is certainly not the most desirable solution. With Mrs. Post's Top Ridge and the Santanoni estates already under State aegis and a long list of tax-exempt properties already off local tax rolls, as university conference centers and religious retreats, serious efforts must be directed toward encouraging continued private ownership by tax reduction incentives and other means of persuasion. . . .

Dr. Harvey Kaiser of Syracuse University has estimated that the Adirondack region still has about fifty so-called "great camps" and about the same number of others of somewhat lesser quality and importance. But until a thorough survey, now under way by the Preservation League of New York State has been completed, nobody knows just how many noteworthy architectural landmarks still exist. It is known, however, that many equally imposing structures have either burned or been torn down for various reasons over the years.

This has been a rather lengthy but necessary preface to the consideration of the "great camps" on the Saranacs, some of which were every bit as luxurious as those in other sections of the Adirondacks. However, since there were so many such impressive and costly structures built from the 1880's onward into the early 1900's, it would take a fairly good-sized book to give them proper coverage. Therefore, except for merely mentioning some of them, attention will be focused on just a few of the particularly noteworthy.

The consensus of those most familiar with the Upper Lake's history is that the largest, most imposing and most expensive of its camps was Prospect Point, built by Adolph Lewisohn, who made his fortune in copper. As Ruth Johnson, wife of Tom who is the director of Young Life, present owner, commented in a thesis which provided much of the information for this chapter: "The extravagance lavished on this camp evokes memories of bygone years; of a time when great wealth was acquired and spent seemingly with ease."

Indeed less than a century ago there were many such millionaires — Rockefellers, Bedfords, Swensons and Earles and others of equally great wealth — who built a cultural equity in landscape. All a part of American cultural development, it constituted a legacy of interior and exterior craftsmanship that can't be duplicated anymore, anywhere.

There are many almost incredible stories about some of the camp-owners. . . .

For example a caretaker, a promoted ex-guide, complained to a friend about a tough situation which recently had to be handled. His problem was that he had to scare up guides, a scarce commodity during a busy season. "You see, the Missus has a rough camp back in the woods where she entertains as many as twenty people at a time. Each week she decides to rough it for lunch at the rough camp. So that morning a maid makes the rounds asking each guest whether they's like squab or filet mignon, and what kind of cold soup and dessert. Next, all this fancy grub is stowed into pack baskets. So I had to find ten guides to tote the stuff so that the twenty guests could rough it!"

Those really were the "good old days" — for some people!

Chapter 26

The Playgrounds of the Very Rich: Camp Wonundra, Later Camp Cork

This "great camp," built by the late William Avery Rockefeller over the period from 1930-33, is unquestionably the most lavish of the present-day privately owned camps on Upper Saranac Lake. While Lewisohn's Prospect Point enclave, now Young Life, was considered to be the showplace of the early 1900's Wonundra represents the finest work of the architect William G. Distin, whose predecessor, William L. Coulter, designed the Lewisohn structures.

The actual building work was contracted by the Blagden Construction Co. who incidentally sold the property, part of their Beaverwood holdings to Rockefeller.

Consisting of seven land acres and two underwater and located at the end of Whitney Point between Bottle and Fish Creek Bays, this rocky, elevated, well-wooded peninsular property affords superb views from many points.

According to T. Robins Brown, consultant in architectural history and historic preservation who made a survey of the great Adirondack camps in 1978, "This picturesque assemblage of buildings, nine in all, exhibit design sensitivity to the woodland setting and carefully executed rustic detailing. The design sources are eclectic, showing Distin's familiarity with the Adirondack camps of William West Durant and with late 19th century Queen Anne and Shingle style buildings."

The main cabin is the focal point of the complex and serves as a multi-purpose structure, a departure from the Durant pattern of separate units. This large one-story building has a grandly proportioned 30 x 50 living — dining room with fireplaces at each end and huge wood ceiling trusses. Radiating from this spacious room are three wings and an unusual octagonal vestibule.

Brown's further description: "This main cabin and the nearby guest cabin are made from Canadian pine and feature numerous rustic exterior details such as a projecting procession of logs suggesting brackets and log railings: details are bold and massive and there are no delicate twig rustic work screens, a hallmark of the Durant-style structures. The main cabin, in particular, gains its main effect from its irregular massing. Broad gables are a major motif. The interiors of the buildings have many interesting features ranging from massive fireplaces, eight in all of native boulders, to custom-made hardware. The ambience is one of casualness and superior quality."

Other buildings in the complex include the typical boathouse, a log lean-to at the end of the Point, a pump-house with 5,000 gal. storage tank, a two-story garage — gardener's quarters and one-car garage, a garage-woodshed and a small saphouse.

Rockefeller, who also owned Bay Pond, near Paul Smith's, finally decided to sell Wonundra and did so in 1969 to Stephen Briggs, Charles McCoy and William Gillespie, Joseph Blagden's step-son. Briggs was the grandson of the founder of Briggs and Stratton Co., and also Outboard Marine. His partner McCoy's father was a former president of the DuPont Co.

The story behind the sale has considerable interest in that it reveals many aspects of

William A. Rockefeller's Camp Wonundra

William A. Rockefeller's personality and character. Apparently the Gillespies and Briggs were at the latter's home in Lake Forest, Ill. one evening. A phone call from Joseph Blagden informed them that a superior camp property on the Upper Saranac was on the market and it was suggested that they come up and look it over pronto. Briggs, who had never been north of Ithaca, Cornell is his alma mater, agreed that even though they might not buy the place, the prospect represented a fun weekend. McCoy was contacted and all three went by plane to Lake Clear Airport, near Saranac Lake.

When they arrived they were met by a man dressed in Ballard woolen trousers held up by suspenders, a rather nondescript shirt and smoking a corncob pipe who introduced himself as Rockefeller. Rather surprised by the appearance of the millionaire, they followed him over to a 1958 or '59 Ford in which he drove the group directly to the camp on Upper Saranac. A personally conducted tour of the property soon convinced them that it was indeed a showplace. Everything was freshly painted, polished and eminently presentable. The prospective buyers were strongly impressed by the attention to details of construction and all of the finest available — special hardware, stainless steel, concealed radiators, four-zone heating, huge closets, copper pipes and gutters hidden in split logs. Everything, according to Briggs, of superior quality and craftsmanship designed for maximum convenience.

What also impressed the new owners, since they closed the deal the next day, was Rockefeller's final gesture: when they moved in that July they found the refrigerator and freezer completely stocked, the shelves loaded with staples and all the oil tanks topped.

188

Shortly after assuming ownership Briggs and McCoy were enjoying the evening scene at the lean-to on the tip of Whitney Point. While celebrating with the customary quaffing of champagne McCoy, reminded by the sight of the cork and the fact that most of the property faced on Bottle Bay, suggested that even though Wonundra, the big beautiful rock nearby was a very good name, that Camp Cork was even better. Motion carried and that became the newer, apt designation of this exceptional, truly Great Adirondack Camp.

At this point I would like to — as a matter of fact I will — add my personal verbal tribute to the memory of the late Mr. Rockefeller. My association with him was also of a business nature and one which has lingered long in my memory.

Over a forty-year period I have supplemented my regular income by selling Adirondack out-of-print books, photographs and vintage paintings — one of which, an exceptionally attractive although unsigned work, attracted the favorable attention of Betty, the third Mrs. Rockefeller. She, however, wanted her husband's approval before closing the deal.

This large, heavy-framed painting, one of the finest of many I had acquired during the days when they were far more plentiful than nowadays, featured a guideboat passing along a broad shaft of late afternoon sunlight. The setting was typically Adirondack — low middle-ground hills, higher peaks in the background, early autumn colors well selected to enhance an already interesting subject.

What made it even more appealing was that as the light intensity changed the pigments seemed to take on almost a modified gamut of varying hues. . . .

When Mr. Rockefeller saw it, leaning against the wall in the back of the shop because it was too heavy for even heavy hooks, he knelt down to inspect it more closely and for several minutes. Betty, who was getting somewhat impatient, finally inquired, "Well, what do you think of it? Do you like it? I certainly do."

"Yes," he said smilingly, "but of course I'm not as impulsive as you." Then turning to me he said, "I'll have to think it over. I'll call you at 10 o'clock tomorrow morning. Please hold it until then."

At 10 on the button the next morning the call came through; he wanted it if it could be delivered that day. Even though a sleet storm developed, my wife and I drove out to Bay Pond, where the Rockefellers met us at the end of the long approach and directed us to their residence.

What impressed me most at that point were the several hundred deer feeding on hay in the shoveled-out areas of deep snow all along the private road and his concern for their welfare.

Once inside and while waiting for Johnson, his superintendent, to arrive, we had the first of several such pleasant conversations about area history and other mutual interests. When Johnson got there we prepared to hang the painting over the door leading to the Bay patio. The stepladder in place I started to climb but Mr. Rockefeller motioned me down. "I'll put it up myself. You two just hold up the painting and steady the ladder."

Knowing that he was over 80 at the time I was a bit apprehensive but Mrs. Rockefeller signaled me to follow instructions and helped by motioning him to move it slightly one way or the other. Mission accomplished to everyone's satisfaction. Several times afterward they remarked on what I've already mentioned — the very pleasing manner in which the painting's colors changed with the changing light during the day.

Three or four other meetings dealing with a possible writing project followed during that year but, since I felt that the assignment was too tough to tackle at that particular time, nothing ever came of it. However, I was able to form a very positive and eminently favorable opinion of him as being reticent, certainly no word-waster but one who got a lot of mileage out of those he did use. An attentive, interesting and interested, no frills, down-to-earth gentleman in the true sense of the word — that is the way I'll always remember him.

My late friend Bill Distin told a rather interesting anecdote about one of his meetings with William Rockefeller. On that occasion, in response to a phone call, the architect went out to Wonundra. Not being able to get an answer at the door he started making a tour of the premises. As he was doing so he noticed a rather nondescriptly dressed man coming up the stairs from the boathouse. Not recognizing him right away Distin called to the other man, "I'm looking for Mr. Rockefeller. Know where I can find him?"

"Nope, haven't seen him. Probably around somewhere though."

By then Distin was close enough to know who it was but went along with the joke so he said, "I got a phone call to come out here to see Mr. Rockefeller. I haven't much time so will you help me find him?"

The owner chuckled, came closer, put out his hand and said, "Hell, Bill, I'm Rockefeller and you know it." Both had a good laugh and then talked business.

Incidentally, one of the reasons — but not the most important — why he decided to sell Wonundra was the increasingly noisy summer Lake traffic, caused mostly by Fish Creek campers and the resulting decrease in privacy. At Bay Pond he had many escape hatches that afforded him all the solitude he desired. . . .

After an ownership period lasting ten years Briggs and McCoy sold the former Rockefeller palatial great camp to Edward C. F. Carter, of Onchiota, who is in the shipping container business.

Chapter 27

Dr. Ely and His Adirondack Map
By George Marshall*

Whenever Adirondack maps are mentioned one almost automatically thinks of Verplanck Colvin, who of course did do much of the pioneer survey work in the period between 1870 and 1897. However, as George Marshall points out in this excellent, thoroughly researched article, the credit for putting the lakes region of the Saranacs literally on the map belongs to Dr. W. W. Ely.

William Watson Ely (1812-1879) was one of the ablest and most beloved physicians in Rochester, New York, during the middle forty years of the last century. Even in his own day, however, his name was known to more people for what he accomplished through his avocation than through his profession — a most immoral thought. For more than a quarter of a century, his "Map of the New York Wilderness" was used by countless Adirondackers who streamed into this extensive and wild region of forests, lakes and mountains following the end of the Civil War and the publication of Adirondack Murray's *Adventures in the Wilderness.* Dr. Ely was born at Fairfield, Connecticut, was graduated from Yale Medical College, and practiced medicine in Rochester from 1839 until the end of his life. He was "a gentleman of modest demeanor, of refined tastes, who did not seek publicity of any kind." He was nonetheless highly esteemed for his various outstanding attainments. He was not only a successful practitioner, but was also an enthusiastic student of natural science. This interest was fostered by his close friendship with his neighbor, Lewis Henry Morgan, a lawyer who became much better known as the "Father of American Anthropology." Morgan's fundamental and detailed studies of the social habits and patterns of American Indians were published in such classics at *The League of the Iroquois* and led to his general theory of primitive man published in *Ancient Society.*

Morgan spent frequent evenings in Dr. Ely's consulting room exchanging ideas on the new ethnography and on various other subjects which absorbed their attention. Morgan, in dedicating his *Houses and House — Life of the American Aborigines* to Dr. Ely, wrote that for more than 25 years he was "my cherished friend and literary advisor and to him I am indebted for many valuable suggestions and for constant encouragement in my labors." When Morgan was working on his pioneer monograph, *The American Beaver and His Works,* he sent specimens from the Great Lakes region to Dr. Ely, who dissected them, and who later contributed the essential chapters and drawings on the anatomy of the beaver.

As a member of the Pundit Club — a rather exclusive group of Rochester's leading intellectuals which met periodically to hear papers on topics regarded as being on the frontier of knowledge of the day — Dr. Ely read several papers including those on: *"The History of Pestilence," "Sanitary Measures of the Age," "The Theories of Insanity with an Exposition*

*Dr. Marshall is an economist. He took his bachelor's degree at Columbia College, his master's at Columbia University and his doctorate at the Robert Brookings Graduate School of Economics and Government. He has been interested in Adirondack history for many years.

Dr. William W. Ely

of the Doctrine of Moral Insanity," and *"Hippocrates."*

Dr. Ely's interest in science beyond the field of medicine was stimulated by the controversy over Darwinism and evolutionary theories. He published an entertaining poem on the subject which began as follows:

Are you the key, O Monkey, to unlock
    The sealed and scientific mystery?
Were the Apes the parents of the human stock,
    Long are the records of primeval history?
What countless ages did it take to span
    The ethnic chasm from baboon to man?

These verses, which went on for many stanzas, were inspired by the Gorilla in Henry A. Ward's collection at the University of Rochester. Roswell Ward in his *Henry A. Ward: Museum Builder to America,* wrote about it as follows:

"What really attracted the people of Rochester and a host of out-of-town visitors was his zoological collection — the stuffed animals and skeletons of birds and beasts, the like of which Americans had never seen. Of course, the Gorilla was the real center of interest, largely because of the hue and cry over the "heresy" of Darwin and Huxley. The *Democrat American* published a poem about it by Dr. W. W. Ely, which was widely quoted."

The Gorilla did not remain long in public exhibition. Possibly it offended the church elements in Rochester, and most certainly it upset the sense of propriety of many people — it too closely resembled a somewhat misshapen man. Charles Ward [the son of Henry A. Ward] remembers, as a very little boy, being bribed by young ladies to smuggle them into Cosmos Hall, to see the Gorilla. When it finally went to Vassar [in 1864] and the Trustees saw it, the Gorilla was forced to submit to convention. For years, it stood in the Vassar Cabinet, modestly clothed in a pair of short pants!

Dr. Ely was an annual visitor to the North Woods, as the Adirondacks were called from about 1860 until the end of his life; and probably went there intermittently from an earlier date. In any case, his enthusiasm for the region was so well known by 1864 that some verses about him by Charles B. Hill appeared that year in one of Rochester's newspapers.

"Who to the Adirondacks went
   On sport and killing deer intent
And there the Summer Solstice spent?
             — The Doctor.

"Who roamed the woods with trusty guide
   With knife and rifle at his side
And ate his salt pork raw or fried?
             — The Doctor.

"Who killed the buck and "took his horns"
   From buck, or bottle, many morns?
(I hope I trod not on his corns)
             — The Doctor.

"Who likes a story when well told,
   And holds true wit as choice as gold,
And thinks mirth good for young or old?
             — The Doctor."

The Doctor described one of his many sojourns in the Adirondacks soon thereafter in a letter written from Saranac Lake, July 17, 1866 to his friend, Lewis H. Morgan.

". . . Yesterday, on my return to Bartlett's [between Upper and Middle Saranac] from a ten days' sojourn in the woods, I found your letter from Marquette, Michigan.

"I left Rochester on the third, just two weeks ago, with G. E. Mumford, W. B. Burke, and Eddie [Ely's 16 year-old son] — took three guides on the seventh and the same night we encamped about 33 miles down the Raquette River in one of the best hunting regions, where I have been twice before. We remained there until Mumford thought he must return. Had plenty of trout and venison, and a good time generally. G. E. M. could not endure the punkies and mosquitoes any longer — although we, who were accustomed to the annoyances, could have borne them indefinitely. I feel well enough to return to business. My health has improved marvelously and my only apprehension is that a return to Rochester and to work will send me back to the old place. I hope you will have a first-rate time, though what is sport to you will be death to the beaver. If you can pickle a head or two for the sake of training, it might be well.

"This is a great country for sport. Where all the deer come from puzzles me. So many are killed at all seasons and still they do not diminish very rapidly. I have not shot any, preferring to have the other members of the party enjoy the sport. Having enough to eat has satisfied me. I went off one night with Eddie and pointed out to him a fine deer. He shot deliberately and accurately and dropped the animal dead where it stood. The boy scarcely ever fired a gun. He caught about 75 trout and we had more than we could eat. . . . I suppose my recreation is ended for the summer and cannot, therefore, accept your invitation to hunt deer on the locomotive — try it yourself."

Six years later (1872), during one of his vacations at Bartlett's, Dr. Ely made the first recorded ascent of Ampersand Mountain. His reasons for doing so were rather more subtle and personal than the oft-quoted reason for climbing mountains attributed to George Mallory. Dr. Ely expressed the manner in which the mountain enticed him as follows, in *Forest and Stream* of September 18, 1873:

Round Lake from Bartlett's

Ampersand Lake

"At Bartlett's "Sportsman's Home,"." . . the mountain is a prominent object. One never tires of watching the contrasts, and varying lights, of the dark evergreen with the hardwood foliage of the intervening hills. Here also, clouds and mist, blue haze, and the purple light of the setting sun, may be seen and enjoyed. . . .

"It is not strange that such an object, habitually seen during visits to the woods, should excite the desire to become more intimately acquainted with it, and with the prospect which might possibly be enjoyed from its summit."

After a preliminary exploration was blocked by precipices and, after "further consultation with an experienced woodsman," Dr. Ely climbed Ampersand Mountain from "near the site of the Philosopher's Camp [at Big Ampersand Pond]. This consumed two days, and was rewarded with the discovery of the highest peak, a flat-topped cone, having a surface 20 ft. wide and 30 ft. in length, from which the view of both sides was found to be of great extent and interest."

He climbed the mountain again on July 31, 1873 from Ampersand Pond, reaching the top at 6 p.m.

"We slept on the summit without shelter, the wind howling wildly over our heads, while drizzling rain toward evening, with a dense fog, seemed as if intended to discourage our efforts. As this visit, however, was intended chiefly to open a path down the north side of the mountain to Round Lake, so that the extended circuit of a southern ascent and its difficulties might be avoided, the unfavorable state of the atmosphere was a hindrance only to sight-seeing. Having previously determined on the course, the path was selected with the aid of the compass, while our man blazed the line and cut out the obstructions. As we were seven hours in making this trail, it may be inferred that it was thoroughly done — two hours now being sufficient for the descent. The trail scarcely deviates from a northwesterly course coming down. It is free from precipices, or difficulties of any kind, except those incident to forest paths and steep ascents."

This extraordinary method of trail building by compass from the top down perhaps accounts for Henry Van Dyke's graphic description in his *Little Rivers,* (published in 1901) of this trail, when he climbed it from the bottom up, starting at the sand beach at the foot of Round Lake.

"This line through the forest was made years ago by that ardent sportsman and lover of the Adirondacks, Dr. W. W. Ely. Since then it has been shortened and improved a little by other travellers, and also not a little blocked and confused by the lumbermen and the course of Nature. . . .

"After about an hour of easy walking, our trail began to ascend more sharply. We passed over the shoulder of a ridge and around the edge of a fire slash, and then we had the mountain fairly before us. . . . This most uncompromising trail proceeded . . . right up in a direct line for the summit.

"Now this side of Ampersand is steeper than any Gothic roof I have ever seen, and withall very much encumbered with rocks and ledges and fallen trees. There were places where we had to haul ourselves up by roots and branches, and places where we had to go down on our hands and knees to crawl under logs. It was breathless work, but not at all dangerous or difficult. Every step forward was also a step upward. . . ."

The trail continued to follow this route until recently. However, logs were removed and, in its heyday when Walter Rice, "the Hermit of Ampersand," was Fire Observer, the climb up the steeper ledges was made "easier" by ladders and steps. This trail may not have been located and maintained in accordance with a trail builder's handbook, but it had character and went through some of the most beautiful woods in the Adirondacks. The

Verplanck Colvin

newer trail has on the whole easier grades, but it is mediocre by comparison.

E. R. Wallace, in his *Descriptive Guide to the Adirondacks,* writing in the purple language of his day, called Ampersand "the Regi of America. A picture of grandeur and loveliness more enchanting than that unfolded at its summit was never conceived in a poet's dream." He described the opening of the trail by Dr. Ely as "a most difficult matter." Not satisfied with building his trail up Ampersand, Dr. Ely decided to clear the top of the mountain for better views, and to erect a shanty for the use of visitors. In this project he was joined by his friend, Dr. William Read of Boston. On August 13, 1873, they climbed the mountain, accompanied by three men. Dr. Ely described their accomplishments as follows:

"The next day our Tip-Top House was completed, being nicely covered with bark, and the chinks filled with moss, so that it subsequently proved a perfect defense against rain. Being 9 feet long, and with an open front and southeastern outlook, a party of six will find it very comfortable and, for the woods, an elegant structure of its kind. A blazing fire at night was seen at different and distant points, and was signaled at Bartlett's by volleys of fire-arms. . . . Our stalwart and obliging men were now set to work with their axes in all directions — on the edge of precipices, and deep gorges, anywhere — as trees interfered with the prospect. We spent three nights on the mountain and three days at this work, returning at the close of the fourth day.

"I may here note that on the second day, a well-known gentleman from Boston, and his daughter, paid us a visit. We were happy to welcome the first lady to the top of our mountain and the shelter of our shanty. . . ."

Verplanck Colvin credited Dr. Ely with giving Ampersand Mountain its name, and honored him by naming the western arm of Ampersand "Mt. Ely." It is not certain whether Colvin did this when he occupied the summit of Ampersand October 10-13, 1873, and cleared the mountain top of its trees to take observations and to set up Trigonometric Station No. 13 of the Adirondack Survey; or whether he did so in 1895 when with "level and rod" he established the height of Ampersand at 3365 feet and of Mt. Ely at 3110. On the first expedition, he and his assistants had to contend with sleet, snow, ice and hunger. On the second, which was a by-product of running the South line of Township 24, they encountered difficult cliffs near Mt. Ely which Colvin described as follows:

"Here the line began to approach the foot of a steep rocky shoulder of Mt. Ely, a

Colvin Surveying Equipment

Ruins of Colvin Homestead on Western Ave., Albany

197

granite buttress which looks down into the valley of Ampersand. Over this fluff, fire, in former years, had swept. . . . The survey party regarded this savage mass of granite with a great deal of trepidation. . . ."

Colvin also gave the name, "Lake Ely," to one of the many ponds discovered in the autumn of 1873 during his exploration of the wilderness between Bog River and Cranberry Lake. It is north of Graves Mt. and now is shown on the U.S.G.S. maps as "Scott Pond."

Dr. Ely's love for the Adirondacks led him to map them. This undertaking helped fulfill his need to use his intellectual as well as his physical capacities while vacationing. This feeling is expressed in a letter he wrote Oct. 20, 1870, two years after the publication of the first edition of his map, to Lewis H. Morgan.

"I have almost nothing to say about myself, except that my visit to the woods resulted as usual in respect to health. Nothing occurred there worthy of note. After getting accustomed to that kind of life it becomes monotonous. The only novelty to me is in visiting some new territory, which would procure but little interest except as it enable me to improve the map. It is necessary for me to keep ahead of the public in these matters, and as far as I find thus a motive to stir about, and gain health thereby, I count myself the gainer, although the labor is gratuitous."

The first known mention of the Map is in a letter to Morgan dated August 19, 1866.

"I shall not admit that the Adirondacks are behind your country. I am ahead of you, for the publishers are soliciting my production — the Coltons have applied for my map and I am playing coy. They want the contribution but do not think the investment would be remunerative, but would publish, if I would give it to them. If they will give me due credit for Authorship, I think I will let them have the map, but not to use for the purpose of compilation and take all the glory to themselves."

The "Map of the New York Wilderness" by W. W. Ely, M.D. was first published in 1868 by G. W. & C. B. Colton & Co. In a fifteen-page introduction, Dr. Ely described the

Mills Blake, Colvin's Chief Asst.

route to some of the more popular points in the Adirondacks, gave a little information about them, mentioned the longitude of his favorite spot, Bartlett's, and calculated that it was 2 minutes 32 seconds slower than Albany. He included the following practical advice on "Outfit":

"Tourists not acquainted with the woods may be informed that large packages and superfluous articles will prove an impediment to a wandering life, inasmuch as the means of transportation is by small boats, or by themselves or their guides, across carries. . . . For individual comfort it is well to be provided with a pair of warm, coarse blankets, an india-rubber sheet, and stout and warm clothing. . . . Good guides can be obtained, with boats, for a reasonable compensation, the usual price being $2.50 or $3.00 per day. . . ."

He also explained how he came to make the Map and what he hoped for it.

"The author of the accompanying Map deems it but an act of justice to himself to state that it was made for his own use without any reference to publications. Having been an annual visitor to the North woods for the past eight years, he has felt, in common with others, the want of a better guide to the territory than is furnished by the State maps, and has thus been led to prepare a topography of the region from his own observations, and information obtained from intelligent guides and residents. . . . It would be a hopeless task to attempt a delineation of its waters in which no deficiencies could be detected; but the writer has endeavored to present something in this respect more original and accurate than has heretofore been accomplished, and he trusts that the general correctness of the Map will be confirmed, and that it will promote the pleasure and interest of tourists and sportsmen."

The following year, Dr. Ely vastly improved his Map. Many more details were filled in. Lakes, ponds and rivers were shown in greater profusion and with more accuracy than ever before in the history of Adirondack mapping. He even charted the course of the windfall of 1845 in the Northern Adirondacks. A large number of the high peaks were located and named for the first time. It may be of some interest to mountain climbers to know that the 1868 Map showed only eight of the high peaks, but gave their elevations in accordance with Emmons' and Redfield's thirty-one year old figures; the 1869 Map showed seventeen, but omitted the elevations of all but two.

The Map was 32 by 28 inches and on a scale of four miles to the inch. It was printed on light paper which was folded and found within cardboard covers which could be carried conveniently in one's pocket.

In a new introduction, Dr. Ely commented:

"One of the most remarkable and interesting features of the Wilderness is its watersheds and river drainage. The number of lakes and ponds distributed over this extensive plateau is scarcely conceivable. The rivers which arise in this region flow to all the points of the compass. At their origin they are sometimes but a few rods apart. . . .

"The map shows, more particularly than has heretofore been attempted, the relations of the waters and the numerous lakes and ponds, by means of which, with occasional "carries," a large portion of the Wilderness is rendered easily accessible.

"The population of this territory is sparse, and is attracted more by the game, and the love of an independent life, than of the prospect of gain from the cultivation of the soil. The chief value of the country lies in its forests. The abundance of pine, spruce and other evergreen timber, renders lumbering a profitable business, and assures a certain amount of employment to residents, who are by turns hunters, guides and lumbermen.

"When the Wilderness began to be visited by tourists and sportsmen, not many years ago, the forests were found stocked with deer and the waters with fish. The vigorous hunting of the last few years has sensibly diminished the amount of game; yet deer are still quite numerous. The moose has nearly disappeared. The forest still furnishes a home for the bear, the wolf, the panther, rabbit, otter, fox, mink and sable, etc.

"The wild and romantic beauty of the Wilderness, and the facility with which it may be explored, make it a popular resort for tourists. . . ."

Dr. Ely's Map went through many editions over the next quarter century. Various improvements, additions and corrections were made from time to time by Dr. Ely and, after his death, by Edwin R. Wallace; but the general appearance and major features of the map remained substantially as they were in 1869.

For a decade or more, the Ely Map can be said to have been "The Map" of the Adirondacks. It appeared just in time to meet an active demand. A special printing of it accompanied the Tourist Edition of Adirondack Murray's best seller, *Adventures in the Wilderness* in 1869. It was folded in back of *A Descriptive and Historical Guide to the Valley of Lake Champlain and the Adirondacks,* published in 1871, and said to have been written by Judge Winslow C. Watson. It was included in a pocket at the back of each edition of Edwin R. Wallace's popular *Descriptive Guide to the Adirondacks* from 1872 through 1897. The editions which appeared after Dr. Ely's death noted that the Map was "compiled by W. W. Ely, M.D.; revised by Edwin R. Wallace."

Plan Showing Method of Mountain Measurement

A map almost identical to Dr. Ely's 1869 Map also accompanied S. R. Stoddard's *The Adirondacks; Illustrated,* the other leading guidebook of the period, from its first publication in 1874 through its 1879 edition. Stoddard, however, gave Dr. Ely no credit for his Map. Instead he stated that the map was prepared by G. W. & C. B. Colton & Co. Good reason had Dr. Ely to worry that his Map might be plagiarized when he was negotiating with the Coltons in 1866. Dr. Ely also must have had some misgivings when he discovered that the only name appearing on the cover of the pocket editions of his Map was the Coltons' and that his name, as author, was relegated to the Map on the inside. Furthermore, after Dr. Ely's death, the unscrupulous publisher stamped in large gold letters on the cover "Colton's Map of the Wilderness."

Although Dr. Ely asserted that he prepared "a topography of the region from his own observations" and other information, it is inconceivable that he was not helped in part by the work of earlier mappers and surveyors. There is no evidence that he copied any part of his map from his predecessors, other than such basic boundaries as the western shore of Lake Champlain, which had long since ben charted with amazing exactitude. However, he must have learned much from them about the existence and the general location of several rivers, lakes, mountains, villages and boundaries.

Unfortunately no history of the mapping and surveying of the Adirondacks has been written. It would be fascinating to know how these pioneer cartographers actually obtained their information and what impelled some of the early surveyors to run lines, often with astounding accuracy, into the heart of what was then a far-off wilderness, and to learn something of their adventures.

However, if one studies a series of maps over the span of ninety-two years between Governor Pownell's map of 1776 on which was written over the Adirondack region, "This vast tract of land, which is one of the four beaver hunting countries of the six nations, is not yet surveyed," and the appearance of Dr. Ely's map of 1868, one is impressed by the gradual filling in of blank spaces, despite many major inaccuracies.

In 1801, Amos Lay's and Arthur J. Stansbury's map showed a few points in the outer Adirondacks like Saranac, Tupper and "Schron" Lakes. John H. Eddy's map of 1818 was greatly improved and added more lakes and township lines and several major rivers. David H. Burr's beautifully engraved and colored maps and atlases kept adding details from the first edition of 1829 to 1849, and showed Mt. Marcy for the first time on the 1839 map of Essex County. A map by J. Calvin Smith based largely on Burr's was published in 1841 and during the following decade by J. Disturnell. However, with all of Burr's improvements, details of lakes, rivers and mountains in the cental Adirondacks remained sparse.

In 1846, Farrand N. Benedict's "Surveys of a railroad and steamboat route from Lake Champlain to the County of Oneida" was published. Within the narrow East-West strip which he "surveyed," the location of rivers and lakes was with remarkable accuracy. The Adirondack region was shown with many gaps and errors in J. F. French's map of "The State of New York" in 1860. This became the basis for Asher's and Adam's "New Map of the Adirondack Regions" of 1870.

The earliest general maps devoted to the Adirondacks which contained an appreciable amount of detail appeared shortly after the end of the Civil War. The first of these was H. H. Lloyd's "New Map of Northern New York including the Adirondack Region" published in New York, 1865. It included all of the Northern New York Counties, showed a number of lakes, ponds, rivers and mountains, but had far fewer details than either of the next two general maps to appear.

It was during the following year that Dr. Ely was "playing coy" over his map with the

Coltons; but, as we have seen, it was not published until 1868.

Homer D. L. Sweet's and Edwin A. Merritt's map of "The Great Wilderness of New York and a Sketch of the Border Settlements Compiled from Actual Surveys" was published by Weed, Parsons & Co. of Albany in 1867. It was drawn to a scale of two miles to the inch and was remarkable in many ways. No one knows how many of the "actual surveys" were theirs other than Merritt's in 1860 "Maps of The Raquet River and Its Headquarters," which probably in part depended upon Benedict's surveys of fourteen years before. Except for a few regions, such as around Lake George, the Sweet & Merritt map included fewer details and had more inaccuracies than Dr. Ely's Map. Because of its larger scale, however, some of the high peak region seems to stand out more clearly on the Sweet & Merritt Map, but it showed only ten of the high peaks. Unlike the Ely Map, those of Lloyd and of Merritt & Sweet went through only one edition, as far as I have been able to discover.

When one matches comparable details on each of these three pioneer general maps of the Adirondacks, one finds so many differences that it seems quite certain that each was made independently of the others.

During the 1870's, when Dr. Ely's Map had its greatest popularity, Verplanck Colvin made his basic explorations, triangulation and determination of elevations in the Adirondacks. Although Colvin published some general small scale maps in his Reports, only samples of his more detailed mapping were published so that his maps in no way competed with Ely's.

In 1880, the year after Dr. Ely's death, Colvin published his first reasonably accurate table of elevations in his Report of his Adirondack Survey for 1874-79. The same year, Stoddard incorporated them in a thoroughly revised and simplified map, which in certain ways because superior to Dr. Ely's. Two years later, Wallace incorporated the Colvin figures in his revision of the Ely Map, but otherwise kept it basically the same through its last edition in the late nineties.

Dr. Ely, during the late years of his life, became concerned with the problem of diminishing game in the Adirondacks and in legislation to stop this trend. He became aware of what was happening between 1866 when he wrote, "So many (deer) are killed at all seasons and still they do not diminish very rapidly," and his writing the introduction to his Map of 1869 when he observed, "The vigorous hunting of the last few years has sensibly diminished the amount of game." The year following, he was working for the passage of a stricter game law. His advocacy of this measure met opposition and on January 13, 1871, he wrote to Lewis H. Morgan: "I have been obliged to follow up the game law. . . . and have had to contend for my points against the Sportsmen's Clubs. . . ." Despite this difficulty, the Legislature passed a strengthened game law in April. It reduced the hunting season for moose and "wild deer" from 132 days to 71, limiting it between September 1st and November 10th.

As Dr. Ely grew older, he became increasingly restive during his Adirondack vacations, which seemed to isolate him from those professional and intellectual activities which he prized most. When he was sixty-three, he wrote to Morgan from Upper Saranac Lake, October 3, 1875:

". . . Mentally I have lived an idle, dreamy existence — passively enjoying the beauties of the scenery which for three-fourths of a horizon is mountainous, and quite interesting from this locality. Then I have forced myself to take a certain amount of exercise almost daily — enough for health, and more than one usually gets in camp. I am only dissatisfied with the mental stagnation of this sort of life, and the fearful arrest of progess in the direction of knowledge."

Forest Surveying

The Great Corner

In his last years, Dr. Ely could review a life of important achievement in a variety of fields. Perhaps he thought especially of 1869, a time when a number of his major successes reached their culmination. This was the year the University of Rochester chose to grant him an L.L.D. degree. It is not known whether it did so because 1869 marked his thirtieth year of distinguished practice of medicine in Rochester, or because this was the year in which his basic "Map of the New York Wilderness" was published and had its first wide distribution, or because his learned work on the anatomy of the beaver was published the preceding year in Morgan's monograph. Likely the degree was given for all these reasons plus the fact that, during the past three decades, Dr. Ely had become one of Rochester's leading scientists and citizens.

His training and practice of medicine led to an interest and participation in other branches of science, especially the history of medicine, natural history and anthropology. His love of the Adirondack Wilderness and his keen enjoyment of hunting, fishing and exploring its rivers, lakes and forests during many vacations led him to work for the protection of its wildlife and to map it with a completeness not previously equalled.

Dr. Ely's map-making was unique in another respect. All of his predecessors and contemporaries in this field were either surveyors or cartographers who made their living by mapping or publishing. Some were aided by considerable budgets, to cover the cost of assistants and other expenses, which were paid out of public or corporation funds. Dr. Ely, on the other hand, was a skillful amateur. His enthusiasm to discover new places, stimulated by a tendency towards vacation boredom, and his desire to put on paper what he found so it might assist him in planning new trips into his favorite country, caused him to make his first map. His feeling that others might find it useful too made him decide to publish it. The splendid response it received encouraged him to revise and improve it and to permit the Coltons to print a new edition annually.

Ironically, Dr. Ely's Map played its part, along with much stronger forces in bringing more people into the woods and thus in helping whittle away some of their extensiveness and wilderness. This has been the fate of many explorers who have made their discoveries public. However, the principal effect of the Map was, through increasing available knowledge, to add greatly to a fuller and deeper enjoyment of the Adirondack wilderness which Dr. Ely loved so well.

Chapter 28

The Hermit of Ampersand Mountain
By Seaver Miller Rice

As a logical follow-up to the Ely map chapter Seaver Rice's touching tribute to the memories of his truly memorable father, his prominent antecedents and his recollections of Saranac Lake and this region away back when, are a valuable and eminently welcome segment of this book.

Now in his 88th year and still in undisputed possession of every one of his marbles, Seaver is unquestionably one of the most fascinating conversationalists it has ever been my pleasure to meet. Hale, hearty and hefty he's anything but "a tattered cloak upon a stick," as William Butler Yeats described the typical relic of life's stresses and storms.

A resident of Southbridge, Mass. since early manhood he nevertheless revisits as often as possible the scenes of his youth. His reminiscences of the long-gone Adirondacks, his perceptive, tempered comments on the passing scene in his adopted hometown were recently published in *Along the Quinebaug*. . . .

High on the eastern slope of Ampersand Mountain, a few yards from the rocky summit and near the observation tower, is a bronze plaque which reads: Walter Channing Rice — "The hermit of Ampersand," who kept vigil on this peak — 1914-1922 — Erected in loving memory by his sons 1928.

Walter Rice was born in Lowell, Massachusetts on April 6, 1851. His father Henderson Ives Rice, a native Vermonter, had taken his family and pregnant wife in 1850 to live with her parents while he took off to seek his fortune in the gold fields of California.

Henderson Rice returned after two years without obtaining his desire, picked up his family including his newly-born son, Walter, and returned to the farm in Milton, Vermont.

In the year 1856, he learned through his friend Paul Smith that there was an opening for a manager of the Franklin Falls, New York, hotel, so "Hand" Rice as he was known throughout life, packed up his belongings and brought his family across Lake Champlain to Port Kent, New York; journeyed on through Ausable Forks to Franklin Falls on the Saranac river, where he managed the hotel for two years.

Young Walter Rice grew up in this wild Adirondack country and developed a love for the unspoiled wilderness and the lakes and streams of this country which in later years would be disclosed orally before assemblies and in the written word.

Walter Rice had only a meager education but his appreciation of literature and a thirst for knowledge spurred him on so in later life, together with a tender passion for nature, he became well versed in the arts.

In the Adirondack country 120 years ago the lakes and streams teemed with trout and the Saranac river was a favorite haunt of young Walter Rice. He often told us in later years of the big catches in the Permit rapids above Franklin Falls. Sixty-five years ago, the Paul Smiths Electric Company dammed its river at the Falls. This created a large lake. It is well

Van Buren Miller   Capt. Pliny Miller

to mention that in the latter part of the 1800's — northern pike, perch, and bass were introduced into our lakes and streams spoiling much of the trout fishing. Walter Rice's disgust at these measures know no bounds. He was first, last and always a trout fisherman.

When he was a lad of 16 he journeyed over to St. Regis Lake where Paul Smith had settled and built his hotel which developed into national prominence. He assisted at the hotel as night watchman, handy-man and in necessity as a guide.

His first job as a full-time guide was for Dr. Edward L. Trudeau at his camp near Paul Smith's hotel. Dr. Trudeau, of course, was the famed physician who helped in the discovery of an arrestment and sometimes cure of tuberculosis. His simple prescription was rest, nourishing food and pure Adirondack air.

Dr. Trudeau was carried on a stretcher, suffering with this dread malady to Paul Smiths in the late 1860's. He lived on for forty years and is known for his manly benefactions to the sufferers of Tuberculosis. With the aid of his moneyed friends he built and maintained the Adirondack Sanitarium in Saranac Lake. Later this institution was known as Trudeau Sanitarium; it closed its doors as such some thirty years ago when the modern miracle drugs practically eradicated the dread white plague.

In 1877, Mr. Rice came to live in the village of Saranac Lake with a sister who had married R. Eugene Woodruff, who had built the Berkeley hotel there and had taken over the management on account of financial difficulties. Woodruff was the contractor who also built the first Harrietstown Town Hall, the Algonquin Hotel on Lower Saranac Lake and the beautiful Church of St. Luke in the village. This church is still in operation after nearly 100 years.

Walter Rice worked in season as a guide on Upper Saranac Lake in a rough tent camp for two maiden ladies from Philadelphia named Dorsey. They were of Quaker extraction.

On October 28, 1885, he married Laura J. Miller, daughter of Van Buren Miller, one of the leading citizens of the community and grandson of Captain Pliny Miller, the first settler of the Harrietstown section of Saranac Lake village. Miller owned 300 acres there and erected the dam across the Saranac river and later a sawmill to aid in his lumber interests.

In 1888, Rice purchased several acres of land from his father-in-law, Van Buren Miller. This land was situated on the west bank of the river across from where the Town Hall is located. On the hill he erected a twenty-five room building in which he boarded some of the health seekers who were beginning to crowd the village. He named the place Villa Dorsey after his employers and friends, the Dorsey sisters, whom as mentioned he had guided for several seasons on Upper Saranac Lake.

Walter Rice soon established himself in the village. In 1892, he cast the first vote in the election to incorporate the village of Saranac Lake. He was a charter member of the Pontiac Club, which maintained an outdoor electric-lighted skating rink combined with other winter sports. He entered a float in the first mid-winter carnival in 1898, with his five young sons dressed as characters from Mother Goose. In 1907, he was elected Tax Collector for the Town of Harrietstown and also served on the Village Water Board, which purchased land around McKenzie Pond and piped water from this little body of water to the inhabitants of Saranac Lake village.

Walter Rice maintained throughout life his love for trout fishing on the streams and lakes of this region.

As a small boy, I remember many trips he took me on to such places as Cold, Rogers,

Walter Rice, The Hermit of Ampersand Mountain

Ampersand and Ray Brooks. On one memorable occasion in 1903, we went on a trip to Chubb River, a few miles south of Lake Placid and stayed in a log cabin with two men who were conducting a charcoal operation. They made charcoal by slowly burning hard wood in cement kilns for several days. I remember meeting a man along the trail who was gathering ginseng roots to be sold in China. The herbs were in great demand by the Chinese for their medicinal properties. As we rounded a bend in the trail, a mother partridge with her brood disappeared magically. The mother ran down the trail dragging a wing as if broken. "Look," I exclaimed "That bird has a broken wing! I can catch her." Father laughed and replied, "This is your first lesson in wildlife survival; that bird is drawing you away from her hidden chicks."

In 1911, after the death of his wife, Walter Rice leased the Villa Dorsey to other interests. He again returned to his old profession as guide, working at Spruce Island on Follensbee Clear Pond, near Upper Saranac Lake.

There was a tent colony on this state-owned land with three wealthy and prominent families who maintained this establishment. It might be well to mention that at that time a permit was not required by the state of New York to erect and maintain a tent camp on state-owned land. The three families included Dr. Richard C. Cabot of Boston; Walter Clark, an industrialist from New York and Dr. Richard Stockton of Buffalo.

In 1913, Rice rented the Hi Benham camp on Fish Creek near Upper Saranac Lake and conducted a resort for paying guests. Fish Creek reservation is now the site of the famed New York State Conservation maintained camping grounds. [Now Dept. of Environ. Conserv.]

In 1914, Rice entered into the happiest period of his life on Ampersand Mountain, located on Route 3 between Tupper Lake and Saranac Lake village. The state had appointed him fire observer at this lovely spot. An incident which happened 16 years before on this mountain identified him and will bear repeating.

In 1898, the Reverend Elmer P. Miller, an Episcopal clergyman from Catskill, New

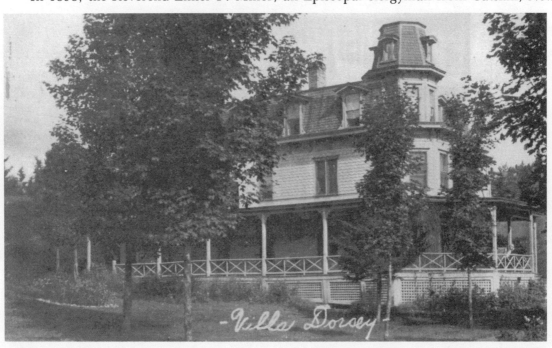

-Villa Dorsey-

Seaver Rice and His Catch of Northerns

York was vacationing at his old home in Saranac Lake. He was also a brother-in-law of Rice. One day late in August, he called at the latter's home and proposed that Rice accompany him in climbing Ampersand. It was mid-day and Rice agreed to go but remarked that it was doubtful if they could make it before sunset.

The Reverend had also made arrangements with his brother Seaver to meet them on the eastern shore of Middle Saranac Lake, at the foot of the mountains, and camp out for the night. The plan was for Seaver to row his guide boat with camping paraphernalia up Lower Saranac Lake, through the connecting river to Middle Saranac, or Round Lake as the natives called it.

The two men trudged up the old state road which connects Saranac Lake with Tupper Lake. This road had been constructed by Van Buren Miller in 1888. Miller at the time was supervisor of Harrietstown in Franklin County. He was also father-in-law of Rice, as previously related.

Late in the day the men reached the path leading up Ampersand and hurried along the rough blazed trail, obstructed by fallen trees and grown-over bushes. Dr. Henry Van Dyke in his book *Little Rivers* has devoted a while chapter about Ampersand and conjectures how the mountain received its name. "It is a mountain. It is a lake. It is a stream. The mountain stands in the heart of the Adirondack Country, just near enough to the thoroughfare of travel for hundreds of people to see it every year. Behind the mountain is a lake which no lazy man has ever seen. Out of the lake flows the stream winding down a long untrodden forest valley, until at length it joins the Stony Creek waters and empties into the Raquette River. Which of the three Ampersands has the prior claim to the name I cannot tell. Philosophically speaking, the mountain ought to be so regarded because it was there before the others existed, and the lake was probably the next on the ground because the stream is the child. But man is not strictly just in his nomenclature, and I conjecture that the little river, the last born of the three was the first to be called Ampersand and then gave its name to the parent and grandparent. It is such a crooked stream, so bent and curved and twisted upon itself, so fond of turning around unexpected corners and sweeping away in great circles from its direct route, that its first explorers christened it after the eccentric

209

Walter Rice and Visitor on Ampersand Mt. 19

Seaver Rice (left) and His Father 1912

210

supernumerary of the alphabet which appears in the old spelling books as &."

The two men hurried along the rough trail, following it for the most part by the blazed trees. After an hour through the hard-wood forest of maple, birch and beech trees, of comparatively easy walking, the trail ascended sharply through spruce, balsam and hemlock trees and an hour later the men emerged on to the rocky summit of Ampersand as dusk was rapidly approaching.

Rice and the Reverend Miller briefly took in the dazzling splendor revealed below. To the north and west could be seen the Lower and Middle Saranac Lakes. The Weller Ponds, Lonesome Pond and dimly seen far to the West were Upper Saranac Lake and the St. Regis chain. To the east and the south was a wild land of mountains — McIntyre, the Gothics, Whiteface and Marcy and more lovely than all was Mount Seward, standing apart from the others and clothed from base to summit in a dark unbroken robe of forest and at its feet the wildest and most beautiful of all Adirondacks waters, Ampersand Pond. "Come, Elmer," said his companion, "Let's hurry back, I doubt if we can make it out of the woods before dark."

The men hurried down the trail. A half mile on, darkness set in. Rice, carrying his rifle, handed his companion a dozen or more sulphur matches to help light the way. They had lost the trail several times and stumbled into the dense forest. The night was of the darkest, the cold mountain air enveloped them and finally Rice spoke up, "Elmer, we are not going one step further. It's useless in this darkness."

He leaned his gun against a tree and began to gather dead branches for a fire. He pulled birch bark from a tree and with his knife he made shavings from dry cedar. He turned to Elmer and said, "Now give me one of those matches and in no time we will have a fire to warm us."

The Reverend fumbled around for a match and couldn't come up with a single one. He had used them all in lighting the way along the trail. "What do we do now?" asked the crestfallen clergyman.

The old woodsman scratched his head and then began to gather the cedar shavings, birch bark and pine needles into one small compact heap. He picked up his gun and exclaimed "Now, Elmer, I am going to fire off this gun into the kindling. I want you to kneel down near the muzzle; when the shot comes out of the gun barrel there will be some sparks. You blow the sparks into the kindling." It worked — and they soon had a blazing fire which warmed them through the long night.

Meanwhile Seaver Miller had reached the camping rendezvous on the shore of Round Lake and set up camp in expectation of the arrival of the two men. As the night wore on, Seaver, then a young man, became almost frantic with fear that some accident had befallen them. Had they fallen off a mountain cliff or met with some other accident?

At last daylight dawned and the men on the mountainside made their way through the woods until they discovered the trail. An hour later they were at the camp-site on Round Lake, where they sat down to a hearty breakfast of flapjacks, bacon and eggs with plenty of coffee.

Sixteen years later Walter Rice was appointed fire observer at the station on Ampersand Mountain, there he spent some of the happiest years of his life. Ampersand Mountain was his mountain. He loved it better than any place on earth. At his death in 1924 his obituary in a Syracuse paper is a splendid tribute to one who grew up and spent his life in the North Woods. I quote from this article: "Walter C. Rice, 72, Pioneer, Woodsman, Guide, Poet and Philosopher died today. He had been in failing health since two years ago when heart trouble necessitated the abandonment as fire observer on the peak of Ampersand Mountain. Mr. Rice's love for the solitude of the Mountain Peak gave him the sobriquet of the "Hermit of Ampersand." But he was not a hermit in the common acceptance of the term! On the contrary, his associations were perhaps more intimate and numerous than any of the old Adirondackers who in recent years have turned their last flapjack, extinguished the embers of their last camp fire and set out with packs lightened of the world's cares and worries over the last long trail.

"News of the death of the Ampersand sentinel will carry a tinge of sadness to distant parts of the country. Hundreds have communed with him in the silences of the Peak above the Saranac chain of lakes. Hundreds have met him with outstretched hand of welcome when rain permitted his leaving the Peak, and hundreds who fished and hunted with him in the halcyon days of the woods will greet him and swap stories in the eternal camp whither his spirit went winging today.

"Walter Rice was a poet, underdeveloped technically, but possessing the fervent love of the beauties of creation and from such well-springs there emerged at intervals his tribute to the wondrous alchemy of nature as he viewed it in blazing trails through the primeval forest, as in mature years he saw it through the windows of his soul from the heights of Ampersand. So deep was his affection for the woods and so frequently did he give oral and written expression of it that year after year visitors to the Saranacs climbed the mountain to enjoy the philosophy of the kindly observer as much as the transcendent beauties sparkling in the vista of the range. He was an observer who looked for more than the outbreak of fire in his beloved forest. He saw not only the misty tops of the mountain at the break of day, the shimmer of the sun on the forest-clad slopes at twilight and the gleam of silver from the Saranac chain at his feet. He saw the entire process of the changing seasons, he watched the buds burst into leafy loveliness and the leaves change to burnished gold and he saw the mating of the birds in springtime and their departure in the fall.

'I never felt lonesome on Ampersand,' he said, with tears in his eyes when he had to abandon his post. 'I have friends up there, a feathered orchestra to wake me in the morning and plaintive song of the hermit thrush to lull me to sleep at eventide.'

"And then Mr. Rice had his books; the works of Dickens, Shakespeare, Robert Burns and O. Henry were encased with others in his rustic bookcase. From these books he garnered embellishments for his homely philosophy which made him a most interesting companion.

"In his last days Mr. Rice set in motion a plan to perpetuate the memory of the Philosophers' camp established a few years before the Civil War on beautiful Ampersand Pond beneath the mountain peak. It was there that Agassiz, Emerson, Stillman, the artist; Senator Hoar of Massachusetts and other great men of letters and accomplishments camped one summer and made the spot historical [1859].

"Mr. Rice suggested that a plaque with their names be placed on the peak of Ampersand to commemorate their visit. He had assurances of support from many people and was working on the plan when he was stricken."

Walter Rice died at the age of 73 on March 15, 1924. At his death he left four sons — Herman M. Rice, Seaver M. Rice, Dr. Irving J. Rice and Sturgis C. Rice. Another son, Walter L. Rice, had died in 1922. And so ended the life of a man who perhaps portrayed the spirit of the Adirondacks, the love of nature and conservation of our heritage more than any other person.

Chapter 29

The Saranac Sojourns of Stevenson and Twain

Although nearly everyone who knows anything about Saranac Lake's past has visited or at least heard about the Stevenson Cottage, surprisingly few people are aware that an even greater writer also sojourned here. Robert L. Stevenson spent the Winter of 1887-88 (actual dates Oct. 3-Apr. 16) in Andrew Baker's little "hat-box on a hill." Samuel L. Clemens vacationed on Ampersand Bay of the Lower Lake during the Summer of 1901 (dates: June 21 to Sept. 19) in a camp to which his pen-name Mark Twain has ever since been associated and which has even superseded that of the rightful owners at that time — the George V. W. Duryees.

Since the two literary geniuses were here during contrasting seasons, it is small wonder that their impressions of Saranac Lake were diametrically different. The great Robert Louis Stevenson reacted to the area in his first month here by stating: "The place of our abode is Saranac Lake in the Adirondacks; it is a mighty good place too and I mean it shall do me good. . . and I am much happier up here. After having gone through a rough, almost arctic Winter, he wrote: "A bleak, blackguard, beggarly climate of which I can say no good except that it suits me and some others of the same or similar persuasion."

In a letter to Henry James, Stevenson commented: "Our house — emphatically Baker's — is on a hill, and has sight of a stream [Saranac River] turning a corner in the valley — bless the face of running water! — and sees some hills too, and the paganly prosaic roofs of

Saranac Lake Village and Lower Lake from Mt. Baker about 1910

Woodcut of R. L. Stevenson by Henry Wolf

Baker's Cottage, Where R. L. Stevenson Stayed in 1887-88

Saranac itself; the Lake it does not see, nor do I regret that; I like water (fresh water, I mean) either running swiftly among stones or else largely qualified with whiskey. As I write, the sun (which has long been a stranger) shines in at my shoulder; from the next room the bell of Lloyd's [his stepson] typewriter makes an agreeable music as it patters off at a rate which astonishes this experienced novelist. From still farther off — the walls of Baker's are neither ancient nor massive — rumors of Valentine about the kitchen stove come to my ears; of my Mother and Fanny I hear nothing, for the excellent reason that they have gone sparking off, one to Niagara, one to Indianapolis. People complain that I never give news in my letters, I have now wiped out that reproach."

Stevenson's wife spent very little time in Saranac Lake because the altitude — and the primitive conditions — did not agree with her. Since his mother and Osborne, his stepson, also went away occasionally the celebrated author was often without company. That gave him plenty of time to concentrate on his writing chores, which were usually done in bed — in a superheated messy room clouded by tobacco smoke. He exercised by taking daily walks or skating expertly on Moody Pond. Then he would come home and rest until dinner-time. Evenings were occupied with card-playing or reading aloud. At ten o'clock everyone hit the sack. Thus did genius "take the cure."

His intense writing schedule left him little time for socializing, even if he had been in the mood to do so; besides, he never cared for chit chat or as Christopher Morley describes such verbal activity, "the subtle discharge of social static."

He apparently enjoyed the company and hospitality of the Trudeaus and the Louis Ehriches, who owned a large comfortable camp on Lower Saranac Lake, because of their informality. Not so pleasant were his visits with the wealthy Coopers who had brought with them all the appurtenances of their city home — silver, china and a butler, whose frosty silence, sphinx-like manner and "power of voiceless condemnation," (Donaldson's wording) both awed and irked the more Bohemian-type Robert Louis Stevenson.

Donaldson also wrote that several attempts at lionizing by the local gentry foiled because the lion "looked, felt and acted more like a sheep." Once or twice he escaped by

Saranac Lake Stevenson Memorial Plaque
by Gutzon Borglum

climbing out the nearest window while the unwelcome adulators were coming in the front door. Understandably that put an effective kibosh on the curious villagers' intrusions.

Donaldson further remarked that on reaching Vailima, his South Pacific final home, the hermit of the North suddenly became a much-changed person, who entertained whole tribes in his home. "Mr. Hyde had blossomed into a Mr. Seek," as Stevenson himself jested. . . .

When Mark Twain arrived on June 21, 1901 he called the camp "The Lair," explaining that no one would know what the word "Thage" meant if he chose that. In a letter to friends he wrote, "Everybody knows what a lair is and it is a good and unworn name. Lairs do generally contain dangerous animals, but I bring tame ones to this one."

A local tradesman once sent a package or communication to the camp addressed to Mr. S. L. Clemens, the Liars, Lower Saranac Lake. Mr. Clemens gleefully accepted the item and enjoyed many laughs during frequent retellings. . . .

Only the preceding Oct. 15 Clemens had been given a great ovation in New York City upon his arrival from England aboard the S.S. Minnehaha. He had just returned from a five-year world tour which had taken him through the Orient and most of the European countries, with months of living in some of them, and featuring magnificent bashes and receptions given him by maharajahs, potentates and kings everywhere.

Return to New York caused him to be besieged by newspapers and magazines for interviews and be much sought as a lecturer. And when Winston Churchill, a young man of 26, fresh from the Boer War, came to America to begin a lecture tour (which netted him $50,000) it was Mark Twain who was chosen to preside. This he did with finesse. But Churchill was thoroughly disgusted with Major Pond, his American manager, who touted him as a hero of five wars, author of five books and "the future prime minister of England," a very perceptive prophecy indeed!

Like Twain, Stevenson had also been overwhelmed by reporters when he arrived in this country from England on September 7, 1887. It was only logical and a mere matter of time before the two literary celebrities would meet and it happened when Stevenson, much improved in health, went to New York en route to San Francisco to board his chartered schooner "Masco" for Samoa. But during that brief stay in N.Y. he met Twain. As wrote Mrs. Stevenson in the biography of her husband, "The time to which he referred with the greatest pleasure was an afternoon spent on a seat in Washington Square enjoying the companionship of Mark Twain. . . ."

The mental picture that Twain painted in a letter to his staunch friend, Rev. Joseph H. Twichell (who had married Clemens to Miss Olivia Langdon at Elmira in Feb. 2, 1870) was halcyonic indeed. Dated "Ampersand," as he did all his letters from Lower Saranac, he expressed his complete pleasure in these words: "I am on the front porch (lower one, main deck) of our little bijou of a dwelling house. The lake edge (Lower Saranac) is so nearly under me that I can't see the shore, but only the water smallpoxed with rain — splashes for there is a heavy downpour. It is charmingly like sitting snuggled up on a ship's deck with the stretching sea all around — but very much more satisfactory for at sea a rain-storm is depressing, while here the effect engendered is just a deep sense of comfort and content. The heavy forest shuts us in on three sides — there are no neighbors.

"There are beautiful little tan-colored impudent squirrels about. They take tea, 5 p.m. (not invited) at the table in the woods where Jean does my typewriting, and one of them had been brave enough to sit upon her knee with his tail over his back and munch his food. They come to dinner, 7 p.m. on the front porch (not invited). They all have one

Mark Twain Camp, Lower Saranac Lake

name — Blennerbasset, from Burr's friends — and none of them answers to it except when hungry.

"We have been here since June 21st. For a little while we had some warm days according to the family's estimate; I was hardly discommoded myself. Otherwise, the weather has been of the sort you are familiar with in these regions — cool days and cooler nights. We have heard of a hot wave every Wednesday, per the weekly paper — we allow no dailies to intrude. Last week brought visitors also — the only ones we have had — Dr. Root and John Howell.

"We have the daily lake swim, servants included (but not I); do a good deal of boating; sometimes with the guide [Frank Davis], sometimes without him — Jean and Clara are competent with the oars. If we live another year, I hope we shall spend the summer in this house."

In a letter to Frederick Duneka, general manager of Harpers Brothers, Clemens stated his "view" requirements in this manner: "It is my conviction that there should always be some water in a view — a lake or a river but not the ocean, if you are down on its level. I think that when you are down on its level it seldom inflames you with an ecstasy which you could not get out of a sandflat."

One of the very few local people whom Twain met during that enchanted summer was an unannounced and unexpected Rev. Walter H. Larom, rector of St. Luke's Episcopal Church in Saranac Lake. The latter recounted that memorable meeting in the *Bookman Magazine* in 1924: "Mark Twain once spent a summer in a modest bungalow [sic — It's a two-story structure and hardly a bungalow] on the shores of an Adirondack lake. During the brief sojourn an entertainment was planned in a neighboring village [Saranac Lake] for the benefit of the public library and the managers of the affair, realizing the immense ad-

217

Mark Twain at Duryee Camp in 1901

The Clemens Family. Left to right — Clara, Jean (standing), Mrs. Clemens, S.L.C. himself (Photo by Fred Rice Sr.)

vantage of 'featuring' the famous author as an attraction, by some process of elimination picked me to call on him and ask him to make a short address. It occurred to me that if I, a perfect stranger, attempted to approach him by way of his front door I might meet with a rebuff (not on the part of Mr. Twain himself — he would be too genial and kindly to do that — but on the part of some domestic or jealous friend).

"So I resorted to strategy and decided to make my attack by water. Boarding my canoe I paddled across the Lake and took the friendly enemy in the rear as it were.

"Mr. Clemens' bungalow was on the very edge of the water. I caught him sitting on this overhanging porch, dressed in the traditional white, and crowned with white hair. In spite of some misgiving on my part he received me most graciously and, without waiting for me to explain the object of my visit, broke into a torrent of appreciation of the beauty of the lake and the mountains, the lights and the shadows, and the wonderful life-giving air of the Adirondacks. When at last I found an opportunity of presenting my plea he replied with great emphasis 'No! No!! No!!! I hate the platform; it scares me. I know it might do good. I might do good to cut off my head too, but I would rather do good some other way.'

"I wish I could remember more of the many things he said in that brief interview. I can, however, recall accurately only his parting words. He was apparently interested in my description of the many canoe trips it was possible to make (with short portages) over hundreds of miles of Adirondack lakes and rivers, and wished that someday he might have an opportunity of making one such trip himself. When I reluctantly took my leave he accompanied me to the end of the little private pier where I had left my canoe in charge of a companion. As we started to paddle away he said, 'I see you do all the work in the bow and stern; well, if I were going along I'd take the middle seat!' "

It is easy to understand why Clemens insisted on maximum privacy. Mrs. Clemens, who all through their married life had recurrent nervous collapses and who died only three years later (June 5, 1904), needed all the rest she could get and that meant an absolute minimum of visitors.

Nevertheless, there was one interesting and untoward interruption in that strict routine. A young newspaper reporter named Northrup came up from New York and requested an interview. Twain was notified and turned him down flat. However, the cub reporter was persistent and devious so he talked with Fred Rice, a photographer and guideboat builder and frequent visitor. The determined newspaperman kept repeating that he just plain had to have that interview. He then explained that he had been promised a job on a big city paper if he could come back with a story.

Rice was moved by the young fellow's plight and decided to intercede for him. He talked with Twain, related the circumstances and pointed out what it would mean for the lad. Remembering that he too in his reporting days had been in the same situation, himself, Twain softened and granted the interview.

Another local man who saw a great deal of Twain during that single summer was Frank Davis, the Duryee's regular guide who had been assigned to work for the Clemens family that season.

In an interview with Bill McLaughlin, printed in the *Adirondack Enterprise* on July 2, 1960, the old guide reminisced about his famous employer. When asked if the celebrated author ever lost his temper, Davis said, "Yup, just once. One of my jobs was to go over to the Ampersand Hotel (just over the Bay) and get the mail each afternoon. One day I met a local drayman named Bern Wilson drivin' Clara Clemens, Mark's oldest daughter, in toward the camp.

"When I got to the Ampersand I found a telegram there telling about the girl's comin' up from the city. You know somethin? She got there ahead of the telegram! And I'll tell you somethin' else. Her father, when he found out, exploded with the finest stream of curses it's ever been my pleasure to hear!!!"

Davis also remembered clearly the family housekeeper, Katie Leary, who usually handed out Mark's coat to be brushed after breakfast each day. She would always wink at him and say, "Smoke up any cigars you find in the pockets!" Frank always figured that Katie had filled the pockets before handing out the coat.

According to Frank, Twain was a heavy smoker so the guide/handyman after each writing session often swept out as many as fifteen cigar butts from the tent floor.

Although Clemens was one of the world's greatest humorists he rarely displayed that inherent gift unless some old friend like Dean Howells joined him at the camp. On such occasions the two men laughed and guffawed over shared remembrances until their eyes filled with tears. But generally, Davis recalled, things were pretty quiet about the premises. . . .

As already noted, Stevenson logged a lot of words during that historic Winter of 1888. According to Sir Sidney Colvin, in his preface to the Saranac Lake letters, they included twelve papers — essays that is — published later that year by Scribners and are generally considered to be among his very best work. "A Chapter on Dreams," "The Lantern Bearers," "Random Memories," "Beggars," "Pulvis at Umbra," "The Christmas Sermon." The other five are inconsequential. His most important project while here and "the hardest job I ever had to do" was *The Master of Ballantrae,* which he got two-thirds through and then put aside and finally finished in Honolulu in Dec. 1888.

Clemens, for his literary labors of that memorable summer, turned out a two-part serial for *Harper's Magazine,* January and February, 1902 issues. This effort, which he called "The Double-Barrelled Detective Story" was originally intended as a parody on A. Conan Doyle's Sherlock Holmes series. It, however, never quite measured up in accomplishing its purpose and therefore can hardly be considered as one of Twain's shorter masterpieces.

Its main claim to fame is one paragraph by which it is likely to be remembered and is a spoof job — a hoax and his last such — on the credulous/gullible reading public. It goes as follows: "It was a crisp and spicy morning in October. The lilacs and laburnums lit by the glory-fires of Autumn, hung burning and flashing in the upper air, as a fairy bridge provided by kind Nature for the wingless wild things that have their homes in the tree-tops and would visit together, the larch and the pomegranate flung their purple and yellow flames in brilliant broad splashes along the slanting sweep of woodland, the sensuous fragrance of innumerable deciduous flowers rose upon the swooning atmosphere, far in the empty sky a solitary oesophagus slept upon motionless wing, everywhere brooded stillness, serenity and the peace of God."

How's that for a one-sentence — except for the short opener — paragraph? And how choice the selection of senseless mood words! The warm light and luxury of this segment of the story are of course misleading but the observant reader will accept the oesophagus as a bird. But it nevertheless disturbed a great many admirers and numerous letters were dispatched Twainward to find out just what it was all about. Some of course spotted the spoof and taunted him with it. The best rise from a reader took this form:

"My dear Mark Twain; — Reading your "Double-Barrelled Detective Story" in the January *Harper's* late one night I came to the paragraph where you so beautifully describe 'a crisp and spicy morning in early October.' I read along that paragraph, conscious only of its *woozy* sound, until I was brought up with a start against your oesophagus in the empty sky. Then I read the paragraph again. Oh, *Mark Twain!* How could you do it? Put a trap like that into the midst of a tragical story? Do serenity and peace brood over you after you have done such a thing?

"Who lit the lilacs, and which end up to they hang? When did larches flame, and who set out the pomegranates in that canyon? What are the deciduous flowers, and do they always bloom in *Fall,* tra la?

"I have been making myself obnoxious to various people by demanding their opinion of that paragraph without telling them the name of the author. They say, 'Very well done' and 'The alliteration is pretty.'

" 'What's an oesophagus, a bird? What's it all mean anyway? I tell them it means Mark Twain and that an oesophagus is a kind of *swallow.* Am I right? Or is it a gull? Or a gullet?

"Hereafter, if you must write such things, won't you please label them?"

Very sincerely yours,
Allette F. Dean

Mark Twain to Miss Dean:

"Don't you give that oesophagus away again or I'll never trust you with another privacy."

He wrote Twichell that the story had been a six-day tour de force, 25,000 words, and he added:

"How long it takes a literary seed to sprout sometimes! This seed was planted in your house many years ago when you sent me to bed with a book not heard of by me until then — *Sherlock Holmes.* . . .

"I've done a grist of writing here [Saranac Lake] this summer but not for publication soon, if ever. I did do two satisfactory articles for early print, but I've burned one of them and have buried the other in my large box of posthumous stuff. I've got stocks of literary remains piled up there!"

Erna Rice, now Mrs. Eskuche, also remembers well certain details of that unforgettable summer in the Saranacs. She especially recalls the Adirondack guideboat built by Fred Rice, her father and Twain's interest in the lake, the islands and the surrounding country expressed while she was rowing Mr. Clemens and, occasionally, his wife around the Lake. Rice, a professional photographer, persuaded Mark to sit for some photos and the great man consented but with one condition — that they never be published or used in any way during Twain's lifetime. The pictures were taken, the promise was kept and here they are to truly enhance this text.

Erna also cherishes memories of the way Twain looked, how he kidded with his wife and how the lively daughters would go over to the famous old hotels for an afternoon of tennis, an occasional tea party and once in awhile an evening's social affair.

Her recollections of the final day are still crystal clear. She had gone over to the camp that morning to take him boating, then she learned that he had received a telegram and had already left on an early train for New York. Shortly thereafter the rest of the family departed and only the newspapers kept the Rice family informed about the subsequent life of their famous acquaintances.

Just before the family left the mountains Twain wrote a farewell bread and butter note to his friends, the Duryees, in which he said, "Hail and farewell! It has been a paradise to us all summer. One doesn't need to go to the Swiss lakes to find that condition!"

That heart-felt tribute to the Saranacs rang down the curtain on a timely, providential interlude in a restless, bedeviled life beset with traumas and tragedies.

Chapter 30

Edward Livingston Trudeau, M.D.
By Gordon M. Meade*

Dr. Gordon M. Meade Birdwatching

It is indeed a privilege and an honour to deliver the first Morriston Davies Memorial Lecture. And it is peculiarly fortuitous that the subject of this lecture should be Dr. Edward Livingston Trudeau, because parallels in the characters and careers of these men are striking. Both were individuals of much promise stricken early in their careers with physical misfortunes which would have overwhelmed men of lesser fibre. Morriston Davies, a brilliant researcher and surgeon, permanently lost the use of his operating right hand through infection; Trudeau developed active tuberculosis. Both retreated to obscure or isolated situations — Davies to a country sanatorium in North Wales; Trudeau to the wilderness of the Adirondack Mountains 300 miles north of New York City. In time both surmounted their afflictions to become outstanding and inspiring leaders in the field of pulmonary tuberculosis. Incredibly, Davies, with his phenomenal determination, drive and energy learned to operate with his left hand and become one of the world's outstanding thoracic surgeons. The story of Edward Livingston Trudeau is our subject for this afternoon.

Trudeau derived from a distinguished and accomplished French family which came to the New World into Canada in the mid-17th century. Soon they made their way to the French colony of Louisiana along the lower Mississippi River, where they developed a long line of respected governors, councilmen, Indian representatives and physicians.

His father was Jacques DeBerty Trudeau — physician, surgeon, artillery officer, painter, sculptor and explorer. In 1841-42, when he was 24 years old, he spent two years with the Osage Indians, where he learned the language fluently as well as their methods of

[1]*This Morriston Davies Memorial Lecture was given at the Annual Conference of the British Thoracic and Tuberculosis Association at Cambridge, England on 29th June, 1972.
[2] From the School of Medicine and dentistry, and the Strong Memorial Hospital, The University of Rochester, Crittenden Boulevard, Rochester, New York, U.S.A.

Dr. Edward Livingston Trudeau 1885　　　　　*Mrs. Edward L. Trudeau 1910*

fishing, hunting and trapping. On his return home his portrait was painted by John Woodhouse Audubon, son of the great bird artist John James Audubon. Later he practiced medicine in New York City, where he married Cephise Berger, daughter of a prominent French physician of New York. At his death he was acclaimed as "one of the most learned, accomplished and many-sided men Louisiana ever produced." The picture hangs today in the home of his great grandson, Dr. Francis B. Trudeau in the village of Saranac Lake, New York.

Edward Trudeau was born in New York in October, 1848. His parents soon separated permanently and he went to reside in Paris with his mother in 1851 at the age of 3. There he was raised and educated — a spirited and mischievous boy. In 1865, at the age of 17 he returned to New York. He then spoke English with difficulty and complained to his cousins that 'Ze English language is a very hard language to prononciate.'

As a youth he had no abiding interests other than amusing himself at sports and with girls — no career inclinations or objectives were evident. For reasons that are not clear he decided to enter the U.S. Naval Academy and to become a career officer.

Just before he was to enter the Academy the first great tragedy and the eventually most decisive event of his life occurred. His older brother, Francis, to whom he was deeply attached became ill in September, 1865 with rapidly advancing tuberculosis. Edward abandoned his plans for a naval career and devoted himself to full-time nursing of his brother — often sleeping with him. There seems little doubt that this is where he acquired his own disease which was to be with him the rest of his life and to dominate his life and career. His brother's death in December, 1865 was a stunning blow. He then drifted, seeking an oc-

The Old Hotel at Paul Smith's in 1884

Saranac Lake Village in 1875 (Stoddard photo)

224

cupation in mining, in a broker's office, and other things spasmodically but succeeding at nothing.

Trudeau was a natural athlete who excelled at rowing, sailing, walking, shooting, boxing and he possessed a congenital love of the out-of-doors and hunting. He was a gregarious, fun-loving person who was attracted to people and they invariably were attracted to him. Having a good time was a major pursuit and he freely admits in his autobiography that after his brother's death he was "fast slipping into a wild mode of life in New York" with his wealthy, care-free friends.

Meeting Miss Lottie Beare was a turning point in his life — his love for her, the family tradition of medicine and the influence of his brother's death brought a decision to study medicine — and a desire to marry and support a wife and family.

In 1868 he enrolled in the College of Physicians and Surgeons of Columbia University, where he was a rather indifferent but adequate student who delighted in pricking the pomposity of too serious superiors. Until now there were no premonitions of greatness.

March, 1871 brought graduation as a physician and a medical post as a hospital resident physician. Marriage to Lottie Beare soon followed in June, 1871 and an almost idyllic life began as he undertook practice with a prominent New York physician and taught classes in chest diseases. A prosperous and successful career in the milieu of New York society with wealthy and influential friends and patients seemed assured. A daughter, Charlotte, was born early in 1872. Life was most satisfying, undisturbed and full of joy and promise.

Unrecognized as the harbingers of a coming disaster were a rectal abscess just after graduation and a cervical adenitis while in Liverpool on his honeymoon. He was advised to paint the glands with iodine, to eat plenty of bacon and to take an iron tonic!

Within a year after marriage he had several occasions of fever — diagnosed as malaria but for which the prescribed quinine was not effective. To the fatigue he was experiencing he paid little attention. A concerned colleague insisted he have his lungs examined but Trudeau at first laughed it off. However, his friend's insistence worried him and he sought Dr. Janeway, who was noted for his skill in physical diagnosis, to examine him. The examination concluded Janeway said nothing. So Trudeau asked, "Well, Janeway, you can find nothing the matter?" Gravely came the reply, "Yes, the upper two-thirds of the left lung is involved in an active tuberculosis process." The effect of this pronouncement is best told in Trudeau's own words: "I think I know something of the feelings of the man at the bar who is told he is to be hanged on a given date, for in those days pulmonary consumption was considered an absolutely fatal disease. I pulled myself together — and escaped from the office, after thanking the doctor for his examination. When I got outside, I felt stunned. It seemed to me the world had suddenly grown dark. The sun was shining, and the street was filled with the rush and noise of traffic but to me the world had lost every vestige of brightness. I had consumption — that most fatal of diseases! Had I not seen all its horrors in my brother's case? It meant death and I had never thought of death before! Was I ready to die? How could I tell my wife whom I had just left in unconscious happiness with the little baby in our new house? And my rose-colored dreams of achievement and professional success in New York. They were all shattered now, and in their place only exile and the inevitable end remained.

"How little I could have realized then how many times it would fall my lot to tell other human beings the same dreadful truth. I think my own experience that day was never forgotten and helped, every time I made a positive diagnosis of tuberculosis, to make me as merciful as was compatible with truthfulness and the welfare of the patient. . . ."

225

This was in February, 1873 and though Lottie realized the ominous import of what Edward had told her, they discussed the future calmly. Since a baby was expected shortly, future plans were postponed. Work had to be abandoned. "Sickness was a new experience for me and I rebelled and struggled against it and was thoroughly unnerved by it. It took me a long time to learn, imperfectly though it be, that acquiescence is the only way for the tuberculous invalid to conquer fate. To cease to rebel and struggle, and to learn to be content with part of a loaf when you cannot have a whole one is good philosophy for the tuberculous invalid. To his astonishment he often finds that what he considers the half-loaf, when acquiesced in, proves most satisfying. When once learned, this lesson made my life fuller and happier. . . ."

His beloved son Ned was born in May, 1873. Meanwhile he was steadily growing weaker and losing weight. Previous hunting and fishing trips in the Adirondack Mountains had instilled in him a deep love for this wild and almost virgin wilderness. His love for the great forest, the hunting and fishing, and the free and wild life drew him there to spend his last days. He felt a longing for rest and the peace of the great wilderness. It was this and not any belief that the climate would benefit him that drew him there in May, 1873. The four-day journey by train, boat and stage-wagon into the forest hostelry of the inimitable mountain guide, Paul Smith, was one of fever and misery. Arriving exhausted, Trudeau had to be carried to his room. A sturdy, giant woodsman took this 6 ft. 4 inch man in his arms like an infant, bore him upstairs two steps at a time, put him gently on the bed remarking: "Why, Doctor, you won't weigh no more than a dried lamb skin." Under the magic of the surroundings he had longed for, hope and appetite began to return. At Paul Smith's, things were very primitive but most comfortable — water in a pail from a spring under the bank — excellent food cooked by Mrs. Smith, and a warm feeling of welcome from all.

The mountain guides were a unique breed — happy, easy-going, at home in the woods, wise in outdoor lore, impecunious, resourceful in emergencies, and good companions. Two of them, Fitz-Greene Hallock and Albert McKenzie became intimate, trusted and lifelong friends of Trudeau and the trust and affection were mutual.

Trudeau, ill though he was, wasted no time in responding to the congenital love of sport in his blood. The day after arrival he hired a guide who arranged a guideboat — a unique craft — with boughs and blankets so Trudeau could lie down, put him in it and they started down the St. Regis River. Soon a deer was sighted on shore 200 yards away. Without sitting up Trudeau rested his gun on the boat side, took aim, fired — and a buck fell. This was a triumphant boost to his spirits. The incident is fundamental in understanding a side of his nature which was to help him over many of the rough roads of his life and to provide him solace and inspiration. The love of the out-of-doors, of hunting and fishing has been a passionate strain in a long line of Trudeaus from the 17th century down to the present generation.

The restful quiet of the woods, the good food of Mrs. Smith, the surcease from the cares of practice and the strains of the big city brought a rapid improvement in his health. In the Fall he returned to New York but by May, 1874 he was back as ill as before. To the distress of his family and friends who felt it was cruel and foolhardy, this time he brought his wife and two small children. His health again improved and the family thrived. By 1876 they had moved to the muddy-streeted, lumbering town of Saranac Lake into a rented house where they lived for 7 years.

From 1874-80 Trudeau did little but rest, hunt, fish and enjoy the fellowship of his fellow townsmen, lumberjacks, guides and tradesmen. Trudeau's warmth of nature, his empathy for his fellow man, and his natural skills with the gun and the rod won their respect.

226

Little by little in this rude village, Trudeau was called by necessity to now and then give what medical care he could to his friends and neighbors. But it wasn't until 1880 that he really returned to the practice of medicine by horse and buggy, sleigh and boat.

"I had almost forgotten I was a physician. I neither read medical literature nor practiced my profession, except on rare occasions when some of the guides were injured or sick or could get no other medical aid. I was so imbued with the idea that life for me was to be a short experience that I had lost all interest in perfecting myself in a profession I should never live to practice. The summer guests at the hotel, however, occasionally needed a physician, so I got a supply of medicine and began to do a little work as time passed."

To this point Trudeau had shown no interest in research, or in the intellectual aspects of medicine.

In the years just before and after 1880 there was a growing flow of tuberculous patients to the Adirondacks, many of whom were seeking Dr. Trudeau. Under this stimulation he began reading everything he could find on tuberculosis. In 1882 he read an English abstract of Koch's epoch-making paper on the 'Etiology of Tuberculosis.' His interest in the germ theory of disease and the new experimental approach to medicine grew and as he said: "The glamour of its possibilities in the prevention and control of disease took a strong hold on my imagination. If I could learn to grow the tubercle bacillus outside of the body and to produce tuberculosis at will in guinea pigs, the next step would be to find something that would kill the germ in the living animal. If an inoculated guinea pig could be cured,

Trudeau on His Way to Visit a Patient

227

Dr. & Mrs. E. L. Trudeau

then in all probability this great burden could be lifted from the human race. Even if this proved impossible, much could be learned as to the best method of preventing the disease, and every fact that could be acquired about this invisible little microbe must prove of immense importance to mankind."

In that statement one sees the genesis of Trudeau as a scientist and the credo that was to be his guiding light and objective for the next 30 years. He could not read German and thus study Koch's paper in its entirety. Of this difficulty he complained to his publisher friend, Mr. Lea, who soon surprised him at Christmas with a hand-written English translation of Koch's paper.

Within a few months he had decided that he was going to try to reproduce Koch's results. "But I knew nothing of bacteriology — had never heard the name before. I lived in a remote region which made access to books, scientific apparatus or other physicians impossible. I had my microscope, however, and I decided the next time I went to New York to devote all my efforts to learning how to stain and recognize the tubercle bacillus under the microscope. I could then test Koch's conclusions as to the presence of the germ in the patient's secretions, and could plan to learn how to cultivate it outside of the body; but the first thing to do was to learn to find and recognize the germ."

On his next trip to New York he sought vainly for someone who was interested in Koch's work and who could teach him what he wanted to know. Finally he found Dr. Mitchell Prudden, who had worked in Koch's laboratory and who, after a few curt instructions, put Trudeau in a corner to struggle. Eventually he mastered the techniques and hurried back to Saranac Lake. Later he and Prudden became warm and respected friends and Prudden taught him considerable bacteriology.

On return from New York with his newly acquired knowledge he began, in the cottage he'd built for his family, to equip his small office as a laboratory with what simple apparatus he could devise and procure. The equipment consisted of a dry and steam sterilizer, an oil stove and a homemade thermostatic box heated by a tiny kerosene lamp which had no regulating device. He had the tinsmith build a series of 4 wooden boxes — one within the other — packed between with wool and sawdust. All had doors so that by opening and shutting these according to the temperature outside the house — 35° below

228

zero is not uncommon in Saranac Lake — he could maintain a fairly regular heat in the inner chamber.

"One of my great problems was to keep my guinea pigs alive in winter. They require a constantly warm place to live. We had no coal in Saranac Lake, and in winter it froze in every house when the mercury fell below zero at night. It became evident I should have to keep my guinea pigs, as I did my potatoes, below ground. I had a big hole dug in my yard, put a kerosene lamp in this little cellar, and kept my guinea pigs in boxes on wooden shelves. It turned out to answer fairly well.

"In the fall of 1885 I began to work. I made examinations of all my cases, and as a result found only one patient in whom, while the symptoms were present, I could never detect the bacillus. I studied this case, found the expectoration would not kill animals, and published a paper in October, 1885 — the first from my little laboratory — as 'An Experimental Research Upon the Infectiousness of Non-bacillary Phthisis!'

"What I craved to do was to cultivate the tubercle bacillus outside of the body and then to produce the disease with it in animals. In the early winter of 1885 I attacked this problem with great earnestness. I had learned from Dr. Prudden how to make artificial media but I knew the first growth of the tubercle bacillus could be obtained only on solidified blood serum, and then with difficulty. I bought a small sheep for 3 dollars and a half, and from it procured the required amount of blood. After many accidents I succeeded in getting some fair slants of blood serum in tubes.

"I made plants on this blood serum from a tuberculous gland removed from one of my inoculated guinea pigs, and put all tubes in my homemade thermostat. For the next two weeks I watched the temperature of my absurd little oven with jealous care, and I remember getting up one very cold night and going downstairs to look at the temperature. After 10 days I still had 4 tubes free of contamination. On the 8th day I thought I detected a little growth on the corner of one of these.

"With my platinum spade I removed a little of the suspected growth, rubbed it on a couple of slides, dried and stained it. My first intimation of success was when one of two large masses on the slide refused to decolourize when treated with the acid. I washed the slide, put it under the microscope and to my intense joy saw nothing but well-stained culture masses and a few detached tubercle bacilli. At once I planted some fresh tubes from the one I had examined, and I knew now I had pure cultures. This little scum on the serum was consumption in a tangible form. With it I could inoculate animals and try experiments to destroy the germ."

As far as can be ascertained, Trudeau was the first in the U. S. to cultivate the tubercle bacillus and to confirm Koch's brilliant discovery.

"As soon as I had pure cultures I began to inoculate rabbits and guinea pigs and started some experiments to try to kill the germ in their tissues with various germicides such as creosote, carbolic acid, etc. They all failed, and I found that the tubercle bacillus bore cheerfully a degree of medication which proved fatal to its host."

"The world has been trying to do for thirty years what I had in view at that time and is still in 1915 as far from success as I was then. But to me the future was full of promise."

From then until a few years before his death, Trudeau's goal was to find a way to eliminate the tubercle bacillus by pharmacologic or bio-chemical means. In his last paper, 'Relative Immunity in Tuberculosis and the Use of Tuberculin' (published shortly after his death in the *British Journal of Tuberculosis* [October 1916], and written while he was suffering his terminal illness, he prophetically said, "My faith in the possibilities of chemotherapy for tuberculosis is based simply on what Ehrlich has demonstrated as pos-

Adirondack Cottage Sanitarium (Trudeau) in 1900 (Stoddard)

Early Saranac Lake from Lake St. Hill

Laboratory at Trudeau in Early Days

sible in syphilis — namely, that a chemical compound could be discovered which would kill the germ without injuring the cell. . . . I see no reason why what has been accomplished in the treatment of syphilis should not be attained in tuberculosis, and such an agent, when properly used, would prove of great value in the treatment of this disease.

"As I was busy all this time working out the application of the new method of treatment in pulmonary tuberculosis on patients at the Sanatorium, I began to wonder how, if the tubercle bacillus had already gained access to the body, a change of climate, rest, fresh air and food could influence the disease. I carried out the following experiment."

"Lot 1: five rabbits were inoculated with pure cultures, and put under the best surroundings of light, food and air obtainable. I turned them loose on a little island [in Upper St. Regis Lake] where they ran wild all summer in fresh air and sunshine, and had abundant food. All but one recovered and survived.

"Lot 2: five rabbits were inoculated at the same time in the same way and put into the worst environment I could devise — a dark, damp place where the air was bad, confined in a small box and fed insufficiently. Four died within three months with extensive tuberculosis.

"Lot 3: five rabbits were put under similar bad conditions as Lot 2 without inoculation. At 3 months all were killed and though emaciated showed no tuberculosis.

"This showed me conclusively that bad surroundings of themselves could not produce tuberculosis, and that when once the germs had gained access to the body the course of the disease was greatly influenced by the environment. . . ."

Almost eighty years later — in 1964 — Dr. Rene Dubos, the renowned French-American scientist-philosopher, stated that this experiment was a great inspiration in his own scientific life. When asked in 1960 what were the great problems of infectious diseases for the future, he began his paper with a restatement of this experiment of Trudeau's. "I believe this experiment represents not a turning point but a landmark in the development of our sciences, and much more importantly it represents the future, the picture of things to come. The conditions under which these rabbits were placed were not too different from those of the unfortunate people of the world today — in India — in the tenements of New York.

"This experiment is a model of enormous importance as it separates clearly the two great components of infectious disease — the role of the microbe and the role of the environment. This experiment has never been repeated. It needs to be — not on 15 rabbits but on 1500 rabbits and many other kinds of animals. It brings us very close to one of the largest problems of the civilized world."

Trudeau was not a prolific writer. During 30 years he published 53 papers. Most of his more important studies saw the light in very short papers in Proceedings or Transactions of medical societies or in not-widely-read journals. Often a 6-8 page paper presented the results of 5 years or more of careful experiments. This fact, added to his not being associated with any great medical faculty probably explains why his scientific achievements made their way slowly. And, too, from 1880 on anything medical which appeared in Virchow's *Archiv* or a standard *Zeitschrift* or *Wochenschrift* commanded many times the attention given to items published elsewhere. When Roemer described the immunization of small animals in 1910 the work was hailed as epochal and even today some citations mention him as the first man to "turn the trick." Yet from 1893 to 1905 and later, Trudeau had been writing about having done the same thing. Roemer added nothing new in the principles of immunization to the discoveries of Trudeau. Trudeau's statements are flawless as regards facts and pregnant with prophecy.

Critical review of the enormous body of work on active immunization during the 1890's will show that Trudeau was the first investigator to grasp the principles of tuberculous immunity — of the conditions under which it occurs. Before 1900 he stated definitely and without equivocation that infection and, as nearly as he could make out, only infection gave rise to the immune state.

His first 18 papers came from the work in his crude home laboratory. Then on a cold November night in 1893, while he was ill in New York with a kidney abscess from which he never fully recovered, came another of the tragic blows with which his life was filled — his home and his laboratory with all its contents and his work were burned to the ground. This calamity came only a few months after the death from tuberculosis of his spirited and only daughter, Charlotte — whom he could not save.

Among the condolences and offers of help that poured in after the fire was a characteristic letter from Dr. (later Sir) William Osler — "Dear Trudeau: I am sorry to hear of your misfortune, but take my word for it there is nothing like a fire to make a man do the Phoenix trick." And Osler's prophecy was soon fulfilled when Trudeau's good friend and former patient, Mr. George Cooper, offered to pay for a new stone and steel laboratory. Thus came into being the Saranac Laboratory from which over the years came the world-recognized work not only of Trudeau but of Baldwin, Krause, Gardner, Steenken, Vorwald and many others. Today it has been supplanted by its direct descendant, the splendid complex of the Trudeau Institute, where Dr. George Mackaness and his staff carry on the work and traditions of the men who went before them.

The whole story is every bit as romantic and some ways more remarkable than that of Koch, the country doctor founding the science of bacteriology in the curtained rear of his office. When Koch discovered tuberculin he had risen to the directorship of a great laboratory in Berlin. At that very time Trudeau was discovering essentially the same substance in his little room in Saranac Lake. (Years later the two men met at an International Congress.)

"I began to realize about this time that the direct destruction of the germ in the tissue by germicides was a hopeless proposition. So I sought to produce immunity in my animals by dead germs, or prevention inoculations of substances derived from the liquid cultures from which the bacilli had been filtered. I published the results of this work in the *New York Medical Record* on November 22, 1890, describing my experiments in detail and giving my conclusions that neither the dead germs nor the soluble poisonous substances derived from liquid cultures of the tubercle bacillus protected rabbits and guinea pigs against subsequent inoculations." This was 3 months after Koch announced that tuberculin would completely protect guinea pigs against subsequent inoculations with tubercle bacilli and would cure the disease in human beings!

Koch's announcement created a world-wide sensation — Trudeau's report not even a ripple of comment.

How can we explain and understand the scientific achievements of this man who had no formal training in scientific research, who was almost 40 before he accomplished any, and who had shown little if any interest in scientific intellectual pursuits until well into adult life? The assessment is best made by a man who knew and worked with him and who was himself a distinguished scientist — Allen Krause.

"Trudeau had little or no scientific training or scholarship. Nor was there much in him of the student in the sense of a man to whom intellectual pursuits and pleasure come first. But he was a supremely intelligent man, of great imagination, with a soaring and extremely active mind, a man of remarkably sound intuition — the intuition which, without knowing much of the complexities of a problem can sense what is essential and go straight to the heart of it. This uncanny ability was often a marvel to many disciplined scientists. He usually planned experiments directed right toward the goal.

"These traits were what made him a greater scientist than was generally supposed. And much greater, indeed, than he himself ever realized — far greater than the medical world then credited him. His range of knowledge of medicine was comparatively limited. He had little if any taste for sustained study, and probably much preferred the rod and gun to the book.

At the same time he had tenacity and determination which kept him steadfast in pursuit of all he could learn regarding tuberculosis. He could not read German and for a long time much of the literature was a closed book to him except what he got from abstracts and reviews in such journals as the *British Practitioner*. But after Dr. Edwin Baldwin came to him in 1882, he kept in close touch with the German work. For years Dr. Baldwin would carry his bundle of literature over to Trudeau's house in the evening and read to him what was going on in tuberculosis in Germany. These two formed an ideal pair for scientific work — complementary in temperament, antecedents, training and point of view, yet as one in their capacity for sacrifice and devotion to an ideal.

Trudeau must be given a place at the very apex of tuberculosis investigators — in both discovery and solidity of performance. And the fact that he was not a professional scientist and worked with slender resources in moments snatched from the cares of practice and the burden of building one of our great institutions put the stamp of genius on his career which we must not forget was shadowed by his own recurring illness."

Trudeau's health was always unstable and the physical enemy that drove him into the woods never retreated for long. For years he suffered intensely from migraine and during his last 20 years chronic cystitis made him miserable, and at times it sent him to bed for weeks. It probably arose from an old prostatic tuberculosis, and it quite possibly contributed to the advance of his pulmonary disease during his last 5 years. Toward the end he submitted to a pneumothorax in an attempt to bring his disease under control, but it was not very effective. I have seen his chest film made on a glass plate and he did, indeed, have extensive disease.

His own pain and suffering shook him — he could bear physical punishment well. Yet when the pain and fever were relieved his bright eyes and enthusiastic view of life returned promptly. People marveled at his wonderfully rapid recoveries from what seemed like serious illness. The explanation was simple: he suffered and enjoyed alike — intensely.

By 1877 Trudeau had proved to himself the value of a restful life, fresh air and good food in the Adirondack climate and environment for the treatment of tuberculosis. His good friend, Alfred Loomis, now was writing articles on the advantages of the Adirondacks for the tuberculous. And as Trudeau saw patients coming into the woods without proper places to live and be cared for, he began to formulate his ideas for a sanitarium based in part on the principles worked out 20 years before in Germany by Brehmer and Detweiler. Thus was conceived the second great dream of his life — a place where the tuberculous ill could get the best in care at low cost. Loomis enthusiastically agreed, promised his support and offered to examine prospective patients free of charge in New York City.

With this encouragement Trudeau set to work to build his sanitarium. In the years when the idea was germinating he had been keeping an eye open for a suitable site. He had long had a favorite fox-run on a level spot on the slope of Mount Pisgah just outside the village — there was a superb view across the river and the valley to the mountains beyond. This was where he would put his sanitarium. His friends, including his closest confidant —

the guide Fitz-Green Hallock — agreed although Hallock thought it was too bad to spoil a good fox-run.

To his great surprise his guide friends purchased 16 acres and presented them to him as a gift of affection and respect. Construction began with one wing of a main building and a small two-bed patient cottage which accepted in February, 1885 its first two patients — two shop-girl sisters from New York City. Alice Hunt had pulmonary tuberculosis and her sister Mary had Pott's disease. Here they spent the rest of the winter with a wood-stove, two cots, a washstand, two chairs and a kerosene lamp. Its total cost was 100 dollars — about 40 of today's pounds. This was the "Little Red" which today stands as a permanent memorial to Trudeau and the movement he began.

For the next 25 years Trudeau's life was that of a "beggar." But a most successful life of mendicity it was. The rich, the powerful and the obscure friends, patients and strangers responded most generously to his needs and requests. Steadily the Sanatorium grew until at his death there were almost 50 buildings on the 90 acres with all facilities for the medical, social and spiritual needs of those who came there to "cure." Patients were never charged the full cost of their care — the yearly deficit was made by Trudeau's "begging." Eventually a substantial endowment came into being.

Trudeau Sanatorium was a unique place with an atmosphere which inspired all who came with hope and confidence — a reflection of the attitudes of its founder. Those who "cured" there came to think of themselves as belonging to a special fraternity. They came away with a new outlook on life which henceforth stayed with them. And over the years more than a thousand of those patients were medical students and young physicians who, as they recovered, were put to work on the staff. Trudeau Sanatorium thus became the spawning ground for generations of America's leading chest physicians, who went out to establish and staff sanatoria all over the country and to become outstanding in research, teaching and clinical practice. For years they dominated the stage and the men they trained are now in the forefront.

Thus the first private tuberculosis sanitarium in America became a model and the stimulus for the development of a vast sanitarium treatment movement. By 1910, 25 years after "Little Red," there were 386 hospitals and sanatoria in the U. S. that owed their inception to Trudeau. And over the next 40 years it grew far beyond that. Now in the past 20 years — since the "Magic Bullet" Trudeau sought was found — they have steadily closed until there are only a handful left. Trudeau Sanatorium, the first to open was, ironically, the first to close — in 1954. Trudeau himself would have thrilled and rejoiced to see the present day.

And by the time of his death Saranac Lake had become a thriving village and a world-renowned centre of medical care, research, study and teaching. Today it is a thriving trading and resort centre and college town. Tuberculosis is no longer its "business."

The oldsters, many of whom had been his idolizing patients, talked much about Trudeau the man and much less about Trudeau, the physician. They would go on for hours about the man who would send the rebellious patient smiling into eternity, the man who would replenish an empty cellar with fuel, and who would set up the stranded widow in some profitable occupation.

His simplicity and genuineness made him highly attractive to men and women of every walk of life. It went far toward inducing the wealthy to help him in building the sanitarium. Details were irksome and often beyond him but he was always prompt to seek advice. He had superior capacity for recognizing ability in others. Those who helped him in his work recognized that if any career were to be enhanced by their contribution it would be

234

Taking The Cure — Rest Period in 1900 (Stoddard)

Exercise Phase of the Trudeau Cure in 1900 (Stoddard)

Three Leaders in T. B. Field — Drs. Brown, Heise and Baldwin

theirs and not Trudeau's. The result was a loyalty no associate or friend ever broke. If there was self-ambition in the man no one ever saw it. Simple; sincere, transparent and enthusiastic he loved praise — it was a manna that stimulated him.

No man was ever freer of class prejudice and consciousness. To the needy he offered his purse, his time and services without stint and from the favoured of fortune whom he attended he sought money for the sanitarium. This was all part of the daily work of an Adirondack physician who never made his own living from the returns of his private practice.

Trudeau was a man of soaring mind, a man of unusual sensitivity — especially to the sorrows and pleasures of human existence; with nimbleness in thought and action, an almost feminine intuition, and an abiding faith in his fellow man. Above all he had an almost excessive capacity for sympathy — simple, unconcealed and impossible of simulation. It was recognized and felt by everyone, sick and well.

Of his many illustrious patients the one who probably made the greatest impression was Robert Louis Stevenson. He arrived in Saranac Lake in October, 1887 and took lodging in a small cottage at the edge of the village. Trudeau says Stevenson was "not really ill." Trudeau had to make few professional calls on him but found him so attractive in conversation that he often went to sit before the fireplace to talk with his famous patient.

Trudeau and Stevenson found each other mutually attractive and stimulating despite their quite different interests and views on life. Trudeau was bound up in the study of facts wherever it might lead. On the other hand Stevenson sought to ignore or avoid unpleasant facts and to live in a beautiful and ideal world of fancy. He wouldn't go with Trudeau to the sanitarium or the laboratory because to him these were unpleasant things. But finally one day soon after he had written *The Lantern Bearers* he consented to visit the laboratory. Trudeau became engrossed in showing off his animals, equipment and experiments.

236

However, he soon noticed that Stevenson had disappeared. Trudeau found him on the porch looking quite ill and distressed. "Trudeau," said Stevenson, "your light may be very bright to you, but to me it smells of oil like the devil." To Trudeau his laboratory represented a vision of relief to humanity from sickness, suffering and death. The light of this vision was so bright to him that he never noticed the smell of oil which overcame Stevenson.

But they were excellent friends who admired and respected each other. They debated and discussed many questions and parted angrily only once — at the end of a heated argument over the trivial question of which was the better system of handling passenger rail luggage — the British or the American.

When Stevenson left Saranac Lake he presented Trudeau with a set of his works specially bound. In each volume he had written in his own hand an original verse dedicating the volume to some member of the Trudeau family, even including Nig, the dog. In Dr. Jekyll and Mr. Hyde he wrote — "Trudeau was all winter at my side. I never spied the nose of Hyde." Tragically these all were lost in the fire of 1893 that consumed the home and laboratory.

In time, over the years, the world of medicine and academia recognized and rewarded Edward Livingston Trudeau with high honours. Honorary degrees were bestowed on him by the universities of Yale, Pennsylvania, McGill and Columbia and of the last he became a trustee. He was a principal figure in the founding of the National Association for the Study and Prevention of Tuberculosis of which in 1905 he was the first president. (This is now the National Tuberculosis and Respiratory Disease Association.) In 1908 he was made Honorary President of the International Tuberculosis Congress. And in 1910 — the highest honour of the medical profession at that time — the presidency of the Congress of American Physicians and Surgeons — was given to him. His inaugural address was entitled *The Value of Optimism in Medicine*. In it he summed up one of the attributes which helped him to survive and create: 'Optimism is the one thing that is within the reach of us all, no matter how meager or obscure and limited careers may be. It was about my only

Trudeau Memorial Statue by Gutzon Borglum

Gloria Victis — Mercié

Trudeau

Trudeau Institute on Lower Saranac Lake (Kirstein photo)

asset when I built my first little sanitarium cottage on a remote hillside in an uninhabited and inaccessible region. Viewed from a pessimist's viewpoint that little cottage as an instrument of any importance in the warfare against tuberculosis must have appeared as a most absurd and monumental folly.

"In a long life, which has been lived daily in contact with patients beyond the reach of human skill who through months and even years of hopeless illness looked to me for help, I have indeed had need of all the optimism I could cling to. It has ever been a precious asset and has never entirely failed me.

"Let us not, therefore, quench the faith nor turn from the vision which, whether we own it or not, we carry, like Stevenson's lantern — bearers their lanterns, hidden from the outer world. Thus inspired many will reach the goal; and if for most of us our achievements inevitably must fall far short of our ideals; if when age and infirmity overtake us, we come not within sight of the castle of our dreams, nevertheless all will be well with us, for does not Stevenson tell us rightly that 'to travel hopefully is better than to arrive, and the true success is in labour.'"

A copy of Mercier's 'Gloria Victis' — the victory of spirit over body — for many years stood in the main hall of the Sanatorium. It meant much to Trudeau and he often referred to it. Now it greets the visitor as he enters the Trudeau Institute, where the spirit and the work of Edward Livingston Trudeau live on.

View West Over Lower Saranac Lake from Trudeau Institute (Kirstein photo)

Chapter 31

They Go To Church By Boat

Every Sunday morning during the Summer months scores of vacationers and year-round residents wend their way by water to a small, rocky, windswept island in Upper Saranac Lake. Their destination — the Island Chapel — is unquestionably one of the most unique and picturesque places of worship in the nation and its interdenominational services attract people of all ages and religious persuasions from nearby camps and campsites, as well as from villages thirty or forty miles away. For many, the Sabbath meetings have become a welcome, distinctly memorable and significant feature of the Northern Adirondack Summer scene.

On a typical fairweather Sunday morning the limited docking area, usually supervised by Emerson Wertz, very nautical and jaunty in his captain's cap, is alive and throbbing with boats of all types — canoes, guideboats, sailboats, outboards and inboards — and an occasional seaplane. As they approach their religious rendezvous, the casually dressed passengers seldom fail to be once more impressed by the sturdy, spired structure whose but-

The Second Island Chapel

tresses blend so well with the rugged setting and its storm-buffeted pines.

On such a Sabbath the little church is soon filled to capacity — about 200; the overflow group and late arrivals seek standing room in the foyer, watch through the windows or listen from seats on the nearby rocks.

On days when the Upper Lake, noted for the intensity of its storms, becomes too boisterous and therefore dangerous for small boats, the Remington's "To-N-Fro" takes over and makes triple its usual number of trips. This sturdy, reliable Richardson cruiser, whose 50th birthday was properly celebrated this past summer (1979), can conveniently carry 20 passengers from the Wawbeek dock, the usual assembly point and one that has probably provided the similar service for eighty of the ninety years that the Island Church (as the natives call it) has been in existence (1889 onward). . . .

What was it like on the Upper Lake before the first church was built on what was then known as Johnson's Island? The most visible and relevant economic feature was the area's appearance. The entire lake region had been extensively and intensively logged — nearly denuded of its towering pines, the multi-purpose "big whites," which were cut down in the Summer months, rafted across the Lake in the Spring and driven down the Saranac River via the outlet dam at Bartlett's, not far from Chapel Island. Incidentally the first recorded log-drive was in the spring of 1847.

The so-called lumber barons were The Maine Co., which operated in the late 1840's and throughout the '50's in what became the Saranac Inn area; Christopher Norton of Plattsburgh, known as the "King of the Saranacs"; the Dodge-Meigs, later called the Santa Clara Lumber Co.; the Baker and Tefft Co. of Plattsburgh and several smaller firms. By 1860 most of the choice available first-growth pines and spruces had been floated downstream to numerous sawmills located at Bartlett's, at Saranac Lake village and all along the lower reaches of the Saranac River to Plattsburgh on Lake Champlain. What you see nowadays are, for the most part, second and third growth evergreens which are nevertheless much easier on the eyes than the logged-over, often burned-over "vistas" which constituted the legacy of the lumbermen.

Soon after the end of the logging era came the first wave of Summer people, some of whom — like the Meigs family — were owners of large tracts of timber on the islands and mainland. Others, mostly prominent professional and business men and friends of the early arrivals — as well as sportsmen previously attracted to the area — came, liked what they saw, bought and built on their property and started the pleasant, eagerly anticipated vacation routine since followed by, in many instances, several generations of the same family. Quite likely an appreciable number of those who later became seasonal residents of the Upper Lake were former guests of the volatile Virge Bartlett, whose renowned Sportsmen's House, located just over the eastern ridge, entertained hundreds of travelers from 1854 until its owner's death thirty years later. It is known that Bartlett's successors, the Saranac Club, provided many church-goers from 1889 until its demise in 1913.

Possibly, too, other later residents first saw the alluring Upper Saranac from the porch of nearby Corey's, (Wardner's after 1896) Rustic Lodge, in business from 1850 until 1911.

The far more luxurious first Wawbeek Hotel, built in 1891 and torn down for scrap lumber in 1914, considerably increased the Summer population. Its replacement — the much smaller present Wawbeek, built about 1922 [burned Mar. 1, 1980) — has also contributed its share of vacationers and Sabbath worshippers at the Island Chapel.

A considerable and concerned number of those summer residents felt strongly that their spiritual needs required no vacations and must be nourished continuously. That conviction prompted them to establish and maintain the small chapel which they, mostly

Presbyterians, built on the one-acre island in 1889. However, at one time Catholic masses were held there and, over the years, Christians of all denominations have been welcomed to the services.

While heretofore largely self-sustaining and therefore nominally independent, the officers of the group now felt it advisable to seek help from the original sponsoring organization — The Champlain Presbytery — and subsequently it became part of the Adirondack Mission, at that time actively supporting the outreach to the lumber camps. Rev. Aaron Maddox of Tupper Lake, one of the several lumber-jack sky pilots, is credited with being largely responsible for his energetic and timely assistance to the Island Chapel as well as founding the Indian Carry Church on the mainland, near Corey's in 1888. Under the reorganization policies the Champlain Presbytery then underwrote most of the chapel's operating budget. Another provision was the directive that the pulpit be available to other than Presbyterians, an enlightened procedure which proved beneficial to the church's revival and survival.

Very likely some unknown clergyman was the motivating force behind the concerted effort to build the little church. It is also quite possible that William Bucknell of Pennsylvania was one of the small group of principal benefactors. Such a supposition is valid considering the fact that he gave so much money to the University of Lewisburg that it was promptly renamed Bucknell. It is also a matter of local oral record that his daughter, Edith, was married on the island shortly after the chapel was built. It is noteworthy that the deed transferring ownership of the Island from Weed and Turner to the Champlain Presbytery was recorded on October 4, 1892 and filed at County Courthouse, Malone, October 26 of that year.

There may have been other wedding ceremonies there too before the well-publicized Marvin-Ferris nuptials of September 10, 1902 but none which were described in such ample glowing details as these:

"Shadows and sunshine chased each other over the waters of Upper Saranac as the canoes and launches approached the little church on the island before the hour appointed for the wedding of Anna Edwards Ferris and Charles Ingalls Marvin. From the pretty camps on the shores of the Lake came many guests, and the "Saranac" brought those who had come from a distance, to the wedding in the woods; so that the pews in the tiny chapel were soon filled. The space behind the reading desk and above the platform was transformed with a chancel of pine and hemlock boughs and screened by those boughs, the violins and organ were invisible as they played softly until the guests were assembled. Then, as an electric launch [Swenson's], decked in the scarlet and green of mountain ash, glided noiselessly up to the dock, the ushers went down to meet it. The first bars of the Lohengrin Wedding March sounded as the ushers turned and led the way over the rocky path under the pines to the church.

"Entering by the two doors, the ushers and the bridesmaids came up the short aisle and took their places in a group on each side of the clergyman, Rev. Dwight E. Marvin, D. D., the father of the groom. The bridesmaids — Miss Cara Marvin, Miss Mary Dwight Ferris and Miss Isabel Stuart Ferris wore pink gowns and wreaths of green, and carried shower bouquets of pink sweet peas and maidenhair ferns.

"The bride entered with her father, Sherwood Bissell Ferris, who gave her away. The bride's gown was of white crêpe de chine, and her veil of tulle over a wreath of white sweet peas, and she carried a shower bouquet of white sweet peas and maidenhair ferns.

"The groom met her at the aisle and Doctor Marvin married them, reading his own service. The groom's brother, Dwight Willison Marvin, was best man and the ushers were

Mr. and Mrs. Charles I. Marvin

The Wedding Party

Baptism of Carolyn Alethea Robinson

Sunday Service in Original Church

John Kilpatrick of New York, Dr. Charles Browne and Archibald D. Davis of Lakewood, New Jersey.

"Immediately after the ceremony the bridal party and guests from a distance took launches to Deer Island, where an informal breakfast was served.

"Mr. and Mrs. Marvin are spending a few weeks in a little log cabin on an island near Mr. Ferris' camp."*

Another auspicious day in the annals of the Island Chapel and the only such occasion in its record was the 1955 baptism of the Remington's grandchild — Carolyn Alethea Robinson. This ceremony represented a red-letter landmark for the descendants of Edmund Lyon and, like the Marvin-Ferris wedding of 1902, it signified a definite turning-point in the Chapel's history — a clear symbol of its solid foundation, its assured acceptance within its dedicated community and visible proof of its renewed spiritual vitality.

Unfortunately, difficult days arrived — the struggling little church had just about realized its potential as a religious institution when the Great Depression overwhelmed the nation and the world. After the trying years following the traumatic stockmarket crash, which peaked on Black Tuesday — October 29, 1929 — the ripple effect took its toll on the Summer population as well as elsewhere. Few camp-owners were financially able to survive without drastic retrenchments and lifestyle changes but fortunately some families, such as the Lyons, continued to maintain their cherished vacation retreats and their Chapel. Eventually, however, declining membership and decreasing financial support forced the remaining concerned members to make the first of what ultimately became two soul-searching decisions.

Meanwhile the indomitable Lyons and their persistent neighbors continued to hold Sunday services at the Island. Since ministerial help was often unavailable the Lyons, their friends and guests not only frequently comprised the entire congregation but also took charge of the service itself, composed and delivered the sermons. On one such occasion Arthur E. Sutherland, then a young man but later a distinguished Harvard Law School professor, assumed the principal spiritual role. Lacking musicians then, Elizabeth Lyon Kidd played the organ while Francis Remington officiated at its pump.

The second of the two major crises — and far more challenging than the decision to seek Presbyterial financial help and its accompanying sacrifice of independence — occurred on an otherwise uneventful day in August, 1956. Whether it was a bolt of lightning or, as was more likely, a fire left smoldering by picnickers, is relatively unimportant in retrospect but the results were destructive and dismaying. In spite of all-out efforts by neighboring camp-owners the cherished little church was soon reduced to charred timber and ashes. Pulpit, bell, Bibles, parquet walls and the handsome pulpit chair given by Rochester friends of Edmund Lyon in his memory — all were consumed by the flames.

It is quite possible that if the fire had happened during the Depression there never would have been a replacement church. But, like the proverbial phoenix another and more substantial structure was erected — but not without the concomitant struggle. The Summer community came through again and the same people who had weathered the previous crisis once more showed their mettle. Just how much the Island Chapel was and is appreciated became known during those dire days that followed.

At a hasty meeting of those most deeply involved rebuilding plans were discussed. There was some opposition from those who felt that the Indian Carry Chapel made a new

* Years later that small island (.67 acres) known as Doctor's island became the property of their son Sherwood Marvin (now deceased), who renamed it "Grey Rocks."

Destruction by Fire of Original Church — Aug. 1956

church unwanted and unnecessary. The dissenters, however, were quickly outvoted and a fund-raising committee organized. Priorities were designated: steeple bell; wrought iron; glass; lumber for pulpit and pews; runners for the aisles; paint, stain and logs for the docks and flying buttresses. The last requirement was readily met by the Farnham Yardley family, who donated the spruce logs milled for that purpose; the Bartlett Carry Co. also gave the bumpers for the docks.

Those people who could not afford to give money were enlisted to help with the work parties — and work they did!

The response was immediate and effectively organized. Among the members of the Rebuilding Committee were the Rev. William Clark, one of the earlier church's most energetic leaders in every respect; Mrs. Francis Remington, treasurer; Mrs. William Butterfield; Miss Dorothy Emerson; William E. Petty Jr. and John Sennott. These people worked diligently to raise funds for the project; they distributed leaflets and solicitations to interested persons and occasional visitors as well. Moreover, they were strongly supported in their campaign by the National Missions Committee; the Champlain Presbytery including the Rev. William B. MacCready, Hardy Sweet, the Rev. David W. Muir and the Rev. William J. Erdmann.

The building, designed by architects William G. Distin and Arthur Wareham of Saranac Lake, was completed within two years during which time Summer services were continued, the congregation seated on the rocks. Providentially, none of these worship meetings was interrupted by rain, apparently an omen of celestial approval.

The first Island Church had been relatively small by comparison. The new structure, while hardly an edifice, was constructed in rustic simplicity in order to blend with its superb

The Island Church in Winter

natural setting. Picture windows provided a modified panoramic view of the long lake and mountain vistas, which engendered wider visual and enhanced spiritual horizons.

The opening ceremony marking the resumption of services in the fine new building was covered by *The Adirondack Daily Enterprise* in an article dated Wednesday, July 23, 1958: "The Presbytery of Champlain is grateful and appreciative of the fine response and help of so many in the rebuilding of the Chapel on Chapel Island.

"Participating in the service last Sunday were: Rev. W. Clark, Chairman of the Building Committee, assistant at the Eliot Congregational Church of Newton, Mass. and Summer supply pastor of Island Chapel and Indian Carry, National Missions Churches of the Presbyterian Church of Saranac Lake, and presiding as Presbytery Moderator at the service; Rev. Alvin B. Gurley, former minister of the Presbyterian Church in Saranac Lake and Chairman of National Missions of the Presbytery when present rebuilding of this chapel began, and now resident Minister of Visitation of the Ridley Park Presbyterian Church, Ridley Park, Pa., Rev. William B. MacCready, pastor of the Adirondack Parish and present Chairman of the National Missions Committee of Presbytery:

248

"The Choir was from the Girl Scout Encampment on Eagle Island with Stephanie Hokuf as director."

Although the chapel itself was now completed, its congregation still lacked several of the important adjuncts of Christian worship but once again the established residents rose to the occasion. Judge John Van Voorhis donated a portable organ which he himself delivered by boat. The stained glass windows in the front doors came from his parents, the Eugene Van Voorhis' home in Rochester, N.Y. Another active Summer community member — Mrs. Grace Grabenstein, affectionately called "Auntie Grace" — furnished the hymnals as a memorial to Rev. Aaron Maddox, lumber-jack sky-pilot and the first ordained minister to serve the Island Chapel.

In 1960 the Lyon twins — Mrs. Francis Remington and Mrs. John Van Voorhis — made a special trip to the Steuben Co. in New York and purchased the unusual altar curtains — spun glass, which does not fade nor become food for moths.

A small birch-bark cross fashioned by Mr. Remington stands in front of the window behind the pulpit. Each of the new pulpit chairs was given by Dr. and Mrs. James Craig Potter — and inscribed — one with the words "In commemoration of the sustained interest of the Lyon family in their chapel, 1958"; the other reads "In memory of Carolyn and Edmund Lyon, from Rochester friends." Thus was the faith and dedication of forty years rewarded and perpetuated.

The story behind the Chapel's bells is also fascinating. Two bells have been used in the church. The first of these, donated by the Corey family, originally saw service on an East River boat in New York Harbor. The Coreys acquired it and used it to call the family to meals and to summon help. Although it was cracked and its voice couldn't carry far, it nevertheless served its purpose for some time.

The next occupant was a locomotive bell, given by the Hardys of Boulder Island. There is a story, without confirmation, that an ancient school bell brought from Canada was also used at least temporarily.

Besides the long-active, stalwart mainstays other members have served the Chapel faithfully and well. Philip Arras, for instance, has been not only a loyal attender for over thirty years but also its effective P.R. person as well. Richard Russ, its treasurer and organist for many years. Major and Martha Day have been willingly and efficiently active. And, according to a 1960's church bulletin Drs. Dunham Kirkham and Richard Loomis, Miss Margaret Vance and Gen. Russell Minty have done their share and then some to keep the church functioning smoothly. The list must be fairly lengthy.

Although the early years' services were usually conducted by Union Theological Seminary students, present-day worship meetings have outstanding ministers such as John Fitch, the coordinator, who has been a welcome and eloquent fixture at the Chapel for eleven Summers, sometimes as often as eight Sundays in the series of services and Rev. Newton Greiner, the alternating occupant of the pulpit for six seasons.

Two young student clergymen who occupied the Island Church pulpit have been Rev. David Cockroft, son of the president of French's Mustard Co. and the Rev. William Hudnut III, son of the well-known Presbyterian theologian.

So much for its truly memorable and, at times, exciting and challenging past-but what does the future hold for the time-and-elements-tested Chapel on the Island? Since experience has shown that the only thing you can be sure of is that you can't be sure of anything, a reasonable assumption should, however, include more than a modicum of optimism based on the anticipated orderly flow of events and current developments.

In recent years Upper Saranac Lake and the Lakes region in general have experienced a rapid and continuous increase in popularity and population. Although the number of very wealthy summer residents has somewhat decreased, the accompanying slack has been considerably counter-balanced by the influx of new property owners and seasonal visitors. Moreover, for a variety of personal reasons — foremost of which are spiraling taxes and mounting maintenance costs — and because of changing vacation preferences several of the more palatial "camps" have been either sold or given to religious and educational institutions for use as retreats or conference centers.

Two examples are Prospect Point, Adolph Lewisohn's former luxurious enclave, later Camp Navarac but now Young Life and Eagle Island, once owned by the Graves family, who gave it to the Essex Co. New Jersey Girl Scouts Council in 1937.

Not so incidentally, over the years the Scouts have, by their choir-singing and eager participation, greatly enhanced the Sabbath services.

Other factors which have added measurably to the number of Summer residents have been the expansion of the Fish Creek Campsite and the accelerated efforts of the State and local publicity agencies.

Question: How will these changes affect the future of the Island Church? Quite likely very little when the limited capacity of both the island itself and the structure are taken into consideration. Then too the transportation logistics virtually preclude a second service. So, it would seem logical that the most feasible and desirable course would be the continuation of the time-tested and convenient status quo.

As David Wade, Jr. who generously provided much of the material in this chapter, perceptively observed: "Surrounded by change in an ever-changing world, evolving itself as its congregation evolves, the Island Chapel nevertheless endures. When the Adirondacks reach their mid-summer peak the little church approaches its seasonal height. The congregations of residents and guests are swelling to their peak. There is a conjunction of spirits, the human joining the natural and both aspiring upward. Within a few short weeks, however, the mornings will get progressively colder and the people will reluctantly leave for home. Silence will return to the mountains and the Island Chapel will also become silent — its walls upright, its bell intact and waiting for the Spring. For, like the camps and the boathouses and everything else constructed by humans, this building is meaningless without the men and women who give it meaning."

Chapter 32

Deer Island

Deer Island, one of the more accessible and attractive islands in the Upper Lake, has seen a lot of history. Originally part of the Col. Christopher Norton timber empire, it was later acquired by the Santa Clara Lumber Co., dominated by the Meigs family after the ill-fated John Hurd of the Northern Adirondack R.R. (later known as the N.Y. and Ottawa) had been bought out. The Santa Clara Co. (named after Hurd's wife as is the hamlet on the Middle branch of the St. Regis River) under Meigs' management once extended along both sides of the Raquette River — from the Cold River country, which includes Ampersand Pond, down to Stony Creek Ponds, plus both the Indian and Sweeney Carries.

Although the headquarters of the logging company was at Axton (Axe-town in the Dodge-Meigs days), the family had vacation retreats at Ampersand Pond (now owned by Avery Rockfeller) and Deer Island.

The Ferrises, related to the Meigs clan and the manufacturers of the ubiquitous "Ferris waist," owned half of Deer Island (a part of which is now owned by Dr. Craig Potter) to which generations of their descendants return year after year, a pleasant addiction understood and indulged by aficionados everywhere in the Adirondacks.

Apparently Alfred White bought part of Deer Island from Meigs because the latter built a spacious "camp" on Big Wolf Lake, near Tupper. The Whites' camp, which they named "Rest-A-While" was designed by Mr. White's celebrated but unfortunate brother — Stanford White.

Probably one of the more amusing incidents during the White occupancy occurred when Bossy, a cow which provided readily available dairy products, decided one day to explore the mainland — a fairly formidable water journey for a bovine swimmer. Whether she was floundering or, more likely, someone on Deer saw the potential AWOL, headed her off and ignominiously towed her back securely tethered to a scow.

Eventually her cowshed on the north tip of the Island underwent a major face-lift and became a studio for June (Linda) Lyon, who had studied at the Arts Students League. Years later the Lyon grandchildren commandeered it and named it "The Three Bears House" because they liked to think that Goldilocks had once lived there. But that's getting more than slightly ahead of the story.

Another Upper Lake summer resident, Dr. L. Emmet Holt, owned a camp on Panther Point. A pioneer pediatrician his book — *Care and Feeding of Children,* published in 1894 and reprinted many times, was every bit as influential among mothers of that generation as have been Dr. Spock's recent day Vade Mecums.

The eminent Dr. Holt introduced Edmund Lyon, a classmate (vintage 1877) at Rochester University and one of that city's most prominent businessmen and philan-

---

* According to Mrs. Sherwood Marvin, whose father was an M.D. and knew Dr. Holt, the latter came to Saranac Lake to investigate and study the so-called milk disease or Summer Complaint which caused severe infant mortality. As a first step in controlling this disease, Dr. Holt prescribed boiled barley water as a more healthful substitute for cow's milk, which apparently became contaminated somehow!

Edmund Lyon

Carolyn Talcott (Mrs. Edmund Lyon)

"Bircholm", Deer Island

252

thropists to the alluring Upper Saranac.

Moreover, Mr. Lyon had also achieved more than a modicum of fame by devising the innovative *Lyon Phonetic Manual*. He and his wife, Carolyn Hamilton Talcott, were the principal benefactors of D.M.I., a school for the deaf in the "Flower City" and were devoted friends of Helen Keller and Alexander Graham Bell.

The Lyons were apparently enchanted by the superb lake and mountain vistas — so much so that several years after Mr. White's death they bought "Rest-A-While" from the widow and, in the Summer of 1917, with their three daughters — Elizabeth, May (christened Carolyn) and June (legal name Linda) — the parents took over the island sanctuary which Mrs. Lyon renamed "Bircholm."

During the early years there was no electricity so the family read by the glow of kerosene lamps and went to bed by candlelight. Rather romantic in retrospect but somewhat hard on the eyes and nose — besides being inconvenient.

Six generations of the Lyon family have been returning to and enjoying Deer Island — the oldest to do so was Grandfather Philo Fuller Talcott, a Captain in the Civil War and an ardent fisherman who strictly observed the Sabbath. On other days the boat could never leave the dock without his being in it. However, his fishing days ended by default when, aged 90, he lost his balance while disembarking from a guideboat. Fortunately, the water was shallow and there were no lingering ill effects, but for valid personal reasons he never went fishing again.

The sixth generation are Linda Lyon Van Voorhis' great grandchildren — John and Michael Hayes.

While the Whites were there they solved their transportation problem by using an oversized guideboat; probably a twenty-two footer, which was equipped with three sets of oarlocks and usually manned by Ellsworth Petty, their guide/caretaker as well as being in the employ of the Lyons in the same capacity for many years.* Not large or comfortable enough for a fairly large family and their guests, this venerable craft was soon replaced by a canopied launch which, because of its spasmodic motor was aptly dubbed "The Chug-Chug."

This staunch launch and its dauntless pilot became part and parcel of the local legend and their shared fame was perpetuated in this segment of Winifred K. Smythe's memorable "Bircholm":

"Every Sunday dear old Chug-Chug took the crowd to Chapel Isle
  Where the organ only wheezed when pumped by hand.
  And the open windows showed a view that tended to beguile
  As they sang their hymns in sight of Ampersand.

"Then later, all the young ones cranked that good home-made ice cream
  With ice that Ellsworth cut in Winter's chill.
  He was indeed a quiet man — one held in high esteem
  And a woodsman of the very greatest skill.

"Now we who warm ourselves today at Bircholm's glowing fires
  Tread in the steps of early counterparts.
  Our joy — with theirs — in staying here inspires
  Toward *all* the Lyons — thanks with grateful hearts."

---

* Other caretakers at "Bircholm" have been Howard Ellithorpe, George Ramsey and — most recently Francis Pilon.

"The Chug-Chug"

Capt. Philo Talcott

Mr. Lyon died April 24, 1920. Ten years later Mrs. Lyon bought an open-cabin Richardson cruiser which, because of its frequent trips back and forth from the camp to the mainland dock/boathouse was appropriately yclept the "To-N-Fro." Capable of accommodating twenty people handily and happily this commodious craft has since seen much service taking the family, friends and other worshippers who required transportation to Chapel Island.

Therefore, it was altogether fitting and proper that the 50th birthday of this sturdy cruiser should be joyously observed this past Summer (1979) by a family picnic on the boat while moored to the dock on Church Island, preceded by a ceremonial serenade tour of the Upper Lake.

In 1936 Mrs. Lyon joined her husband in "that land that is fairer than this and by faith one can see it afar." As Mrs. Smythe remarked in another portion of her poem:

"My memories of Mrs. Lyon throughout all the years
Overshadow all the things I'd love to say.
Her gracious charm and thoughtfulness *so* often reappears
And I feel her spirit here in camp today!"

Professor Hocking, the renowned philosopher and teacher, in his valedictory lecture before leaving Yale to go to Harvard, was asked to give his definition of beauty, "Beauty, I believe," he said, "is one means of anticipating the achievement which all of us hope for at

Mr. Lyon and His Three Daughters

255

Lisa R. Dietal and Her Mother, Mrs. W. M. Dietal

the farther end of eternity — the complete subjugation of matter to the uses and ends of the spirit. Here in what is beautiful we see that attainment before our eyes and its presence sustains us in the long journey."

To me that expresses and epitomizes the finest of human and great Nature's attributes and attitudes, our and her graces and glories. "What oft was thought but ne'er so well expressed," as Alexander Pope so perceptively remarked.

Seasonal and seasoned exposure to such visual delights as offered by Deer Island and other comparably scenically endowed locations — and there are many along the Saranacs — cannot help but elevate our thoughts and enhance our all-too-human perceptions and spiritual values.

Celebrating the 50th Anniversary of "The To-N-Fro"

256

Chapter 33

Church of the Ascension — Saranac Inn

There were two places of worship on the Upper Saranac — The Island Chapel, already covered, which was at the south end of the Lake and The Church of the Ascension at the north end, near Saranac Inn. Each has an interesting history.

It is evident from notes written in the Parish Register that sometime in the year 1905, efforts were made to put together a record of the early beginnings of the Church of the Ascension. In a letter from Mrs. Frederick H. Gibbens, dated November 12th 1905, she quotes the following from the diary of her husband:

"Saturday, September 5, 1885, The Church finished tonight.

Sunday, September 6, 1885, Go to the first service in the little log church on the hill.

   Mr. Dotten performed the service."

"Thus began the life of the Summer church, here on Upper Saranac Lake, which has continued every summer uninterrupted for more than eighty years. The site for the church was a choice of Mrs. Edward L. Trudeau, at which time the trees now surrounding the church were either non-existent or small saplings. It was possible to see a large part of the lake from the church, and a stairway up the hill was used by many of the members who came to the church's lakeside landing at the foot of the hill.

Mr. W. Quincy Riddle, Mr. Daniel W. Riddle, Mr. C. W. Chandler, Mr. Thomas Blagden, and Dr. William R. Dunton, in the summer of 1882, interested guests of the Inn

Church of the Ascension in 1893 (Frank Firth photo)

in providing funds for the erection of the church. There is evidence that some very informal worship services were held in the unfinished church as early as 1884 — there being "one bare room with chairs. The missionary at Saranac Lake included the Inn and Paul Smith's in his work and held services at the Inn, "whenever he found sufficient time," according to a letter from Dr. Trudeau. When completed, it was less than half the size of present building, and from the beginning there seems to have been a proprietary tie between the owners of the Inn and the church.

Ten years after his first Summer as rector, Mr. Dotten wrote, in 1905, about his past congregation "the names of all of them are a fragrance in my memory." During this early period, a Sunday school class was run by the Misses Eastman and Mrs. Peabody; and it gave to the church the brass vases and book rest still in use.

In 1904, (for a total price of $1188) the church building was extended 24 feet; four windows and the robing room were added. This expansion coincided with enlargement of Saranac Inn and was undertaken to accommodate the increased number of summer guests. At that time, the Upper Saranac Association built the Rectory which was leased to the "Church Committee" for seventy-five dollars per annum. The church building itself was leased annually for a nominal figure. Some fifty years passed before the Saranac Inn Chapel filed a certificate of incorporation, in 1935. In 1947 the rectory was purchased by the Corporation, and in 1952, the Corporation purchased the land on which the church was built, from the Saranac Inn Company. In 1964 the church purchased four and three-quarters acres of woods adjoining the church grounds."

A letter from Mr. Frank J. Firth, at a very early date, states, "Nor was the Inn Co. then willing to acknowledge any Episcopal Diocesan authority. The chapel was simply a free chapel subject only to the control of the Company (so far as it cared to control) and of those people who had been most active in building it, who were mostly Episcopalians." It is evident from the records that clergy of the Episcopal have always officiated at the services.

The Clergy

The Rev. Milton C. Dotten	1885, 1887-1891
The Rev. Montgomery Throop, Jr.	1886
The Rev. Walter H. Larom	1892
The Rev. Richard L. Howell	1893-1897
The Rev. Dr. Leonard W. Richardson	1898-1929
The Rev. Dr. Edward S. Travers	1930-1931
The Rev. Dr. Henry Darlington	1932-1936
The Rev. Canon George A. Robertshaw	1937-1964

"Other clergy who have taken services as guest preachers have been Bishop J. I. Blair Larned, Bishop Robert F. Gibson, The Rev. Dr. Arthur Lee Kinsolving, The Rev. Professor William Lyon Phelps, The Rev. Dr. Albert J. M. Wilson. In 1964 The Rev. Edward B. Pollanick took a number of services, and in 1965 The Rev. Charles A. Perry, The Rev. Dr. J. Burton Thomas, and the Rev. Warren G. Davis took Summer services.

"The employees about the place are mostly Catholics and for their accommodation the use of the building is given to the nearest resident priest of their denomination for an early morning (6 o'clock) service which is held every Sunday and for which he comes from Saranac Lake Village distant about twelve miles. At eleven o'clock there is a service conducted by a resident minister, the present incumbent being a minister of the Protestant Episcopal Church and the service conforms to the simplest requirements of that denomina-

Rev. Dr. Leonard W. Richardson (Firth photo)

Elizabeth Morgan Serving Tea at "The Birches", 1904

"The Birches" Main House (Firth photo)

259

Duncan LeClaire, Capt. of "The Saranac"

John Clark, Mate of "The Saranac"

"The Saranac" (Stoddard photo)

tion. It is arranged and conducted in a spirit of true brotherly love and Christian family devotion, with charity each towards the other; considering as of prime importance those matters and beliefs wherein all intelligent Christians unite and nevertheless important matters wherein they differ. It is therefore a happy, united Christian family, and the Sunday gatherings are looked forward to with pleasure and broken with regret. There have worshipped in this harmony members of Presbyterian, Methodist, Episcopalian, Baptist, Unitarian and Catholic denominations, most of whom have also found it possible to commune together with gratification and benefit.

"Ministers as well as laymen are found in the congregation and unity in communion. The young people are as much interested as are the older ones.

"The Minister and family have the use of a comfortable rectory on the shore of the lake nearby the church and are members of the Summer colony. The church is open during the months of July, August and September. It is a free church, wholly supported by voluntary offerings made at the Sunday morning services and these offerings have always paid for maintenance and all current expenses.

"When it was desired to enlarge the church in the 1920's the Minister read a brief notice of the fact that $1200 was needed for this use and on the conclusion of the services the subscriptions were offered. The list opened with subscriptions of one hundred dollars each and every denomination represented among the worshippers was so on the subscription list. One of the employees subscribed a day's wages in memory of his wife and no subscription on the list was more highly valued. The entire amount was raised, the building enlarged and on the day of the accounting it was a gratification to those in charge to be able to submit their report and vouchers showing all bills paid and no call necessary to provide any increased cost such as is so often found in church and other building work. This church has never had under its Church Committee Management a deficit on any of its construction work or in the conduct of its services. . . .

"About two years ago (1907) the Minister stated that no trace had been found of a man who had been lost in the woods a short time before and made an appeal for help for his widow and two small children. A fund of nearly $350 was at once raised and placed in the hands of two trustees to disburse as seemed to them likely to be most helpful.

"This Church Committee also conducts a service in the guide house on Sunday evening for the guides, maids and employees, care being taken to make it such a non-sectarian service as will be acceptable to all and give no cause for objection to any priest or minister whose people attend."

During the 1920's the church was enlarged to its present size, and in 1948 the trustees met with an architect to consider plans for further enlargement. At that time it was not unusual for the church to be crowded with extra chairs down the aisles and anywhere from 35 to 50 seated in the woods outside. Faithfully over several decades the boys from "Hank" Blagden's Camp LaJeunesse arrived by open trucks and walked up the hill to occupy the first dozen or so pews on the gospel side. When this boys' camp closed its operations in the early 1950's and sale of the Inn resulted in a greatly reduced number of guests attending the church, plans for enlargement were not carried out.

Forty-three children have been baptized in the church. Ten marriages, five confirmations, and four burials have taken place during the life of the church to date.

The following notes are of historic interest:

"On Wednesday morning, August 15, 1945, a service of Thanksgiving was held in the Chapel, at which time more than 250 members of the Congregation offered their thanks to Almighty God for the termination of the war with Japan."

"In 1952 following purchase of the land from the Saranac Inn Co., the name of the Church was again restored. It was originally called The Church of the Ascension, given that name by the Inn's Church Committee 'inspired by the grand view from the hilltop,' changed to Saranac Inn Chapel about 1920, and in 1952 renamed and incorporated "The Church of the Ascension."

In view of the unusually long association each man had with the Church of the Ascension, it is appropriate to include these few words about Dr. Richardson:

At the time of Dr. Richardson's retirement many tributes were spoken and some printed. He had been a Professor at Trinity College and later at New York State College for Teachers — "its most respected and best loved Faculty member." It is clear from the records of thirty-two Summers that this high opinion was fully shared by all members of his congregation.

And about Dr. Robertshaw:

"His influence permeated the lives of the young and the old and continued to influence those who were young in 1937 as they grew older. Whether it was in the pulpit or on the golf links or at a picnic, he reached out and touched those who were with him and made them happier and better for the experience. Throughout the tremendous upheavals in this period in the type of the community on the Lake and the removal of the dominance over the everyday lives there of the Inn, he maintained steadfastly the character and position of the Chapel. People who through much of the year were too lazy or too indifferent to go to religious services on Sundays at home uniformly went to the services he conducted. He appreciated the physical beauty and peace and spiritualness of the place and he helped others towards such an appreciation. As he became more and more a very real part of the community, he led others into the life of the spirit wherein his was dedicated.

"But, first and foremost, our Summer Rector was a Priest of God. The members of his congregation knew this was the source of the inspiration for his leadership and few indeed failed to respond." [the foregoing taken from a minute adopted at a special meeting of the Board of Trustees in 1965]. . . .

Of the ten marriages which were solemnized at the Church of the Ascension the best documented was that of Arnold Harris Hord and Annie Robb Firth which took place in October 1, 1903. The bride was the daughter of Frank J. Firth of Germantown, Penna., the president of the Anchor Steamship Line, who had vacationed in Saranac Inn in 1890 and who in 1895 built "The Birches," the first of two cottages erected by him on property purchased near Saranac Inn.

What made that particular wedding of unusual interest was the fact that most of the party came up from Philadelphia aboard a small private train consisting of a combined parlor/baggage car, a sleeper, and a dining car.

The accompanying zeroxes provide the train schedule and the personnel of the wedding party.

Following the ceremony John S. Trower, a Philadelphia caterer who had brought his staff and equipment up from that city for the occasion, served lunch at "The Birches." Music for the gala event was furnished by Franz Rath, a graduate of the Vienna Conservatory, and his orchestra.

One of the highlights of the festivities was the cruise around Upper Saranac on the sleek 70 foot steamboat, "The Saranac," which was chartered for the afternoon by the bride's father. This rollicking ditty, composed by three members of the joyous group, sounded the appropriate keynote to what must have been a truly memorable Autumn interlude.

Arlo Flagg

Jim Patterson

Duck Derby

Jim O'Malley

Earl Torrence

Bert Chase

Schedule For The Trip

Lv. Broad Street Station, Philadelphia .... 3:50 P.M. Sept. 29th
Arr. Jersey City .... 5:38 P.M. Sept. 29th

A dining car will be placed on the train at Jersey City and dinner served between Jersey City and Newburgh.

Lv. Jersey City (Via West Shore R.R.) .... 6:18 P.M. Sept. 29th
Arr. Newburgh .... 8:07 P.M. Sept. 29th
Arr. Albany .... 10:50 P.M. Sept. 29th
Lv. Albany (N.Y. Central) .... 11:05 P.M. Sept. 29th
Arr. Saranac Inn .... 6:50 A.M. Sept. 30th

The Buffet porter will serve coffee, eggs and rolls, to anyone wanting them, before leaving the car at Saranac Inn Station Wednesday morning. Please give the order the night before, if convenient. As the sleeping car will be left at Saranac Inn Station, you will not be hurried in leaving the car in the morning.

Return Trip

Lv. Saranac Inn (Via N.Y. Central)....................... 9:20 P.M. Oct'r. 1st
Arr. Albany.. 5:15 A.M. Oct'r. 2nd
Lv. Albany, via West Shore special for Kingston .... 5:20 A.M. Oct'r. 2nd
Arr. Kingston .... (?)
Lv. Kingston, (Via West Shore) .... 6:50 A.M. Oct'r. 2nd
Arr. Jersey City .... 9:35 A.M. Oct'r. 2nd

Buffet breakfast will be served on the car between Albany and Jersey City.

Lv. Jersey City (Via Penna. R.R.) .... 10:32 A.M. Oct'r. 2nd
Arr. Philadelphia (Broad St. Station)................... 12:29 Noon Oct'r. 2nd

Thursday October 1st 1903
Wedding party left Phila 3⁵⁰ P.m. Sep 29
Arrived Saranac Inn 8 A.m Sept 30—
Left   "   " 9²⁰ P.m Oct 1st

Party

Charles E. Morgan jr   *—
Lillie M. Morgan   *   ⎫ Remained on
Silas Casey Jean H. Stuart U.S.A.— ⎬ until Saturday
Sophie D Casey   ⎪ night Oct 3rd
Sophie Pearce Casey   ⎭
Elizabeth M. Morgan ✗
C. E. Morgan 3rd

John D. Browne
Alice E. Browne.
Wordruff Jones.
Sara E. Jones.
Sara Elizabeth Jones—
Mary Carpenter Jones—
A. Robinson McIlvaine —
Elizabeth E. McIlvaine
Fm D. Young
Mary R. Young.
Francis R. Strawbridge
Anna Estes Strawbridge—
Edith Keel
Mrs Joseph M Shumaker—(Annie M Shumaker)—
Mary Janet Miller.
Edw. Mellor
Deborah Wharton Mellor.
Wm Brevard Gilpin
Elizabeth D. Chandler.
Edwin T. Evans
Frances Eagle McIlvaine

265

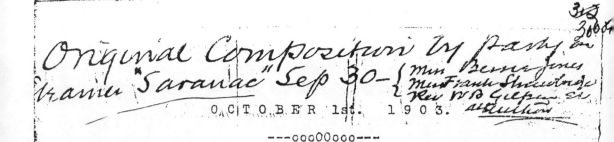

Original Composition by party on Steamer "Saranac" Sep 30—
{ Miss Bessie Jones
  Miss Frank Shrewbridge
  Rev W B Gilpin &c & children }

OCTOBER 1st. 1903.

---ooo00ooo---

Here's to Mr. Firth Drink her down etc.
Thanks for all this joy and mirth Drink her down etc.
Heres to Bride and Groom Drink her down
May they ne'er know any gloom.

The ceremonys o'er let the bells ring loud
Joy is to the fore--Merry is the crowd
Bride and Groom three cheers
Gladness be your lot
Far away be tears and forget us not.

Wedding bells, wedding bells ringing all the day
Wedding bells, wedding bells hear their joyful lay
Wedding bells, wedding bells ringing all the day
Wedding bells, wedding bells ring through life's long way

We've been travling up the railroad all this weary way
We've been travling up the railroad to see the Bride to-day
See, Oh see, the couple beaming--May their joy be long
Happiness be theirs forever--Our blessing through this song.

This good old autumn day--This good old autumn day
Gathered here at Saranac to see the Bride away
We've come from far to wish her joy and that's no idle lay
Gathered here at Saranac on this their wedding day.

The time has come to leave us
This parting greatly grieves us
You go where love has called you
We pray all joy before you
Farewell, farewell our own true friends
Farewell, farewell our own true friends.

HOBBLE GOBBLE ---- RAZZLE DAZZLE
ALL ABOARD
MR. AND MRS. A. H. HORD.

266

Chapter 34

Boat Races and Such on the Saranacs

Although regattas and other entertaining events traditionally rang down the seasonal curtain on both the larger Saranacs, the following report, supplied by Bill Hord, furnishes the results of the nautical extravaganza held on August 19, 1911 on Upper Saranac.

Not so incidentally, Bill also was the source of the information about his grandfather, Frank J. Firth, and the marriage of his (Bill's) parents, as well as providing most of the photos in the preceding chapter.

The "Eagle's" Great Leap

"Mr. Graves threw the full power of his engines, which are said to develop about 250 horse, into the task and the "Eagle" made a great leap to the right missing the "Perhaps" by a short foot. Instantly the "Eagle" straightened in the course and shot away down the lake. The other boats got under way at the same time and for a few moments the spectators saw four powerful boats abreast, cutting and dashing Saranac's waters into the fury of a hundred storms. While the "Ketchup," the "Palmer Singer" and the "Perhaps" dug into the water and covered their drivers with foam, the "Eagle" lifted and, under the tremendous energy of her great horse-power, darted to the front and gained a positive lead.

In the first mile, ending at Ward's point, the "Eagle" had gained 500 feet over the "Ketchup," her most dangerous rival. Mr. Graves smiled, signaled to his engineman and the latter cut down the power of the engines. At no time again in the race were the "Eagle's" engines called upon to do their utmost and the "Eagle" settled down to calmly negotiate the many turns. The "Eagle," however, made the first round at the rate of 35 miles an hour. Her speed was gradually diminished as the sun went down and the light faded from the course. She made a fine sprint at home stretch and was a mile ahead of the "Ketchup" at the finish. When he stepped from his boat, Mr. Graves received an ovation for his splendid exhibition.

The "Ketchup" and the "Palmer Singer" were both disqualified for fouling buoys and the "Perhaps" was awarded second place.

The Guides' Race

R. Shean won the guides' race handily and carried off $25 for his effort. The start of this race was on the beach at Saranac Inn and the course included a turn around Goose Island. H. Sweeney started to go the wrong way around the island and this may have cost him the race. He finished second.

In the burling contest Guy Dennicore of Tupper Lake rolled his rival, Paul Marlow, off the log twice. Dennicore got the first fall, Marlow the second and Dennicore the next after some very fast foot-work. The winner got $25 and the second man $10.

A greased pole contest for a purse of $25 went to Marlow. This followed a struggle between guests and campers which had been won by Douglass Blagden.

Probably the Way "The Eagle" Flew

Saranac Inn Dock on Regatta Day

Douglass Blagden's "Albatross" Winner 8/10/07

Frank Firth's "Nan" 8/10/07

Wide-Open Inboards on The Lower Saranac

The summaries follow:

Sailing Race — Douglass Blagden, first; S. M. Colgate, second; Joseph Lewis, third.

50-Yard Swim — R. H. Johnson, Jr., first; T. V. Stillwell, second; J. T. Thayer, third.

20-Yard Swim — Duncan Graves, first; Junior Benning, second.

Diving Contest — J. T. Stillwell, first; R. H. Johnson and Calvert Holt tied for second place.

Obstacle Race — Douglass Blagden, first; S. S. Large, second; Francis N. Bangs, third.

Hand-Paddling, Canoe Race — (Doubles) — R. H. Johnson and Donald Blagden, first; the Messrs. Thayer, second; Holt and Stillwell, third.

Tub Race — Donald Blagden, first.

Tub Race, for Girls — Katherine Bulkley, first; Sally Humason, second.

Burling Contest — Guy Dennicore, first; Paul Marlow, second.

Greased Pole Contest — Paul Marlow, first; Sam Shaw, second.

Greased Pole Contest for Guests and Campers — Douglass Blagden, first; Calvert Holt, second.

Tilting Contest — won by S. S. Large and J. T. Thayer.

Guides' Race — R. Shean, first; H. Sweeney, second; Thomas McDonald, third.

Mixed Double Boat Race with Coxswain — Miss Ina Wincherly and LeRoy C. Lane, Mr. Cameron, Coxswain, first; Miss Evelyn Holt and Calvert Holt, J. A. Brooks, Coxswain, second.

Two-Paddle Canoe Race — Fox and Thayer, first; Fisk and Johnson, second.

Launch Race — A, Handicap Race — Won by Donald Blagden, in the "Petrol."

Launch Race — B, Handicap — Won by Donald Blagden in the "Brunnhilde."

Incidental Intelligence

(1) The Upper Saranac Lake Property Owners' Association was organized September 2, 1901 with E. P. Swenson as chairman and John G. Agar, secretary.

(2) The Guidehouse Library at Saranac Inn was started September 3, 1901.

(3) Saranac Inn Post Office was renamed Upper Saranac Post Office October 30, 1906.

(4) How to Cook a Loon: Cook the bird in water for 12 hours. At night pour off the water and cook the loon overnight. In the morning toss in a sizeable piece of grindstone. When you can stick a fork into the stone, you'll know that the loon is ready to be eaten.

Memories of a Classic Regatta

The following article by Bill McLaughlin, clever columnist and good friend, is a welcome and appropriate tribute to an annual tradition that enlivened the vacation scene

"Adios II" on Lower Saranac in 1922 Race (Kollecker photo)

on Lower Saranac but is now only a pleasant and lingering memory for many area and Summer residents.

"One of the more sparkling nautical Adirondack extravaganzas now relegated to the discard was the Saranac Lake Boat and Waterways annual Summer's end regatta.

It gained peak momentum in the years following World War I and signified the closing of the vacation season on Lower Saranac Lake.

Classic inboards belonging to the various camps were pitted against each other in handicap races over a 6 mile course and rivalry was extremely keen . . . so keen in fact that South Adirondack challengers began to look forward to the Saranac Lake Regatta with competitive zeal in hopes that they could crown a champion from outside.

The regatta was widely publicized around the state as early as 1922 with the dominant figure John I. Kane, whose mastery of his boat "Adios II" over the 6 mile course established him as the favorite for several years.

Adios II, a 22 foot 2000 pound Fay-Bowen with long slim lines, gave competitors anywhere from 2 to 4 minute handicap allowances and was still able to come in first under the wire.

In the first years two boats that challenged with perennial optimism were E. L. Gray's "Let-er Go" and "Muguet" owned by Mrs. C. M. Hyde and driven by C. C. Harris. These boats were constantly in danger of collision as they jockeyed at high speed for the inside corner advantage.

Outboards were also vying for regatta honors at a mile and two miles. Dorothy Sim-

"Adios II" with Mrs. J. C. Kane, Pilot and Mrs. Charles C. Harris (Kollecker photo)

"The Poker Dot", Mrs. Charles C. Harris, Pilot

mons' "Poker Dot;" "Chief Elto," owned by Leo Maas and Rev. E. P. Miller's "Louise" usually fought for honors against Selwyn Wood's "Skip" or John A. Galloway's "Balbridge."

Over a period of time John A. Galloway, who ran the Chevrolet agency, became enamored of the bigger inboards and gradually emerged as the pioneer promoter of hydroplane racing on local waters.

Whether he had smelled enough exhaust as an also-ran in the outboard classes or simply had a yen for power and lightning speed can only be surmised but by the year 1925 John A. Galloway was becoming famous throughout the state for his performances in a big inboard christened "Miss Chevy."

Commodore Charles Harris and Rear Commodore Matt Davis usually laid out the official regatta course so that it would be completely visible from any point in the vicinity of the Algonquin landing or the Crescent Bay boathouses.

Others besides Galloway were seeking regatta honors in Saranac Lake. Outstanding contenders were "Oh Boy," a Baker and Hill entry; "Tinker Bell," owned and driven by D. C. Arnold; and "Wisp," another Baker-Hill hopeful.

By that time Mrs. C. M. Hyde had added a second "Muguet," christened "Muguet II," to her stable of inboards but was running consistent thirds and fourths in spite of added mechanical innovations.

"Hoodoo," a crowd-pleaser driven by C. J. Swain, Jr., was always a threat but it wasn't until the sudden appearance of "Sally Waters" on August 15th, 1927 that inboard racing really became the showcase event of the northern Lake Country.

"Sally Waters" was Galloway's answer to second and third place finishes. She boasted a 151 cubic inch displacement engine in a hull of the newest hydroplane design. She won easily at Tupper Lake on August 25th against boats from Quebec, Ontario and New York State racing centers.

The engine was broken in slowly to prevent piston damage and eventually the speedy craft was taking every cup and crown in sight. Galloway was selling Chevrolets as fast as they arrived from the factory with the publicity generated by "Miss Chevy" bolstered by the outstanding performances of "Sally Waters."

Galloway then groomed his daughter Hope for additional family honors and she soon had her own boat, "Happy Days," roaring around the lake.

A strong nucleus of local promoters had already laid plans for an officially sponsored Adirondack Racing circuit. They included George Billings, H. W. Lockwood, Freeman and Frank Baker, Livingston Chapman, E. L. Gray, W. G. Distin, C. J. Ayres, R. W. Steel and W. H. Pilcher. All of them exerted influence to set the Saranacs apart as special inboard racing waters.

Eventually the clear dominance of the hydroplanes and the phasing out of the Fay-Bowens terminated the regatta on Lower Saranac but the memory is still strong among boating enthusiasts who lived through that special era."

Dr. Albert Einstein on Lower Saranac Lake 1936

Sailboat Race on Lower Saranac Lake c. 1920 (Kollecker photo)

Chapter 35

La Jeunesse, Premier Boys' Camp and the Blagdens

"An institution is but the lengthened shadow of a single man." That perceptive observation by R. W. Emerson represents a valid assessment of the influence of Henry H. Blagden, the founder and guiding force behind one of the nation's most successful summer camps — La Jeunesse. Located on Fish Creek Ponds off Upper Saranac Lake, this exceptional "foundry," as the owner aptly called it, started slowly in 1916, gained momentum rapidly and flourished until 1954 when, for health reasons the dominant factor decided to retire. However, the story of the intervening thirty-eight years is particularly significant because of the indelible and immeasurable impression the camp made on well over 2,000 discerning adolescents from some of America's most influential families.

Henry Harrison, or Hank as he insisted on being called — even by the boys and without an iota of disrespect — was one of five sons of Thomas Blagden, whose extensive holdings on the northwest shore of Upper Saranac dated back to the earliest years of the Prospect House, later known as Saranac Inn.

Born in Washington in 1853 to a family which gave Rock Creek Park to the capital city, the elder Blagden made his first trip to the Adirondacks in 1870, when Ed. Derby was manager of Prospect House. Feeling a strong affinity for the alluring region he shortly afterward built "Camp Alpha," (also called Camp Sunrise) near the Inn, more widely renowned twenty years later as the President's Cottage because Grover Cleveland honeymooned there. More recently known as "The Cabin" this cottage is now the property of Mrs. Frederick W. Lincoln.

Subsequently Mr. Blagden built "Camp of the Winds," now owned by George Bissell, Jr.; still later, to provide room for his expanding family, he put up "Deerwood" and "Land's End."

Another smaller Blagden camp of that period was labeled "Sunset," on Back Bay, formerly the property of Littman, who once owned the Golf Course.

The last of his camps, aptly named "Omega" was where, aged 85, he died of a heart attack 10/3/38. . . .

Like father, like son is a quotation that exacts a certain degree of credibility and is certainly applicable to the males named Blagden. Augustus, during a lifetime that lasted eighty years, became, in turn and sometimes simultaneously, the president of numerous national corporations, the last being an eight-year tenure at The Federal Machine and Welding Co. of Warren, Ohio. Ben, another son, headed The Blagden Construction Co. which built among others "Beaverwood" and Rockefeller's "Camp Wonundra" on Whitney Point. Donald and Thomas Jr. were both successful corporation executives. All five sons are no longer in the land of the living but their descendants, still yielding to the potent spell of the Saranacs that first affected their grandfather, consider that section to be very special country indeed.

Although each of his four brothers was influential in his own way, the consensus is that

Thomas Blagden and Sons. From left to right: Augustus S., Benjamin D.S., Donald P., Henry H., Thomas Jr. & Thomas Blagden Sr.

the personality of Henry, or Hank the preferable greeting, undoubtedly made the profoundest and most significant impression. Everyone who ever knew him for an appreciable length of time agreed that he was their most unforgettable character. The story of La Jeunesse, his achievement, provides remarkable evidence that this was an exceptional individual. And since such successes or accomplishments don't just happen there has to be a fascinating story.

In 1940 Sam Bodine, the editor of "Smoke," the La Jeunesse "Old Timers Association" newsletter, prevailed upon its founder, Hank, to write up the history of the camp. He complied and in the resulting chronicle furnished a detailed coverage of the camp's first quarter-century.

Asked how it all started he remarked: "To begin with I developed bad eyes at the age of 16 and from then on they proved to be quite a handicap. I was forced to give up Yale just as I was about to enter. Understandably this was a tremendous disappointment and I — though I hated to do so — was forced to give up all eye-work and devote years to outdoor life. This, by the way, turned out to be a blessing in disguise because it fitted me for my life's work.

"Eventually the doctor proclaimed me fit to resume a business life so I started as an apprentice in a relative's malleable iron firm. Everything went well until I worked up to a place of responsibility. Then I had a general break-down and my eyes, my weakest point, gave out again. Dr. De Schweinitz, of Philadelphia, examined them and said, 'You must take to the open again and this time take my advice and stay there for good!'

"My next step was to go to Pinehurst, N.C. to visit my old tutor and friend, Eric Parson, who was then starting a school there. The climate of that place was just what I needed and my health came back quickly. Living in the school with the boys became very interesting, and Eric Parson suggested my becoming a master. I had some camp equipment in the Adirondacks and Eric Parson had the experience and the boys. So we combined forces and organized the Adirondack Summer Camp of Pinehurst School. We put up a tent camp and a lean-to at the head of Big Square Pond in Township 20, Franklin County, N.Y. We opened camp July 1, 1916, with 15 boys, one guide, a cook and two monitors. That year a bad infantile paralysis epidemic broke out and no children were permitted to travel until freezing weather. In order to get away from everyone, we went to Fish Pond and camped there until about the 15th of October. I decided definitely at that time that I wanted to go on with boys' work and joined Eric Parson as a master in the Pinehurst School.

During this period of time, the First World War was on, and the U. S. was being more and more entangled. When the Spring of 1917 came I found that Uncle Sam could not take me on for fighting due to bad eyes, flat feet and what not. I definitely wanted to go on with a camp, and after looking over various sites, decided to buy the land where the camp is now located, on the north shore of the First Fish Creek Pond, in Township 20, Franklin Co., N.Y. I bought the property from Mrs. John Benham. Her husband had used the property for a hunting camp. The only means of getting to and from camp at that time was by a winding, rough country road, and by water from Saranac Inn. It was a common sight in those days to see the deer feeding around the shores of the pond, and beaver had their houses and dams on the Second Fish Creek Pond, while at the head of Big Square Pond one could see the beaver at work.

"Now that I definitely owned property for a camp, I was anxious to give it an Indian name. After an extensive search, with no luck — my mother suggested La Jeunesse, and that name stuck. The camp, as it stood, took care of the 1917 group which just filled one table in the dining-room shack. Due to the war, we had military training, which was a

Mr. and Mrs. Joseph Blagden at Beaverwood Cabin

grand success and the boys liked it. When 1918 rolled around the enrollment was more than doubled, so we enlarged the dining-room to take care of two more tables, and bought the Fortune camp, which stood where the Lodge now stands. The weather was cold and wet that summer and we found ourselves very much in need of an infirmary to isolate colds, etc. Jim Kellogg, the camp's first head monitor, quietly went to work and interested a number of boys' parents and they donated enough money to plan and start construction on the Ritz. This name was given the building because it was the only place boys could have a hot bath and sleep on a spring bed.

"The Spring of 1919 found us with our enrollment doubled again, which meant enlarging the dining-room and kitchen, and putting in running water, which was a great luxury and comfort. As each Summer came and went, it seemed to be better in some way than the last. My brother Ben came back from the War in 1920, and while he was waiting for a job, he worked with us, and we were very lucky to have him as he is a wonderful mechanic. While he was here in 1921 we built the large lean-to and the work-shop. The boys helped with the construction of both these buildings.

"During the Summer of 1922, we all gathered in the lean-to, and I was asked to tell a story. It was a special occasion and as we had an exceptionally congenial group, I somehow started dreaming out loud; and as I gazed into the fire, I mentioned how nice it would be if we could some day have a Lodge or Log-house of some sort, where we could get together in years to come. On the night of the banquet of that year, I gave out the cups and prizes and the boys made their speeches. After we were all through the program, the smallest boy in camp, "Baby" Grand, got up and made a very good speech, giving me an envelope saying 'Hank, this is something from us all to start a fund to build the Lodge you were talking about.' As along as I live I will never forget the thrill it gave me to receive that check for

278

$300 that these boys had raised to start the Lodge Fund. I was so choked up it was all I could do to make my speech. That was the beginning of the "Lodge Fund" which has carried on ever since.

"1926 found us wanting a tennis court, so in the spring of 1927 we cleared ground and built the first concrete court. Tennis proved very popular and in 1929, we had the very good fortune of having another court presented to us by Mr. Poyntell Johnston, of Wilmington. The tennis courts, by the way, were built partly on the Bliss property. Mr. and Mrs. C. N. Bliss, old friends, built their camp when their sons "Bobby" and "Tony" attended the camp. In the meantime, La Jeunesse was growing so, I made them an offer which they accepted. Every year, I paid something on account for the property. The property was only half paid for when on May 5, 1925, a wonderful letter came from Mrs. Bliss, deeding the property to me.

"Soon after that, the State Highway Route No. 10 went through — an advance of civilization that almost broke my heart. Next, the State Public Campground started. All this made the west end of the camp too public and noisy so I built a large storage shed along the west line and started the Stockade Trading Post to take care of the tourists' needs. This killed two birds with one stone by keeping the tourists out of camp and enabling us to get our gas and oil and food wholesale. The store also gives seven or eight young men employment for the Summer. The profits go into the Scholarship Fund.

"The next big improvement was installing electric lights in the dining-room, workshop, office and Ritz in 1930. When the Old Timers came and saw the lights they

"The Cabin", Also Known as "Camp Alpha" and "President's Cottage"

laughed and said we were getting soft. They did not realize what great fire insurance it was and what a lot of worry the electricity took away. With the old lanterns and lamps we never knew when a boy might upset one or the other. 1931 was a big year, too. Mrs. J. Lloyd Coates gave us two Old Town war canoes. It was a wonderful gift, and we have had no end of fun and healthy exercise with them. Each canoe holds twenty-two boys. This same year the old timers presented me with a fifty-pound Old Town canoe for tripping. I am still tripping with that canoe and it is one of my most valued possessions. During this year, too, Toto Walker, head monitor at that time, through his efforts raised money to build the splendid playground. It is the center of all sports, and I don't know what we would do without it.

"1932 proved to be the peak year for gifts, as an anonymous contribution added to the "Lodge Fund" built up by the boys and made it possible to build our "Air Castles," "the Lodge." This building provides a comfortable home for me and quarters for Old Timers when they return to visit the camp. "The Lodge" was completed during the Summer of 1933. At that time, I personally thought, "Well, this is the peak because I have a snug place to spend the last of my days, the boys can come up and visit me and everything will be fine." Little did I know what was around the corner in the line of a snow-capped peak. I always laughed at the idea when anyone spoke of a ring in my nose. It happened, however, in September, 1935, when Miss Mary Bradley, whom I had known from the time when she was a little girl, came up for a camping trip at Fish Pond. Yes, on that trip we found we were wasting time apart and we were married that November 28th — the biggest day of my life. Yes, sir! As the mountain climbers say "we topped out" and now I really know what it is to reach the peak. With Mary, that something that was needed came into La Jeunesse — the feminine touch.

"The Lodge"

280

La Jeunesse 1951

"The Old Timers presented the camp with another light Old Town canoe for tripping which we named the 1933. Frank Lloyd presented the camp with a light canoe which we named "Most Ponder." This canoe is used by the monitor in charge of the Most Ponds Club each Summer. I forgot to mention the fact that in 1932, out of a clear sky, a very handsome and wonderful R.C.A. radio came to me for Christmas with an engraved plate on it which reads "Henry H. Blagden, Christmas, 1932, from Anonymous Half-Bakes of La Jeunesse." The present was wonderful and still adds much to my happiness.

"So it goes on from year to year, right up to the present time 1940. During one of the first Summers of the camp, I was busy working with the boys organizing a camping trip, packing up, etc. When I was through, and the boys had gone off in the truck in a cloud of dust and yells for Fish Pond, to my great surprise I saw seated on the steps a man I had worked with in the iron business, so I greeted him and we sat down for a talk. He said to me, 'Blagden, I envy you this life, because you are doing such a worthwhile work. As I sat here watching you, I said to myself there is the same man I saw last in an iron foundry moulding iron. Now he is moulding lives.' Having him say that made me think and realize, more than I ever had, what I was doing and ever since then I have called my camp "my foundry." I have stuck to one ideal formula in the mixture of iron and steel we have been turning out, and I am happy to say I am now seeing very good results. Each year, I take in as many boys who have not the necessary cash to take them to camp, as the camp can afford, and mix them with the boys who have everything. For the former, the camp is a great experience as a general rule and their enthusiasm and interest carries the boys who have everything and are inclined to be lackadaisical, along with giving them that something they need. Mixing this way, their friendships grow and they help each other all the way through life. I am seeing this work out now and it is a great satisfaction to me. My greatest satisfaction, however, as I review the years of La Jeunesse history, is the wonderful friends I have made in you boys. You have paid me back "tout-a-fait" for the effort I have expended in these twenty-five years that have passed so quickly. It is thrilling to find ourselves to be such

"Hank" and Mary Blagden at Fish Pond Nov. 1955
(Bodine photo)

The Harry Blagden Family (Christmas card)

a large, strong, healthy, and enthusiastic family. My dream now is to live long enough to see you boys so strongly organized that this wonderful, useful spirit will carry on indefinitely, and that your sons will have the same enthusiastic loyalty for La Jeunesse that you have.

"In closing it is interesting to note that we find ourselves looking at a barometer that says we must prepare for war, as that was the reading of the glass when we started. We are planning to have military training in 1941, as we did in 1917, and I am all for it, as I think we all need more discipline to awaken us to the responsibility of life. For the past ten years I have noticed a growing tendency to a lack of responsibility. I therefore think that a definite tightening up with more discipline and military training will help us all."

That, then, is the story of the first twenty-five years at La Jeunesse. The next fourteen followed very much in the same pattern even with a World War II interruption. The issues of "Smoke," the camp newsletter, carried stirring accounts of the activities — and many instances of heroism by the "Old Timers" in the several branches of military service. Moreover, the ranks of the "graduates" were diminished appreciably by the twelve who made the supreme sacrifice.

Just how much of a sacrifice it was was later recounted by Rupert Brooke, who also did not survive the conflict, in this passage from one of that tragic era's most eloquent poems:

"These laid the world away; poured out the red

Sweet wine of youth, gave up the years to be

Of work and joy, and that unhoped serene

That men call age; and those who would have been —

Their sons — they gave their immortality."

Most interesting and poignant of all were the many letters to Hank from those in uniform who invariably credited their very survival to the rigorous and vigorous training and experience provided by the camp program. Such testimonials were particularly pleasing to Hank because they epitomized incontestably the values which he had engendered into the grateful human products of his unique "foundry."

After Hank's stroke and heart attacks which sidelined him permanently, the camp operated on a reduced scale through two more seasons before it closed down for good in 1956.

Henry Harrison Blagden's — Hank's physical existence ended but his spiritual legacy still flourishes evergreen in the memories of those who were fortunate enough to have known him. Truly a most memorable man — a statement undoubtedly true of all the Blagden men but particularly applicable to the founder and main motivating force behind La Jeunesse.

"Camp of the Winds"

Chapter 36

Deerwood

The Adirondack region boasts many fine estates but, as in any locality, only a few can be so outstanding as to be considered showplaces. Deerwood was one of those lavish camps which lined the shores of Upper Saranac and helped make the region so special.

This impressive enclave was the second such built by Thomas Blagden, who had also owned neighboring "Camp of the Winds," constructed apparently in the 1880's and now the property of the Bissell family.

Research indicates that Deerwood went on the tax rolls in 1910 so logically it had been constructed just previously on a forty-acre property, much of it heavily wooded. Thirty-five of those acres were used as a deer park for a large herd of those animals which necessitated that the area be completely fenced. For guests at nearby Saranac Inn these graceful animals represented a fascinating phase of the Summer scene.

The three-story main building erected on a stone foundation, an unusual feature in itself, was planned for year-round use and occupied for several years by one of its owners in all seasons. Another feature was the abundance of picture windows which framed the ever-changing vistas of forest, lake and background mountains.

Other interesting but smaller log structures on the property were "the Lodge," located at the entrance, and the "Cabin in the Woods," which served as Blagden's escape hatch. Furnished with comfortably appropriate yet rustic carpentry creations and enhanced by a superb collection of trophies and sportsmen's paraphernalia, this was the favorite haunt of the succession of owners.

The three-story boathouse had a lounge or ballroom on the second floor. This well-equipped room had a large brick fireplace and windows on all four sides.

A wide porch or veranda extended entirely around the four-slip building. On the third floor was a guests' dormitory, large enough to accommodate six persons.

So far I have been unable to find out whether there was an intermediate owner between Thomas Blagden, Sr. and John L. Severance, the Cleveland philanthropist who endowed the Cleveland Symphony Orchestra and built Severance Hall to house that famous organization.

The noted benefactor's interest in music undoubtedly was the dominant factor in the establishment of Deerwood — Adirondack Music Center in 1941. According to one of its early brochures "At Deerwood talented students and a distinguished faculty are brought together in this loveliest of natural settings. Talent and personality can develop here in an atmosphere of artistry, sympathetic understanding and zestful living.

"A season at Deerwood means living a life of music study in the great outdoors, with companions from all over the country. . . . Orchestra and choir rehearsals, private lessons with famous teachers, music history, appreciation and theory classes, recording hours,

Thomas Blagden in Whimsical Mood

A Blagden Picnic
Back: Miss Sara H. Dorsey and Miss Mary L. Lloyd. Front: Mrs. Joseph Washington and Mr. and Mrs. Thomas Blagden.

286   *(Frank J. Firth photo)*

Aerial View of "Deerwood"

"Deerwood" — Adirondack Music Center

drama rehearsals, dance rehearsals, preparations for recitals and concerts — all combine to form a musical life stimulating beyond words.

"In one Summer at Deerwood you will accomplish the equivalent of at least two years of high school or general college music. You will take home with you wonderful memories of friendships and experiences that last a lifetime. It is unusual indeed when a Deerwood student does not declare his Summer 'the happiest one of my life!'"

While the Deerwood program was eminently successful and provided incalculable cultural entertainment for the entire North Country, it nevertheless was not altogether a financial success. Very few artistic individuals also possess pecuniary acumen and the administrators of Deerwood were no exception. As a result the place went into heavy debt — so much so that at the request of its numerous creditors there was a sheriff's auction which attracted almost as many people as Charlie Vosburgh's extravaganzas at Saranac Inn.

After the contents had been auctioned by Girard the buildings were sold to Alfred and George Bissell, who hired a Malone salvager named Wood, who demolished the structures in piece-meal fashion, as requested by interested buyers, over a two-year period — 1958-9.

Very few traces are left to indicate that an imposing private camp, later converted into an internationally known music center, ever occupied the premises. It now lives only in the memories of the many students who summered there on the spacious shores of the Upper Saranac.

Boathouse at "Deerwood"

Chapter 37

The Psychology of the Lost

Although what follows does not deal directly with the Saranacs, it nevertheless puts into focus many situations and tragic incidents that could very easily — and undoubtedly did happen more often than we would like to think about — here and everywhere in the wild country.

As the curtain-raiser for these dramas there's a story of a stranger far up in the Canadian bush who casually remarked to his guide: "All the Indians around here Ojibwa, I understand."

"All but a few," replied the guide. "There is, however, another tribe too — the Hellarwes."

"Hellarwe?" repeated the stranger. "Never heard of them."

"They're nomadic people," the native explained. "On the move constantly. Never stop more than a day or two at any one spot. And each time they get ready to move on, the chief of the tribe climbs the highest tree. Then he shades his eyes with his left hand while hanging onto the tree with his right and peers intently out over the landscape in every direction. Finally and querulously he shouts down to the rest of his people: 'Anybody down there know *where* the *Hellarwe??*' "

Then there's the mossy chestnut which sums up succinctly the situation in which many of us — at any rate those who have spent considerable time in bush — in wilderness country — have found ourselves more often than we'd care to admit. Like the befuddled Redskin — "Injun not lost! Wigwam/tepee lost!" And by such easy rationalization a lot of self-respect is thereby salvaged. "Me *lost?* Nope, just temporarily confused!" is after all just a euphemism whose purpose is hopefully to dispel the knowing, sometimes sympathetic but more often incredulous looks on the faces of those who are aware of the predicament. Moreover, anyone who states emphatically and straight-facedly that he or she has never been lost or even slightly bewildered in the woods is a downright terradiddler, which translated means low-grade liar.

Henry Abbott, in his excellent Birchbark book which he called *Psychology of the Lost**, which title I borrowed for this article, opened his small opus with a story about a drunken man who thought himself lost while actually under a tree right in front of his own house. A patrolling policeman found him sitting morosely there, his arms wrapped around the tree, hat and coat on the ground nearby, and muttering away to himself, "Lost! Lost in an impenetrable forest!" The obliging officer recognized the besotted one, steered him to his own front door (less than thirty yards away), located the keyhole for him — and then left him to the "tender" ministrations of his impatient, much-enduring spouse.

Nor is it essential that an individual get spiffed, crocked or plastered as a prerequisite to becoming lost. Sane and sober people have also lost their lives in the forest. Abbott also

---

* Abbott, Henry *Psychology of the Lost* New York: 1930 privately printed

Easy Country to Get Lost In

related the plight of a man who got caught in a blizzard on Orange Mountain in New Jersey, lost his way in the woods and died from fear and exposure on a spot that in daylight was well within sight of his own home. A stone monument memorialized the tragic incident.

Countless lives have of course been lost in raging snowstorms when all familiar landmarks have been obliterated, but many non-fatal though nevertheless nerve-wracking experiences have been caused by heavy fogs on Adirondack lakes. Moreover, the body of water need not necessarily be large. In fact two men found that it could provide them with all the bewilderment they wanted and then some. Even though they had fished there for many years and were therefore well acquainted with the place, their situation was complicated by the fact that the shoreline was densely wooded and hilly and there were many jagged rocks and shoals that could stove in the guideboat. The fog blanket became so thick that the men couldn't even see each other, so even when they reached shore they were unable to locate anything that might set them on the right course. Since neither had a compass all they could do was grope around in the whiteout and hope to land at a recognizable spot.

But they were not that lucky and kept traveling around in circles until nearly daylight, when the fog finally lifted enough for them to get their bearings. But they were on the water nearly seven hours! Almost unbelievable but nevertheless true, that such a thing could happen on South Pond near Long Lake!

Todd's *Long Lake** contains two accounts of lost men that are just about as vivid and moving — tearjerkers in fact — as anything I have ever read. They are excellent examples of what it meant by stream of consciousness reporting. As Todd stated: "The sensation of being lost in a vast forest is horrific beyond description. No imagination can paint the bewilderment and terrific sensation which you feel when you are alone and fairly lost. I ex-

---

* Todd, John *Long Lake*, Pittsfield, Mass., E. P. Little 1845

perienced them once and can say that it is as near derangement as can be — if there is indeed any difference.

"I remarked that only one of the settlers had found a grave — that is still true, and yet there are two graves there. One containing the daughter, and the other the brother of one of the settlers who had come in to visit his brother. After being there several days he went out on the mountain west of the Lake, all of which are covered with mighty forests. He took a dog with him. The night came and he returned not; the next day and no tidings of him. They then began to search for him. They fired guns, kindled fires and searched but to no good end. At the close of the third day the dog returned home with his throat partly cut. They then understood the whole. The poor man was lost — was starving — and had tried to kill the dog for food; but the dog was too strong for the starving man and had got away alive. They continued the search day after day but with no success. The ice covered the Lake and Winter came on — went past — and Spring returned. Then they found the lost brother. He had wandered no one knows whither, and had just enough strength to drag himself down to the Lake, where he lay down and died of starvation and exposure (hypothermia). . . .

"Nor is it strange. Once lost in that forest I should have very little expectation of ever finding my way out. Even when we were in the wilderness this Summer (1843), a man was

Part of a Search Party

lost and was dying of hunger within four miles of us. His body has since been found. The reason is obvious. When you have once entered the wilderness there is no such thing as seeing anything for 30 rods before you. A mountain might be just by you yet it could not be seen, and after you are confused there is no recovering self-possession. No one should venture beyond Long Lake — or any Adirondack lake for that matter — without an experienced guide.

". . . Some years since, Will Wilson, our guide was trapping on the headwaters of the Beaver River. The ice had broken up so that his little bark canoe would float. Just at night as he was pushing his boat into a small pond, seeking beaver signs, he heard something walking in the water. By the heavy splashings he concluded that it must be a moose. The rifle was carefully laid before him and his noiseless paddle shot his light boat speedily forward.

"As he rounded a point he saw two white legs. A few more strokes and the human form was seen! It was a man without any hat — his clothes nearly gone — his legs lacerated and naked, while he kept striding on in the icy water. He was muttering to himself. As the silent boat shot on it came up to him before Wilson spoke. The moment he did, the wild eyes and the startled look showed that the man was deranged. By the kindest tones of voice — and few voices were ever softer than his — he coaxed the poor emaciated creature to pause, and finally to get into the boat. Wilson then asked permission to camp in his company. The poor creature, as it afterward appeared, had been out and lost 13 days. He had gone out with his gun and dog to hunt, near his father's house. He had got lost — had lost his gun — had killed and eaten his dog — all save a few bones which he still had in his bosom, and which he gnawed more or less. But great kindness and effort he was made to reveal the place of his home. It was far down on the Black River.

"He was a young man of liberal education and fine promise. I believe he once before had a turn of being mentally deranged. But on the morning of leaving his home he was perfectly sane. With great skill he was made to believe that our guide was going to the place where he lived and, as a particular favor, desired his company. This the man promised. So he ate and camped and traveled with his new friend. When he got near his father's house he said, 'That is the house!' — and then put off at a speed almost too great to be followed. When he reached his home and the mother saw him, how she rushed to him and lifted up her voice and wept!! How she poured out her heart in thanksgiving, praise and tears!

"It seemed that there were 50 men in the wilderness seeking him but they had not met him. What a picture for a painter! The father, pale and haggard, was just dismounting from a fruitless search. The emaciated son in his rags, the mother in her tears. The hunter-guide with his long unshaven beard, swarthy appearance, hunter's dress but with a heart that made him weep for joy that he had saved a human life and restored to his family the son who was lost. He told the story with entire simplicity as if it were nothing that he did — and he took no reward for his deed. He spoke of it as a pleasant remembrance and I tried not to let him see the tears I dropped into Tupper Lake as I sat paddling and listening to his story. Was I mistaken in supposing that the reader would thank me for preserving it?". . .

The purpose of these incidents is not to show how stupid people can be but rather to indicate how easy it is for the average, reasonably intelligent individual to lose his bearings and go astray — become écarté, as the French term it. But the really regrettable factor is that much of the suffering and tragedy could have been prevented if the people concerned had known even a little about psychology and could counteract those first overwhelming feelings of fear.

Some people who suddenly realize that they are lost allow themselves to panic and

Lost In a Snowstorm

quarrel with the compass. An example of the latter was told to Stoddard[*] by one of the
Negroes who went to North Elba after the colonizing effort by Gerrit Smith and John
Brown had failed. "The ole fella went out huntin' one day in Wintah an' got lost in the
woods. He had a compass with him but when they found him they found whar he had sot
down on a log an' picked his compass to pieces. Den he sot on the log 'til he froze to
death!" . . .

It is a well-known fact that people unused to the woods will become so completely
befuddled and "turned around" that they will be certain that their compass points the
wrong direction. They will even distrust the sun itself if it happens to be in a different position from where they think it ought to be. Moreover, many rattled people forget that during the early afternoon — between two and four — the sun is in the South and not in the
West.

Even though the compass itself can become notoriously inaccurate near iron deposits,
or even metallic objects such as knives and axe blades, it is under most other conditions
reasonably dependable.

Many able-bodied individuals have lost their lives unnecessarily by yielding to instant
fear. Even though well-armed and supplied with enough food to last a week, too many inexperienced hunters have lost their cool and self-control so completely that they have run
headlong through thickets and swamps until they dropped dead from fright, hunger, ex-

* Stoddard, S. R. *Old Times in the Adirondacks* Saranac Lake, N.Y. Adirondack Yesteryears Inc., 1971 and originally appeared in his
Adirondacks Illustrated Guidebook.

haustion and exposure. What should have been only an exciting adventure all too often ends in needless tragedy.

Nessmuk (George Washington Sears) repeated in his classic *Woodcraft* the well-authenticated story of an Oswegatchie guide who perished the same way. Even guides are not infallible and many of them, although they would be very reluctant to admit it, have been in the same predicament themselves — and probably more than once, especially in a strange region.

Therefore, if you are traveling through a dense woods on a cloudy day and suddenly see the sun break through in the Northwest about noon, there is no reason to become frightened. All is not lost, the end is not near; you have just become mixed up. Although you meant to be heading south you have veered away to the northwest. What happened was that you had unintentionally started swinging southwest, then west and then northwest. If you had kept on until you were heading north you could then rectify your course by going straight south. Still confused? So am I!

Constant reference to the compass will correct the natural tendency to deviate from a straight course — especially when the person convinces himself that he is indeed lost. Why that instinctive deviation is almost always to the right is hard to understand. The most logical answer is that most people take a longer step with the right foot than with the left. To compensate for that tendency the bewildered individual will unconsciously take a bigger stride with his left foot. At least that's one theory that has been advanced.

In Donald MacKay's *The Lumberjacks* the following incident rather wryly describes an unusual but certainly understandable dilemma.

"The trouble with people is that they panic. You could go a long time — a week — or more — without food, if you just sat down and made a fire and thought things out.

"A timber cruiser once found a lumberjack lost in the snowy New Brunswick woods. He asked him, 'When you found out that you were lost, why didn't you follow your backtracks out?'

"The man replied, 'Goddammit! I've been hunting for them all day!'

"So the cruiser took him by the shoulder, turned him around and said, 'There they are, damn it; they must have been following you all day!' "

F. H. Buzzacott provided some very sensible advice in his frequently reprinted *Complete American and Canadian Sportsman's Encyclopedia of Valuable Instructions*: "When you realize that you have lost your way, don't lose your head — keep cool and try not to let your brains get into your feet. By this is meant don't run around and make things worse by tiring yourself out. Sit down and think. Cool off, then climb a tree or hill and try to locate some familiar object so you can retrace your steps. When it gets dark build a rousing campfire. Ten to one you will have been missed by then (if you had told someone your plans) and your fire will be seen by the searchers.

"Give distress signals — three blasts on a whistle, three spaced shots — but don't waste all your ammunition. Build a shelter, keep the fire going for warmth and assurance, keep a reasonably clear head and make the best of the situation. Chances are that a night's rest if not sleep will enable you to get an early start and a safe trip back on your own. If not, by staying put, the search and rescue party will appreciate the shorter, less burdensome mission."

In retrospect I can honestly say that nearly all my own so-called adventures and misadventures were not really so venturesome or accidental — they were actually the results of carelessness and poor planning.

Very likely others who have been lost in the woods and lived to tell the story of their mishaps will agree.

294

Chapter 38

Seneca Ray Stoddard, Versatile Camera — Artist

Three of the greatest 19th Century photographers, pioneers in their craft, were born in the Northern New York — Brady, Jackson and Stoddard. One of them, Seneca Ray Stoddard, bequeathed to following generations a priceless treasure — the photographic record of the Adirondacks, its people and its customs.

Two generations ago the name of Seneca Ray Stoddard was recognized throughout the East as synonymous with superb outdoor photography. Testimonials from nearly every reputable writer, traveler and authority on the Adirondacks proclaimed in print that his illustrated guidebooks and maps were the most popular and reliable such sources available. Audiences in cities all over the country heard his lectures, illustrated by his unique and carefully tinted stereopticon slides.

He was also a talented artist with ink, oils and watercolors; an inventor; a poet; a writer and one of the most widely-traveled men of his time (1844-1917).

Unlike his more aggressive, publicity-minded contemporaries — W. H. H. Murray, Verplanck Colvin and Harry V. Radford — Stoddard never sought success quite as ardently or as persistently as they. Therefore, his importance was almost entirely either overlooked or undervalued by the historians of his time.

The older generation of campers on Adirondack lakes have always valued their Stoddard photos, albums, guidebooks and maps.

The features of such famous guides as Alvah Dunning, Paul Smith, Bill Nye, Mitchell Sabattis and Old Mountain Phelps were perpetuated in oft-reprinted pictures by Stoddard. The patriarch of Keene Valley, Orson (Old Mountain) Phelps, depended on the sale of Stoddard's likenesses of him for a considerable part of his livelihood in his declining years. He photographed the steamboats and guideboats on the lakes and rivers, the ruins of the old forts, the crowded stagecoaches, the toll gates, the survey parties, the lumbermen, the clothing worn, the architecture and furnishings of the luxurious camps and posh hotels — even the musical instruments and the sporting equipment.

The numerous night scenes taken by Stoddard are of special interest. Most of these were taken by the intense light generated by magnesium flare powder, a technique that required considerable skill and practice and which occasionally resulted in injury, disfigurement or worse. Once such experience, while he was making a night study of the Washington Memorial Arch at the lower end of New York's Fifth Avenue, was nearly fatal for Stoddard.

Another remarkable night view, now considered a classic, was that of the Statue of Liberty. Its sculptor, Bartholdi, declared this was the only photograph which did it justice.

Among his more familiar nocturnal Adirondack masterpieces were the firelight scenes of the open camps at the Sagamore on Long Lake, the Antlers at Raquette Lake, Camp Phelps on Upper Ausable Lake; the perennially popular poker-playing guide scene, the

Female Golf Form Then and Now

Now

Running the Rapids Between Middle and Lower Saranac

Kiddies' Day at The Loon Lake House

297

party of hunters and their dangling deer, and the Colvin survey party at Long Lake in 1888.

They remind one of the work of another celebrated northern New Yorker, William H. Jackson of Peru, whose famed Western camera artistry bracketed him with Stoddard as being among the three best photographers of their time. Matthew Brady, of Civil War renown, born in Warren County, was the other member of this group.

Very little is known about Seneca Ray Stoddard's early life. He was born on May 13, 1844 in the Saratoga County hamlet of Wilton. His parents were Charles and Julia (Ray) Stoddard. The family lived on farms in several sections of this state before the father moved to Hartford, Michigan where, at the age of 50, he was killed by a falling tree.

Seneca Ray was largely self-taught.

Leaving home at the age of 16 he worked for the next four years, at the starting pay of $3.00 per week, painting numbers on freight cars and decorative scenes on the interior of passenger coaches. At twenty he moved to Glens Falls. His first pictures were small views and stereopticon scenes of the Hudson and the town.

He journeyed on foot, bicycle and train to Lake George, Luzerne, Ticonderoga, Crown Point and Lake Champlain. In the early 1860's he took pictures of Ausable Chasm.

Meanwhile Stoddard had started his guide book series; his first were of Saratoga Springs; then, from 1873-1877, he published annual revisions of his *Lake George-Luzerne-Schroon Lake* — and *The Adirondacks*. From 1878-1888 the title was changed to *Lake George and Lake Champlain*. The series called "The Adirondacks Illustrated" came out in 1873, following Stoddard's first trip through the mountain region with Charles Oblenis, his brother-in-law (The Professor of the series) as his companion. The series was revised and reprinted until 1914.

The incredibly industrious photographer also became a competent civil engineer under the tutelage of his half-uncle, Hiram Philo, a well-known Glens Falls surveyor. While he was writing his two sets of guidebooks, he was also busy making maps, first of Lake George, then of Lake Champlain and, still later, of the Adirondack area.

Undoubtedly the most useful map ever prepared by Stoddard was his Lake George hydrographic survey of 1906-08. This, reprinted in 1951, became almost indispensable for boatowners and fishermen.

The first of several such long trips away from his home base came in 1883. Having become a good canoeist by constant practice on Lake George, Stoddard and Charles Burchard, secretary of the American Canoe Association, started on the first leg of what became a five-stage cruise from the mouth of the Hudson river along the New England coast to the head of the Bay of Fundy.

In 1892 Stoddard went to Alaska with Burchard again as his companion.

Early in 1894 he traveled south to Florida, the Gulf States and Cuba; later that year he went across the continent and photographed the Bad Lands of Dakota, the Yellowstone Park, the cliff dwellings and the Grand Canyon in the Southwest, California's Yosemite Valley and the Pacific Northwest.

In 1895 he sailed to Bermuda, the Mediterranean countries, the Holy Land; then went north from Italy through Switzerland, France and home again from a British port.

In 1897 on board the "Ohio" he went to England, the Orkney, Faroe and Shetland Islands, Iceland, the North Cape, Norway, Denmark, Russia and Germany. Accounts of this and the preceding trip were published in profusely-illustrated volumes entitled *The Cruise of the Friesland* and *The Midnight Sun*.

His final European voyage was made in 1900.

Blue Mt. Lake Hotel

Prospect House, Blue Mt. Lake

"Homeward Bound" Lake George 1879

Seneca Ray Stoddard (1844-1917)

Each of these long journeys resulted in illustrated lectures. Although greatly impressed by Europe, Stoddard still considered American scenery the best and the most varied. As he often stated, the most satisfying vistas of them all were those to be found in his own Adirondack region.

His favorite and most popular lecture was called "The Hudson, from the Mountains to the Sea." Typical of audience reaction to this program was the account printed in the Mail and Express (New York) following a Chickering Hall appearance on April 25, 1893.

"Probably never before have such pictures been thrown upon a screen than those 250 marvelous delineations of Adirondack scenery and life. Nor ever were scenes more delightfully described than in his lecture, which corruscated with eloquence, poetry and wit.

"Mr. Stoddard took his audience through the wonderful Adirondack country. He took them into the forest's depths, across carries, into club preserves, up mountains and down rapids. He hunted with them, fished with them, introduced them to camp life, lumber and mining camps, to the noted guides."

"Through his maps, his guide books, his photographs and more recently his lectures, Mr. Stoddard has done more than any other man to popularize this marvelous region and to make its beauties and advantages known."

The most effective lecture on the Adirondacks was that given on February 26, 1892 in the Assembly Chamber of the State Legislature in Albany. Under the auspices of the Forest Commission, Stoddard had been invited to show the legislators and their guests the condition of things "up in the woods." The real purpose of the meeting was to obtain favorable action on pending legislation which would create the Adirondack Park.

A reporter for the *Argus* described the program as follows: "No similar event ever given in Albany has attracted the very general interest displayed in the lecture given last night by S. R. Stoddard, the famous Adirondack artist, who with a few words of explanation, gave a public exhibition of 225 colored stereopticon views. The lecture was exceedingly interesting, and among the large and representative audience present many assemblymen and senators were noted. . . .

"The 'drowned lands' of the Raquette River valley came in for particular attention because it showed the incalcuable damage done by the reckless damming of the streams by the lumbermen. What had once been one of the most beautiful valleys in the Adirondacks is now a scene of malodorous desolation. . . .

"Evidently the lawmakers who saw this program were greatly impressed by it, and it is hoped that it will have a salutary effect on the legislation which will be considered during this season."

The same lecture was repeated in most of the larger cities of the state. Then, on the following May 20th, the long-awaited law was passed. What Stoddard showed had its desired effect.

The Forest Commission, the Adirondack Park Association and various other organizations and individuals engaged in protecting the Wilderness were quick to acknowledge his valued services.

In 1905 Stoddard embarked upon another venture — publication of his *Northern Monthly*. This magazine was planned to continue some of the crusading work started by the youthful Harry V. Radford in *Woods and Waters*. The first issue of the *Monthly* came out in May, 1906.

The early copies of this full-sized magazine were full of Adirondack articles and his photographs. They contained powerful attacks against the despoliation of the mountains by the lumbering and power interests, against land grabs, pollution and corrupt politicians. He lashed out against lax enforcement on the game laws.

His special target was the needless and senseless slaughter of humans that cast its pall over every hunting season. It distressed him so that he even advocated hounding the deer, a method outlawed in 1902, if that type of hunting, which he deplored, would save the life of even one man.

Such outspoken opinions won the aging editor (then 64) few friends and many foes. The magazine became smaller in size as its circulation shrank. In September 1908, the publisher reluctantly printed the valedictory issue. He died in Glens Falls April 26, 1917.

Margaret Sidney, author of the *Three Little Peppers,* in her book *An Adirondack Cabin* used Stoddard's photographs as illustrations. In acknowledgement she wrote: "Mr. Stoddard, as is well known, has done more by his pictures and his pen than any other person to open up the great Adirondack wilderness to the notice of the public."

Adirondack Hunters

Wild Adirondack Game

Chapter 39

William Kollecker, Adirondack Photographer

Judged by the twin criteria of quantity and quality S. R. Stoddard was unquestionably the preeminent Adirondack photographer. However, there were several other camera artists whose work commanded attention and popularity. Among these were George Baldwin, Fred Hodges (my father-in-law), Irving Stedman — and William Kollecker. As far as local importance is concerned Kollecker was definitely one of the very best recorders of the passing scene and, as such, certainly rates much more than mere mention and a brief obituary. That recognition I consider to be not only overdue but an important item in my priority schedule.

Born in Brooklyn on April 15, 1879 Kollecker apparently came to the Saranac Lake area in Jan. 1896 for health reasons. Before coming he had been an employee of a Wall St. brokerage firm. A patient of Dr. E. L. Trudeau he worked for board and room at the Fletcher farm near Bloomingdale and also for a Summer as a bellhop at Mrs. Chase's Loon Lake House.

Although it has not been established exactly how and when his interest in photography started, it is known that he worked briefly in Lake Placid for a combine that called itself

Fletcher Farm, Bloomingdale, N.Y.

Mr. and Mrs. William F. Cheesman

Cheesman Store Interior, Kollecker Behind Counter

Kollecker in 1933

Kollecker Message on Lake Placid School Blackboard 1903

Hannah Clarke, The Teacher-Sweetheart Kollecker Never Forgot

Kaiser and Brownell. Henry J. Kaiser of course later achieved fame and fortune — understandably after his marriage to an heiress whom he had met at the Lake Placid Club — as the head of Kaiser Industries, manufacturers of cement, aluminum, steel, W.W. II Liberty ships and, for a short while, automobiles.

Kollecker's next employer was William F. Cheesman and the story of their meeting is rather interesting. One day in a Lake Placid barbershop Kollecker told the tonsorial expert that he was looking for work. Cheesman overheard, struck up a conversation with the attractive young fellow, found out that he had some photographic training and offered him a job in his own studio and store.

The relationship proved to be mutually advantageous for both parties because, and for Kollecker it served an even more important purpose — it probably saved his life. Mrs. Cheesman, a very motherly and compassionate woman, nursed him through his recurrent lapses of health, took him into their — the Cheesman family — and treated him like one of their own.

When the young man had recovered sufficiently and had acquired, with Mr. Cheesman's help, further photographic skill, Kollecker announced that he would like to go into business for himself in Saranac Lake. However, there was one major obstacle: he had no capital to start with. Obligingly, Cheesman advanced him $200.00 and Kollecker set up shop in a small store on Main Street in Saranac Lake in Nov. 1904.

At that time the photographers did not send away their negatives to be processed and printed but did all their own work. The resourceful Kollecker came up with an innovation that brought him almost overnight success. He conceived the idea that mounted Adirondack scenes would be greatly enhanced by the addition of an attached calendar. His creation went over with a proverbial bang and the young entrepreneur was well on his way to success.

In 1920, when business started to flourish, Kollecker moved next door, into larger quarters which were then occupied by Carey's Jewelry Store and are now the Saranac Lake Jewelers — 73 Main St.

The Kollecker Kodak and Gift Shop eventually became one of the largest of its kind in Northern New York, and its success enabled its owner to travel abroad as well as providing ample time to thoroughly document photographically the changing local scenes in prints that are of exceptional quality.

The Saranac Lake Winter Carnival edition of the *Adirondack Daily Enterprise,* dated February 4, 1915 paid verbal tribute to Kollecker who, over the years but not annually as some misinformed people maintain that the extravaganza has been held, turned out literally thousands of parade pictures. Headlined as Kollecker's Karnival Kodakery the encomium reads as follows:

"The enterprising work of W. F. Kollecker, the photographer, attracted much attention during the Carnival in Saranac Lake. Mr. Kollecker made over three hundred photos of the parade which opened the Carnival on Tuesday and had prints on sale that same evening. The photographs attracted instant attention and sold like hot cakes. His were the first on sale. Many of those that illustrate this issue of the *Enterprise* were made by him. They speak for themselves."

Since Kollecker never married and although he was thought to have had at least one brother and a sister, his lawyer, Bud Edelberg, was unable to locate either. The fact that he died on August 22, 1962, without leaving a will complicated the settlement of his estate. He was buried in the Cheesman lot in the North Elba cemetery.

The disposal problem was unfortunately settled. Many of his proof albums — the large

306

display items especially — were donated to the Saranac Lake Free Library but the bulk of the vast and impressive trove of prints and negatives of various sizes, the collection of black and white movie films and all the assortment of photographic paraphernalia had to be moved fast to make way for another occupant. Orders were given and the clearing-out process began. Dump trucks moved as close to the building as possible, and shovels were manned; Kollecker's memorabilia were tossed out the windows or chucked down the shute, higgeldy-piggeldy.

Some of it had already been taken to the dump before an enterprising young local resident went into action. Realizing the importance of the huge collection and its potential resale value he paid the obliging truckers a pittance a load for several loads of the valuable — to him but not to them — cargoes of so-called junk. And because of his fortuitous intervention, many other appreciators of first-rate photographs have been able to build up their own collections of prime vintage prints.

Moreover, the salvage action has helped round out the pictorial history of this incomparable region while, at the same time, reviving the fame — réchauffer la gloire the French call it — of a truly outstanding Adirondack camera artist.

The accompanying miscellany will provide visual proof of Kollecker's skill and sense of history. . . .

There is a lot more to the Kollecker story than the relatively short article just concluded, but the material which would justify more in-depth coverage was not readily available. However, recently, the wherewithal surfaced with the discovery and purchase of nineteen diaries, ledgers and other fascinating information which provide the necessary first-hand personal details and revelations to round out the picture.

Of particular importance are the diaries of the Hannah Clarke, the one great love of Kollecker's life, for 1904 — a climactic year in the lives of both because of its bittersweet blend of rapture and suffering.

Since Kollecker was so well-known in the area, this trove of memorabilia should not be withheld but told, nevertheless, in a straight forward manner which respects the personalities and reputations of the principals.

Serious consideration will be given to publishing a volume which will do justice to the memory and achievements of a remarkable man.

A Kollecker Miscellany

Mouth to Mouth Resuscitation

Four of a Kind: Riverside Hotel in Background

A Girl and Her Friends

Come A Runnin'

Cats Aren't the Only Curious Creatures

Almost September Morn

In the Good Old Summer Time

There's Nothing Like a Picnic

That Guy on The Right

Croquet Adirondack Style

Much Ado About Something

Aeroplane vs. Automobile
Oct. 6, 1912

Loon Lake House in 1920's

Index

ABBOTT, Henry 289
ABENAKI (Indian Tribe) 102
ADIRONDACK CABIN (book) 94, 302
ADIRONDACK COUNTRY (book) 13, 113, 138
ADIRONDACK DAILY ENTER-PRISE (paper) 82-85, 88, 219, 248, 306
ADIRONDACK FOREST PRE-SERVE 62
ADIRONDACK FRENCH LOUIE (book) 13
ADIRONDACK LODGE 30, 164
ADIRONDACK MUSEUM 130, 133
ADIRONDACK PARK AGENCY 68, 88
ADIRONDACK PIONEERS (book) 46, 53
ADIRONDACK READER (book) 13
ADIRONDACK ROMANCE (book) 94
ADIRONDACKS, THE BOOK 13, 142
ADIRONDACKS (Indians) 101
ADIRONDACKS ILLUSTRATED (book) 42, 63-4, 201, 298
ADVENTURES IN THE WILDER-NESS (book) 18, 31, 191, 200
ALBANY ARGUS (paper) 301
ALONG THE QUINNEBAUG (book) 205
ALEXANDER HOUSE (Hotel) 41
ALEXANDER, Jabez 45-6
ALEXANDER, Percy 45-6
ALFORD, Charles 58
ALGONKIN (Indians) 101
ALGONQUIN HOTEL 45-51, 81, 206
ALTEMUS, Frederick 79
AMERICAN ANGLERS BOOK 27, 140
AMPERSAND BAY 32, 39, 41, 104, 152, 213
AMPERSAND GOLF AND COUN-TRY CLUB 104-9
AMPERSAND HOTEL 23, 41, 42, 81, 104
AMPERSAND HOTEL FIRE 42-3, 81
AMPERSAND MT. 195-204, 208-12
AMPERSAND POND 195, 211, 251
ANCIENT ADIRONDACKS (book) 13
ARCHEOLOGICAL HISTORY OF NEW YORK STATE (book) 100
ARCTIC VILLAGE (book) 160
ARNOLD, Elisha 39
ARNOLD, Silas 39
ARRAS, Philip 249
ASSN. OF RESIDENTS OF UP-PER SARANAC 81
AUSTIN, Harold 133
AUSTIN, Merle 114
AXTON (Axe-town) 63, 102, 251

BACHE, Julius 184
BAKER, Roy 107
BALDWIN, George 172, 303
BALDWIN, Dr. Edwin 236
BARNETT, Lincoln 13
BARNUM, P. T. 86
BARTLETT CARRY CLUB 62, 76
BARTLETT CARRY CO. 260
BARTLETT GOLF COURSE 65
BARTLETT, Virgil 37, 51, 53
BARTLETT'S HOTEL 31, 32, 34, 37, 116, 161, 167, 193
BEARE, Lottie (Mrs. E.L. Tru-deau) 225-7
BEAUCHAMP, William 100
BENEDICT, Farrand 14, 201-2
BENHAM, Hi 277
BIG CLEAR POND 20, 75
BIG TUPPER LAKE 32, 92, 94, 155
BILLINGS, Albert 114
BIRCHBARK BOOKS 289
"BIRCHES THE" 262-5
BIRCHOLM (camp) 97, 251-3
BIRMINGHAM, Stephen 180
BLACK, Gov. Frank 75
BLAGDEN, Augustus 275
BLAGDEN, Benjamin 275, 278
BLAGDEN CONSTRUCTION CO. 187, 275
BLAGDEN, Donald 270, 275
BLAGDEN, Douglass 267, 269
BLAGDEN, Henry (Hank) 261, 275-283
BLAGDEN, Joseph 278
BLAGDEN, Thomas, Sr. 257, 275
BLAKE, Mills 198
BLISS, Mr. & Mrs. C.W. 279
BLOOMINGDALE, N.Y. 71, 83, 152, 303
BLUM, Sarah 180
BODINE, Sam 277
BOSSY (cow) 251
BOSTON DAILY ADVERTISER (paper) 20, 32
BOWLES, Ralph 87
BRADLEY, Mary (Mrs. Henry Blagden) 280, 282
BRADY, Matthew 295, 298
BRANCH & CALLANAN 67
BREWER & LEWIS CO. 80
BRIDGMAN, HELEN B. 94
BRIGGS, STEPHEN 187-9
BROWN, George 107
BROWN, John 154
BROWN, T. Robins 179, 187
BRYAN, Charles 102
BUCKNELL, Edith 243
BUCKNELL, William 125, 131
BURCHARD, Charles 298
BURGER, Bill 154-7
BURNS, Fred 133, 135
BURROUGHS, John 13
BUTTERFIELD, Mrs. William 247
BUZZACOTT, F. H. 294

CAMERON 104-6
CAMP ALPHA 77, 275, 279
CAMP CORK (Wonundra) 187

CAMP DeBAUN 97
CAMP NAVARAC 180
CAMP OF THE WINDS 275, 285
CAMP OMEGA 275
CAMPS AND TRAMPS IN ADKS. (book) 20
CARE AND FEEDING OF CHIL-DREN (book) 251
CARY, Reuben 114
CARY'S (Forked Lake) 32
CHAMPLAIN PRESBYTERY 243, 247
CHAREST, Raymond 96
CHASE, Caleb 113-5, 123
CHASE, Mrs. Mary H. H. 38, 55
CHATEAUGAY RAILROAD 75
CHEESMAN, Clyde 306
CHEESMAN, William 306
CHEESMAN, Mrs. William 306
CHITTENDEN, Lucius 30, 55
CHUG-CHUG, THE 253
CHURCH OF THE ASCENSION 103, 257
CLARK, A. C. 38
CLARK, Herb 142, 164-66
CLARK, Rev. William 247-8
CLARKE, Hannah 305, 311
CLEMENS, Clara 217-8
CLEMENS, Jean 217-8
CLEMENS, Olivia (Livy) 216-7
CLEMENS, SAMUEL L. (Mark Twain) 120, 213-21
CLEVELAND, Pres. Grover 77, 154, 275
CLOUGH, Capt. 116
COATES, Mrs. J. Lloyd 280
COCKROFT, Rev. David 249
COLE, Warren 114
COLTON & CO. 198-204
COLVIN, Verplanck 31, 86, 153, 191, 196, 202, 295
CONQUERING THE WORLD (book) 94
COOK, Marc 138
COREY, Henry B. 249
COREY, Jesse 31, 53, 63-5, 101-2
COREY, Marion 63
COREY'S (Rustic Lodge) 32, 64-7, 102, 167
COVILLE, Oatman A. 92-3
CONSTABLE, William 16
COULTER, William (architect) 171, 179
CRAYON, THE (periodical) 27
CRUIKSHANK, E. A. 57
CRUIKSHANK, Warren 57
CRUISE OF THE FRIESLAND (book) 298

DACEY, Kate 150
DAVID HARUM (book) 86
DAVIS, Frank 217, 219
DAY, Major and Martha 249
DEAN, Alletta 221
DEER ISLAND 97, 169, 251-6
DEERWOOD 275, 285
DEERWOOD-ADIRONDACK Mu-sic Center 285-88
DELAIR, Ronald 170
DELAVAN, Dr. J. Savage 38

DEPT. OF ENVIRON. CONSER. 83
DERBY, Ed 69-72
DERBY, Mrs. Ed. 72-3
De SCHWEINITZ, Dr. 277
DICKERT'S TAXIDERMY 105
DICKINSON, James 90
DIETAL, Lisa 256
DIETAL, Mrs. W.M. 256
DISTIN, William G. (architect) 67, 170-3, 190, 247
DISTIN, William L. (photographer) 170
DONALDSON, Alfred L. 13, 113, 116, 154, 172, 176, 215-6
DOOLITTLE, Susan 83-5
DOOLITTLE, William 82-3
DOUBLE-BARRELED DETECTIVE STORY 220-1
DOUGLASS, B. 60-1
DREXIE, Mrs. Chase's parrot 54
DUKETT'S HIAWATHA LODGE 32
DULEY, Robert 82, 88
DUNHAM, Harvey 13
DUNNING, Sam 138-45, 142
DUNTON, Dr. 75, 257
DURANT, Kenneth 13, 111-2
DURANT, Thomas 175
DURANT, William W. 175-77, 187
DURYEE, George V. W. 120, 213, 221
DUSO, Harry 61-2
DUSO, Kim 83

EAGLE ISLAND (Lower Saranac) 53
EAGLE ISLAND (Upper Saranac) 75
EATON, Charles M. 42, 44, 107
EDWARDS, Lt. Col. H. B. 97
EINSTEIN, Albert 273
ELY, Dr. William W. 191-204
EMERSON, Dorothy 247
EMERSON, Ralph W. 14, 212
EMERSON, Wallace 114
EMMETT, Dan 102
EMMONS, Ebenezer 14, 199

FAY-BOWEN (launch) 271, 273
FERRIS, Anna Edwards 243-4
FERRIS FAMILY 251
FERRIS, Sherwood B. 243
FETHERSTONE, E. 58
FIELDS SARANAC CO. 80
FIFTY YEARS IN A HEALTH RESORT (booklet) 137
FIRE PROTECTION (Algonquin Hotel) 49
FIRTH, Frank 257-267
FISH ROCK (or Sekon Lodge) 86, 88, 184
FISHING AND SHOOTING SKETCHES (book) 77
FISKE, F. P. 57
FITCH, Hedding 58
FITCH, John 249
FITCH, Theodore 58
FLOWER, Gov. Roswell 75
FOLLANSBY POND 53
FOREST AND STREAM (magazine) 20, 30, 194

FOREVER WILD: THE ADIRONDACKS (book) 13
FOSBURGH, Pieter 13, 139
FOWLER, Geo. 58-60
FRANKLIN, Benjamin 16
FRIBBANCE, Mallie 97
FRIEDMAN, Dr. 45
FROST, A. B. 55, 95

GAISMAN, Henry 97
GILLESPIE, William 187
GIRL SCOUTS (Eagle Island) 241
GINGER AND PARFY (cats) 108
GINSBERG, A. J. 95-6
GOLDMAN, Frank 97
GRABENSTEIN, Mrs. Grace 249
GRANTS 114, 123
GRAVES, Henry 250, 267
GRAVES HOTEL (Big Tupper Lake) 32
GREEN, Willard 158
GREENE, Caroline (Mrs. V. Bartlett) 38, 54-5
GREINER, Rev. Newton 249
GREY ROCKS OR DOCTOR'S ISLAND 246
GUIDE TO THE ADIRONDACKS (Wallace's) 31, 41, 45, 63, 92, 196
GUIDEBOAT DAYS AND WAYS (book) 13, 111
GURLEY, Rev. Alvin 248

HALE, Ed. 97-8, 131
HALEY, Bartlett 54
HALEY, Tom 54
HALLOCK, Charles 20, 142
HALLOCK, Fitz-Greene 226
HAMILTON, Alexander 16
HAMMOND, Samuel 20, 138
HANES, William 46-7, 50
HANMER, Bessie 124
HANMER, Henry 114
HANMER, Theodore 123-26
HANMER, Truman 124-5
HANMER, Willard 123, 126-30, 133
HANNA, Mark 107
HARDING, John 45-51, 121
HARDING, Watson 47-50
HARPY LAND JOBBERS 16, 18
HARRIETSTOWN 18, 54, 209
HARRIS, Charles 272
HARRIS, Mrs. Charles C. 46, 184, 271
HATHAWAY, Carl 114, 131-35, 169
HAYES, John 253
HAYES, Michael 253
HEADLEY, Rev. Joel 14, 20, 30, 142
HEALING WOODS, THE (book) 118, 136-7
HERBER, Dr. 124
HERMIT OF AMPERSAND, THE 228, 239-248
HEWITT, J.N.P. 100-103
HEYDAYS OF THE ADIRONDACKS (book) 91
HIGH SPOTS (periodical) 100, 160
HILL, Charles B. 224
HISTORY OF THE ADIRONDACKS (book) 13, 116, 172

HOCHSCHILD, Harold K. 13
HOCKING, Prof. 255
HODGES, Fred 150, 303
HOFFER, Art 106
HOFFMAN, Charles F. 14, 30, 55, 138
HOFFMAN, Ed. 107
HOLT, Dr. L. Emmet 251
HOMER, Winslow 55
HORD, Mr. & Mrs. Arnold 262
HORD, William 267
HOUGH, Daniel S. 32
HOUGH'S HOTEL (Saranac Inn) 32, 69
HUDNUT, Rev. William III 249
HUGHES, Gov. Charles E. 75-6
HUNKINS, Laura (Mrs. Wm. Martin) 38, 55
HURON INDIANS 101
HYPOTHERMIA 291

INDIAN CARRY 67, 92, 103
INDIAN CARRY CAMP 68
INDIAN CARRY CHAPEL 103
INDIAN PASS (book) 51
ISLAND CHAPEL (church) 96, 241-50

JACKSON, William H. 295, 298
JACOBSEN, Anna Rice 120-1
JAMES, Henry 213
JAMES, William 14
JAMIESON, Paul 13
JENKINS, Alfred B. 60
JOHNSON, Mother 31
JOHNSON POYNTELL 279
JOHNSON, Ruth 186

KAHN, Otto 97
KAISER, Dr. Harvey 185
KAISER, Henry J. 306
KANE, John 271-2
KEESEVILLE, N.Y. 31, 56, 89, 160
KELLER, Anton 107
KELLER, Helen 253
KELLER, Ludwig 107
KELLOGG, Jim 278
KELLOGG'S HOTEL (Long Lake) 32
KEOUGH, Chas. 123, 126
KERST 114
KIDD, ELIZABETH L. 246
KIRKEBY, A. L. 78
KIRKHAM, Dr. Dunham 249
KNOLLWOOD CLUB (Lower Saranac Lake) 120, 163, 171, 185
KOLLECKER, William 303-313
KRUMHOLZ, T. Edmund 92, 115-6

LA JEUNESSE 261, 275-83
LAKE OF THE CLUSTERED STARS (Lower Saranac) 27
LAMSON, Sarah (2nd Mrs. Wm. Martin) 38, 55
LANG, J. W. 82
LANMAN, Charles 30, 138
LAROM, Rev. Walter 217-8
LEAGUE OF THE IROQUOIS (book) 191
LEWISOHN, Adolph 171, 174-83
LINCOLN, Mrs. Frederic 27, 275

LITTLE RED 234
LITTLE RIVERS (book) 56, 195, 209
LITTMAN, Harry 88, 275
LOEB, John L. 131
LONG LAKE (book) 291-2
LONG POND 157
LONGSTRETH, T. Morris 13
LOOMIS, Dr. Alfred 233
LOON (steamboat) 94
LOON LAKE HOUSE 38, 42, 48, 69, 78, 81
LOWELL, James R. 24
LOWER SARANAC LAKE 18, 20, 27, 31, 36, 104, 116, 161, 162, 209, 216
LOWER SARANAC LAKE HEALTH RESORT 45
LUMBERJACKS, THE (book) 294
LUNDY, Rev. John P. 32, 37, 102, 139
LYON, Carolyn H. Talcott 246, 249, 251-5
LYON, Edmund 246, 249, 251-5
LYON, June (Linda) 251-3
LYON, May (Carolyn) 251-3
LYON PHONETIC MANUAL (book) 253

MACCREADY, Rev. William 247-8
MACKAY, Donald 294
MACE, Willie 104-6
MACOMB, Alexander 16
MACOMB PURCHASE 16, 18
MCCAFFERY 114
MCCORMICK, Daniel 16
MCCOY, Charles 187
MCKENZIE, Albert 226
MCKILLIP, J.K. 91
MCLAUGHLIN, Bill 219, 270-3
MCLENATHAN 115
MADDOX, Rev. Aaron 103, 243
MAHONEY, Daniel 82-3
MAINE COMPANY 18, 242
MAINE MILL 18
MALONEY, Gardner (guide) 71-2
MARGATE 18
MARSHALL, Bob 142, 164-6
MARSHALL, George 153, 163, 191-204
MARSHALL, M.O. 77
MARTIN, Henry 37, 142, 146-9
MARTIN, Homer 55
MARTIN, Laura 37-8
MARTIN, Stephen 37, 53
MARTIN, William 27, 32, 33-39, 51, 115-6
MARTIN, Willie 110-114, 158
MARTIN'S HOTEL 23, 27, 33-39, 41, 45, 49, 155, 159, 161
MARVIN, Charles Ingalls 243-4
MARVIN, Rev. Dr. Dwight E. 243
MARVIN, Sherwood 96
MARVIN, Mrs. Sherwood 251
MATHEWS, S.D. 44, 107
MAYO, Amory D. 23
MEADE, Dr. Gordon M. 222-240
MEIGS, Ferris 96
MERRILL, John 91
MERRITT, Schuyler 77
MERRITT & SWEET MAP OF ADIRONDACKS 235-6
MIDDLE SARANAC (Round Lake) 31, 51, 56, 116, 137, 161

MIDNIGHT SUN, THE (book) 298
MILLER, Rev. Elmer P. 209-10
MILLER, Laura (Mrs. Walter Rice) 239
MILLER, Milo B. 39
MILLER, Capt. Pliny 27, 51, 207
MILLER, Seaver 243, 245, 246
MILLER, Van Buren 207, 209
MILLS, Harrington 77-9, 126
MINOT, H.D. 149
MOHAWK AND MALONE R. R. 75,
MOODY, Harvey 14, 51
MOODY, Mart 32, 51, 77
MOODY'S HOTEL (Big Tupper Lake) 32
MOOSE 155-7
MORGAN, Lewis H. 191, 198, 202
MORRIS, Thaddeus 27
MORROW, Ralph 133
MORTON, Gov. Levi P. 75
MUIR, Rev. David 247
MURRAY, Lady Amelia 14
MURRAY, Rev. William H.H. 18, 21, 30, 31, 33, 55, 86, 138, 155 191, 295
MURRAY, Rush The 36
MURRAY'S FOOLS 21
MUTUAL INSURANCE CO. 69

NATURAL THING, THE (book) 13, 139
NEMEROFF, Bernard 68
NEW YORK EVENING POST 24
NEW YORK HERALD 34
NEW YORK MAIL AND EXPRESS (paper) 321
NEW YORK TRIBUNE 20
NEW YORK WEEKLY 71
NESSMUK, (G. W. Sears) 114, 294
NEWMARK, Morris 44
NILES, Carrie 54
NOAH J. RONDEAU, ADIRONDACK HERMIT (book) 103
NORTH COUNTRY LIFE (periodical) 123, 154
NORTHROP, A. J. 20, 30
NORTON, Christopher F. 18, 69, 89-92, 242, 251
NOWAKOSKI, Gregory 68

OBLENIS, Charles 150
OHMANN, Dick 83
OJIBWA (Indians) 101
OLD FORGE 30, 49
OLD MILITARY TRACT 14
OLD TIMES IN THE ADIRONDACKS (book) 293
OLD TIMERS 277, 283
O'MALLEY, Pete 142, 150-2
OSAGE INDIANS 222
OSLER, Sir William 232
OUTCALT, George 133

PALMER, Cyrus 113
PARKER, Arthur 100
PARSON, Eric 277
PARSONS 114, 123
PAUL SMITH'S COLLEGE 96, 157
PAUL SMITH'S HOTEL 20, 21, 23, 31, 32, 48, 51, 68, 105, 226
PEABODY, Mrs. Charles 75, 258
PEACOCK, Thomas 153-9
PEARSE, Edward 71

PEOPLE'S FOREST (book) 164
PETTY, Archie 65, 169
PETTY, Clarence 65, 101,169
PETTY, Ellsworth 142, 167-9, 258
PETTY, William 65, 169, 247
PHELPS, Orson (Old Mt.) 30, 138
PHILLIPS, Tom and Judy 131
PHILO, Hiram 298
PHILOSOPHERS' CAMP 27, 145, 195
PIERCE, Capt. James 88-9
PINE BROOK 75
PINE KNOT 171, 176-9
PINEHURST SCHOOL 277-8
PLUMLEY, Honest John 31
PLATTSBURGH SENTINEL (paper) 90-1, 148
POINT OF ROCKS (Lake Champlain) 32
POPE, Alexander 14
PORTER, Eliot 13
POTTER, Dr. & Mrs. Craig 249
PRESERVATION, League of N.Y.S. 179, 183-6
PROSPECT HOUSE (Hough's) 31, 32, 69
PROSPECT POINT CAMP 174-83
PSYCHOLOGY OF THE LOST (book) 289
PURCHASE, Harry 96-7

RADFORD, Harry 167, 295, 301
RAMSEY, George 253
RAQUETTE FALLS LODGE 102
RAQUETTE RIVER 63, 92, 100, 155, 193, 209
REARDON, R. H. 95
REBEN, Martha 118, 136-7
REED, Charles 58
REMINGTON, Francis 169, 246
REMINGTON, Mrs. Francis 247-8
REST-A-WHILE (camp) 169, 251
RICE, Ana 120-1
RICE, Erna 221
RICE, Fred M. 118, 136-7
RICE, Fred W. 1116, 118-121, 219
RICE, Seaver 104-06, 205-212
RICE, Walter 195, 205-212
RICE, William M. 120
RICE, Institute 120
RICE'S HOTEL (Lake Clear) 97
RICHARDS, Orson 18
RICKETSON 114
RIDDLE, Daniel 73-7, 257
RIDDLE, Quincy 75, 257
RITZ, THE (nightclub) 107
ROBERTSHAW, Rev. George 262
ROBINSON, Carolyn A. 245
ROCKEFELLER, Betty 189
ROCKEFELLER, William A. 89, 187-190
ROCKWOOD, Caroline 94
ROMEYN, Dr. J. R. 38, 54, 56-7
RONDEAU, Noah J. 102-3
ROOSEVELT, Theodore 75, 146, 149, 155-8
RUSHTON AND HIS TIMES (book) 13
RUSHTON, J. Henry 13, 113
RUSS, Richard 249
RUSTIC LODGE 31, 63-7, 97, 242

SABATTIS, Mitchell 113

SALISBURY, Herbert 123
SANTA CLARA LUMBER CO. 242, 251
SANTA, CLARA, TOWN OF 80, 86
SARANAC, THE (steamboat) 94
saranac club 57-61
SARANAC EXILES (book) 32, 102, 139
SARANAC GUIDES 30, 49-50
SARANAC INN 21, 31, 48, 69-88, 154, 157
SARANAC INN LAKEFRONT ASSN. 81
SARANAC LAKE HOUSE (Miller's) 39, 81
SARANAC LAKE VILLAGE 37, 42, 47, 75, 155, 172, 205-7, 213, 228
SARANAC RIVER 18, 51, 148
SCHUTZ, Ed 123
SCOPES & FUERSTMAN (architects) 203
SELIGMAN, Isaac 88
SENNOTT, John 247
SEVERANCE, J.L. 285
SEYMOUR, Gov. Horatio 14, 24
SHARING OF JOY (book) 118, 137
SHARPE, Mrs. Evelyn 79, 80
SHATLUCK, M.L. 82
SIDNEY, Margaret 94, 302
SIMMONS, Grant 81
SISTERS ISLANDS 53
SLAUGHTER, Laurence 78
SMITH, Apollos (Pol) 69, 295
SMITH, Clyde 13
SMITH, Everett 135
SMITH, Geoge 136
SMITH, L.L. 91
SMITH, Lydia M. (Mrs. Paul Smith) 38, 55, 226
SMITH, Phelps 55
SMOKE (periodical) 277
SMYTHE, Winifred 253
SOUSA, John P. 116, 118
SPORTSMEN'S HOME (Bartlett's) 51, 60, 195
SPRUCE ISLAND (Follansby Clear Pond) 208
ST. GERMAIN OR SANJEMO CARRY 20
ST. LAWRENCE UNIV. 97-9, 131
ST. REGIS GOLF CLUB 104
ST. REGIS LAKES 31, 231
STAGECOACH 31, 32, 45
STAINBACK, Thomas 155-8
STALLKNECHT, Frederick 142
STANTONS 114
STAUTNER, Ernie 107
STEARNS, Eleanor R. 46
STEVENSON, Robert L. 213-16, 220, 236-7
STILLMAN, William 27, 53, 55, 212

STODDARD, Charles 298
STODDARD, Seneca Ray 31, 63, 86, 150, 152, 202, 293, 295-303
STONY CREEK PONDS 34, 63-4, 101, 209
STREET, Alfred L. 14, 51, 55, 63
SUMMER BIRDS OF THE SARANACS (book) 149
SUMMER GLEANINGS (book) 101
SUTHERLAND, Arthur E. 246
SWAIN, Charles 272
SWEENEY CARRY 89, 92, 155
SWEET, Hardy 247
SWENSON, E. P. 65-8, 186
SWENSON, S. A. 65, 106

TAIT, Arthur F. 55
TALCOTT, Capt. Philo F. 253
THOREAU, David 13
TITUS, John 46-7, 53
TODD, Rev. John 14, 20, 101, 113 290-2
TO-N-FRO (launch) 242, 255-6
TOTTEN-CROSSFIELD PURCHASE 16
TOWNSHIP 20 18
TOWNSHIP 24 18
TOWNSHIP 34 (book) 13
TREACY, Carroll 82
TROMBLEE, Oliver 92
TROMBLEY, H. M. 149
TRUDEAU, Dr. E.L. 123, 157, 206, 222-40, 303
TRUDEAU INSTITUTE 50, 240
TRUDEAU, Ned (Edward) 226
TRUDEAU SANITARIUM 206, 230-4, 238-9
TUPPER LAKE HERALD (paper) 95
TWAIN, Mark (Samuel L. Clemens) 120, 153, 216
TWICHELL, Rev. Joseph 216

UNCLE PALMER'S (Long Lake) 31
UNION THEOLOGICAL SEMINARY 247
UNITARIAN REVIEW (periodical) 73
UPPER SARANAC ASSN. 75, 258
UPPER SARANAC LAKE 18, 31, 51, 53, 63, 68-9, 75, 86, 95, 161, 169, 171, 180, 206, 242

VANCE, Margaret 249
VANDERBILT, Frederick 149
VANDERWELL, Herman 44
VAN DYKE, Dr. Henry 56-7, 138, 145, 195, 209
VAN HOEVENBERGH, Henry 30
VAN NESS HOTEL (Burlington Vt.) 47

VAN VOORHIS, Eugene 249
VAN VOORHIS, John 169, 249
VAN VOORHIS, Mrs. John 97, 131, 169, 249
VAN VOORHIS, Linda Lyon 251-3
VASSAR, Ted 114
VERMONT, THE (Burlington, Vt. Hotel) 47
VILLA DORSEY 207-8
VOSBURGH, Charles 80-8, 288
VOSBURGH, Donald 80
VOSBURGH, Georgina 88

WACHUSETT 20, 32, 36
WADE, David, Jr. 250
WALLACE'S GUIDE TO THE ADIRONDACKS 31, 63, 92, 200
WARDNER, Charles 65-8, 97
WARDNER, James 101
WAREHAM, Arthur 170, 247
WARNER, Charles D. 30, 138
WASHINGTON, George 16
WATER LILY (steamboat) 116-18
WATERTOWN TIMES 131
WAWBEEK HOTEL 23, 81, 89-99, 150, 242
WAY OF THE WILDERNESS (book) 118, 137
WE THE PEOPLE 155
WEBBER, Charles 55
WEBB'S GOLDEN CHARIOT ROUTE (railroad) 75, 138
WELCH, Fay 101
WELLER POND 118, 137-8, 211
WERTZ, Emerson 241
WEXLER, Saul 82
WHITE, Alfred 169, 251-2
WHITE, Stanford 251
WHITE, William C. 13, 113, 138
WHITEHEAD, Charles 24
WHITNEY, Carlos 101, 167
WILDERNESS CURE, THE (book) 138
WILDLIFE BULLETINS 75
WILLIAMS, Roger 100
WILLY, Mladek 180
WILSON, Alex (architect) 171
WILSON, Will 292
WITHERILL, Col. S.P. 131
WONUNDRA (camp) 89, 187, 275
WOODRUFF, R. Eugene 206
WOODS AND WATERS (book) 63
WOOD'S FARM 30
WOOLSEY, James, Jr. 82

YARDLEY, Farnham 60, 247
YARDLEY, Fran 57, 62
YARDLEY, Jay 57, 62
YOUNG LIFE (Prospect Point Camp) 183, 186-7

"We never sleep."